Future-Proofing the State

Future-Proofing the State

Managing Risks, Responding to Crises and Building Resilience

Edited by

Jonathan Boston, John Wanna, Vic Lipski and Justin Pritchard

Australian
National
University

PRESS

ANU PRESS

Published by ANU Press
The Australian National University
Canberra ACT 0200, Australia
Email: anupress@anu.edu.au
This title is also available online at http://press.anu.edu.au

National Library of Australia Cataloguing-in-Publication entry

Title:	Future-proofing the state : managing risks, responding to crises and building resilience / edited by Jonathan Boston, John Wanna, Justin Pritchard and Vic Lipski.
ISBN:	9781925021516 (paperback) 9781925021523 (ebook)
Subjects:	Forecasting.
	Precautionary principle.
	Crisis management.
	Emergency management.
	Political planning.
	Strategic planning.
	Geopolitics.
Other Authors/Contributors:	
	Boston, Jonathan, 1957- editor.
	Wanna, John, editor.
	Pritchard, Justin, editor.
	Lipski, Vic, editor.
Dewey Number:	320.6

Cover design by Nic Welbourn and layout by ANU Press

Contents

Foreword

Allan Fels and John Wanna

The aim of this foreword is to introduce the rationale and main themes of this volume. When we at the Australia and New Zealand School of Government were planning this research initiative, we were confronted by an avalanche of momentous events—especially crises and natural disasters. We had just gone through the Global Financial Crisis of 2008–09; Australia had just endured seven years of incredible drought; we were then hit by massive bushfires across southern Australia (in Victoria and Western Australia); then by a series of major floods across Queensland, New South Wales and Victoria over three successive years; then the massive Canterbury earthquakes occurred from September 2010 to June 2011, destroying much of Christchurch; and following that some huge cyclones wiped out entire communities in northern Queensland. Many of these disasters came at the cost of a substantial toll in human lives. We had also been impacted by many health scares: Severe Acute Respiratory Syndrome (SARS) and bird flu in the early 2000s; the H1N1 influenza; and the equine or Hendra virus.

Elsewhere, the communities of South-East Asia had been decimated by the Asian tsunami in 2004, leaving more than a quarter of a million people dead; the south-eastern states of America were severely damaged by Hurricane Katrina in 2005, flooding New Orleans and closing much of the city; the capital of Haiti, Port-au-Prince, was devastated by a catastrophic earthquake in 2010, killing hundreds of thousands of residents; much of Europe was covered with volcanic ash from Iceland's Eyjafjallajökull volcano in May 2011, causing massive disruption to air transport; and in the same year the Japanese island of Honshu experienced a massive undersea earthquake that caused a huge tsunami onshore, which resulted in a series of nuclear meltdowns contaminating vast tracts of the coastal plains.

Discussing these events, we were aware of a growing literature on disaster and crisis management—some of whose leading thinkers appear in this volume; but as nations we still seemed unprepared and underprepared, even ill prepared, for such eventualities.

We were also conscious that trans-Tasman governments and their organisations had undertaken a substantial body of reform over many years and that they were now in better shape than previously to meet pending challenges. They have been reformed by New Public Management, have introduced better business systems and processes, have used markets and other sectors to improve delivery; and have attempted to embrace whole-of-government responses to problems, and talked about including more citizens' engagement in forming policy and guiding its delivery.

Consequently, without being overly triumphalist, we were prepared to accept that governments *do some things very well* and are *doing some things to the best of their ability*. They are particularly good at dealing with the predictable, the expected, the routine and issues of business continuity. They can be good on occasions in recovery and rebuilding when disasters strike.

There are, however, other things governments are *not doing well at all*—and these issues are what we have turned our attention to.

Governments are not good at precautionary management and preparing for the future; they are not good at thinking through and taking the necessary preparations; they are not good at anticipation and planning, and managing for future risk; sometimes they are not even good at collecting or analysing the information necessary to prepare for future events. And this, we might say, is when they can reasonably predict future events. As Jocelyne Bourgon argues in Chapter 4, governments and their public sectors are not good at dealing with things 'beyond the predictable'.

In short, governments are not (yet) good at future-proofing the state or their societies. Moreover, to the extent that governments consciously think about these issues, they get sidetracked by expedient and short-term concerns and bogged down by the hegemony of immediacy and political time frames.

We know that Australia will experience bushfires again—possibly up to two to three major ones every decade—yet we continue to allow people to build and live in bushfire-prone areas. We know floods and cyclones will regularly recur, but do we take adequate precautions about the known risks? On both sides of the Tasman we continue to build in earthquake-prone areas, and do not require buildings to meet exacting standards.

Too often the best intentions of governments, and normative considerations of what best they should be doing, are outweighed by immediate political, economic and social pressures and the existing array of vested interests calculating their partisan advantage or minimising their disadvantage.

In this volume we do not just focus narrowly on natural disasters—their occurrence was merely one catalyst to encourage us to explore these themes. We have chosen a much wider lens.

We focus on four broad groups of complex future challenges, each with different and particular drivers. Throughout the volume, we consider

- population-based and demographic changes that place huge stresses on global systems—these challenges relate to population size, growth, their impacts on resources, food shortages, problems of ageing and long-term health care, social movements and social dislocation

- environmental problems and challenges from climatic changes—these involve the known and unknown, the acknowledged or agreed and disputed effects of threats to the global environment, and what we can effectively do about meeting these challenges

- our increased susceptibility to natural disasters that may be occurring and recurring at more regular intervals and with greater magnitude; we are interested less in disaster response and crisis management and more in *readiness* and how to *rebuild recoveries* to minimise future risks

- crises we inflict on ourselves: human-induced problems emerging from the economy and from changes in society—local, national, regional and global— these are varied in form and cause and include anything from financial crises to civil unrest and terrorism, risks to technological and security systems as well as cyber attacks, conflicts between minorities and majorities, and conflicts over social values and problems of social integration, bred by social and political divisions.

And although the volume is entitled *Future-Proofing the State*, we are also interested in how society future-proofs itself, and how it develops its capacities for resilience.

To future-proof societies calls for different thinking about our management of complex problems. Building solutions will necessarily have to involve multiple actors and agencies, be focused across policy fields, involving cross-disciplinary approaches and mutual trust and resilience. We will have to find ways to gain political 'buy-in' for longer-term solutions and turn the attention of our politicians to issues beyond the immediate and the predictable.

If we look back, we have historically dealt with problems of *market failure* (usually by seeing the state step in to provide, insure or regulate); then we have dealt with problems of *state failure* as government over-reached itself and unleashed perverse effects (usually by refocusing the state, deregulating and transferring functions to non-state providers); and now we are arguably facing *community failure*, a failure of local communities to retain social capital, to maintain robustness and systemic resilience. These are new challenges.

To explore these issues we ask four questions.

1. What are the long-term challenges we are likely to face, and how can we predict, estimate and anticipate our future better?

2. How can we transform our political, economic and social institutions to ensure that long-term issues receive proper attention, and that our policymakers in

government, in the community, in the non-governmental organisation (NGO) sector and in the private sector address these future issues more seriously?

3. What learnings from previous crises, disasters, failures and looming time bombs can be extracted to enable us to better manage as we go forward and meet similar but different challenges?

4. How can we work together to rebuild and reinforce some of the important mortar of our societies: trust, respect, awareness, societal resilience, and above all capacities to act and respond to whatever challenges come along?

It is worth remembering, however, that governments cannot exclusively commit to future-proofing. We ought to recognise that our governments do contradictory things—they are not just committed to incubating resilience but simultaneously to breeding dependencies and reliance among clients and constituencies; they are extending statist regulations and nanny-ing at the same time as they are preaching the virtues of self-reliance; they are still engaged in various forms of social engineering and orchestrating social outcomes while wanting communities to be more resilient and cognisant of managing future risks. It can be a difficult political environment in which to build future-proofing.

Finally, we began this project with the proposition that governments were not good at future-proofing and preparing for future challenges. We then identified the major problems and impediments that prevented them from doing so. But identifying problems and labelling them were the easy parts of our analysis; finding effective solutions was the much harder component of the exercise—the rationale for this volume is precisely to discover the effective solutions for future-proofing our states and societies.

Professor Allan Fels, AO (Inaugural Dean, 2002–12)

Professor John Wanna

The Australian National University

Canberra

July 2013

Contributors

Jonathan Boston is Professor of Public Policy in the School of Government, and Director of the Institute for Governance and Policy Studies, Victoria University of Wellington, New Zealand.

The Honourable Jocelyne Bourgon has served at the highest levels of the Canadian Public Service and was clerk of the Privy Council and secretary to the cabinet for five years.

Rachel Brookie is a policy analyst with the International Strategy and Policy Team at the New Zealand Customs Service.

Henry Broughton is Sector Manager, Parliamentary Group, at the New Zealand Office of the Auditor-General and was previously a senior performance auditor in the Performance Audit Group.

Neil Comrie is a former chief commissioner of Victoria Police. He conducted reviews into official responses to Victoria's Black Saturday bushfires of 2009 and the floods of 2010–11.

The Honourable Sir Michael Cullen, formerly minister of finance and deputy prime minister of New Zealand, is Chair of New Zealand Post and a member of the New Zealand Government's Constitutional Advisory Panel.

Nicole Eastough is an Assistant Director with the West Australian Department of Treasury.

Allan Fels is Professor and Inaugural Dean of the Australia and New Zealand School of Government.

The Honourable Bill English is the Minister of Finance and Deputy Prime Minister of New Zealand and Deputy Leader of the National Party—positions he has held since 2008.

Bruce Glavovic is the Earthquake Commission Fellow and holds the Chair in Natural Hazards Planning at Massey University and is Associate Director of the Massey-GNS Science Joint Centre for Disaster Research.

Paul 't Hart, formerly professor of political science at The Australian National University, is Professor of Public Administration, Utrecht University, The Netherlands.

Peter Ho (Hak Ean) is Senior Advisor to the Centre for Strategic Futures and a Senior Fellow in the Civil Service College, Singapore. He is Adjunct Professor at the S. Rajaratnam School of International Studies at Nanyang Technological University and Chairman of Singapore's national planning authority.

Bridget Hutter is Professor of Risk Regulation, Director of the Centre for Analysis of Risk and Regulation and Head of the Department of Sociology at the London School of Economics and Political Science.

The Right Honourable John Key is Prime Minister of New Zealand, a position he has held since 2008. He first entered parliament in 2002 and became leader of the National Party in 2006.

David Kirk is Managing Partner of Bailador Investment Management, Chairman of Trade Me and Executive Chairman of the Hoyts Group. He has also been an advisor to the New Zealand Prime Minister.

Robyn Kruk recently retired as CEO of the National Mental Health Commission and was formerly a departmental head of Australian Government departments for the environment, arts, heritage and health. She co-chairs the Western China taskforce of the China Council for International Cooperation on Environment and Development.

Vic Lipski is a professional editor and research assistant in the Institute for Governance and Policy Studies, Victoria University of Wellington, New Zealand.

Jim McGowan is Adjunct Professor in the School of Government and International Relations at Griffith University and former director-general of three community and emergency services departments in the Queensland Government.

Peter Mumford is a Director in the Ministry of Business, Innovation and Employment and Principal Advisor in the New Zealand Treasury, focusing on regulatory issues.

Andrea Neame is Sector Manager, Local Government, in the Office of the Auditor-General. She was previously an audit manager at Audit New Zealand.

John Ombler is New Zealand Deputy State Services Commissioner and was responsible for coordinating the public service response to the Canterbury earthquakes.

Murray Petrie is a member of the International Monetary Fund's Panel of Fiscal Experts and has participated in many missions to IMF member countries. He is also Deputy Chair of Transparency International New Zealand.

Justin Pritchard is a political science honours graduate and research assistant in the Australia and New Zealand School of Government.

Lyn Provost is Controller and Auditor-General of New Zealand and is a Fellow of the Institute of Chartered Accountants of New Zealand (ICANZ).

Adam Rogers is a Director in the Strategic Policy Division at the Queensland Department of Transport and Main Roads.

Pierre-Alain Schieb is Counsellor in the Directorate for Science, Technology and Industry in the Organisation for Economic Cooperation and Development (OECD), which manages the International Futures Programme, the OECD's strategic foresight unit.

James Smart is an analyst at the New Zealand Treasury and former research assistant in the School of Government, Victoria University of Wellington.

Brian Walker is an Honorary Research Fellow with CSIRO Ecosystem Sciences and Chair of the Board of the International Resilience Alliance, a research group working on the sustainability of social-ecological systems.

John Wanna is the Sir John Bunting Chair in Public Administration in the Australia and New Zealand School of Government at The Australian National University.

Sally Washington is Principal Analyst in the Corporate Sector of the State Sector Performance Hub, a joint New Zealand policy team of the Treasury, State Services Commission and Department of Prime Minister and Cabinet.

Part 1: Governing for the Future

1. Governing for the Future while Meeting the Challenges of Today

Jonathan Boston

The world we have made, as a result of the level of thinking we have done thus far, creates problems we cannot solve at the same level of thinking at which we created them. (Albert Einstein, quoted in MacHale 2002)

Powerful global forces will reshape the context ... over the next few decades. They include increasing international connectedness, geopolitical power shifts, rapid technological developments, demographic changes, climate change, growing resource scarcity and changing values ... Together they are creating a world that is fast-paced, heterogeneous, complex and unpredictable. (Gill et al. 2011:29)

The Nature of the Problem

We live in the midst of significant social, demographic, economic, technological and environmental changes and challenges. In tackling these, governments need to focus simultaneously on issues of immediate, practical concern and those of a longer-term, more enduring or fundamental nature. Moreover, in responding to the pressing problems of today, policymakers and public managers must keep a watchful eye on the issues of tomorrow, including how the short-term policy 'solutions' they adopt will affect future risks, challenges, opportunities and capabilities. Put briefly, this means *governing for the future*. Governments must take a long-term view—looking out over decades, if not centuries, not merely a single electoral cycle of three or four years.

A crucial goal of such an approach is *future-proofing the state*—that is, anticipating and preparing for foreseeable challenges, managing and mitigating risks, building resilience and reducing future vulnerabilities, thereby ensuring a better, more sustainable tomorrow. These tasks, of course, are complex and hard—conceptually, analytically and, above all, politically. A range of possible futures needs to be imagined. Potential risks need to be identified and assessed. Judgments must be made about what level of risk is socially acceptable. Difficult policy trade-offs must be confronted. Intergenerational costs and benefits must be calculated. Ethically justifiable discount rates must be applied. And in the midst of all this, governments need to be constantly mindful of the likelihood of surprises, including rare, unpredictable, high-impact events—what are now referred to as 'black swan events', as discussed by Peter Ho in Chapter 5.

To undertake all these tasks competently requires astute leadership, foresight and wisdom. It also depends on robust evidence and excellent science. Some of these ingredients are often in short supply. Yet frequent calls are made for 'better future-proofing' as governments attempt to manage in the aftermath of crises and disasters; this applies not only to natural disasters such as earthquakes, floods and fires, but also to financial crises, pandemics, technological failures, moral panics and the unintended, damaging consequences of the state's own actions. So how can we improve the *future-proofing of the state*?

The 2012 Australia and New Zealand School of Government (ANZSOG) Annual Conference held in Wellington, New Zealand, brought together leading thinkers and expert practitioners to consider various dimensions of future-proofing, including the following.

1. What does the future hold, and can we predict and manage it better? What long-term challenges are likely to confront our political systems and how can we identify them and prepare for them sooner rather than later?

2. Can we realign or transform our political context—which is dominated by the tyranny of the urgent, short-term policy imperatives and the pervasive effects of the electoral cycle—to ensure that long-term problems and risks receive adequate attention and thereby prepare ourselves to meet future challenges? And what institutional mechanisms might be available to increase the incentives for policymakers to take long-term issues more seriously?

3. What can we learn as policymakers and public managers from our region's recent experiences in recovering from major natural disasters? Such learning may involve rethinking our practices of public management (including the processes of inter-agency collaboration), getting better at anticipating, managing and sharing risk (at individual, local community, national and international levels), and using recovery strategies to enable communities to withstand better the turbulent times that lie ahead.

4. How do we (re)build trust and foster resilience, which holds our nations and communities together, in the face of significant challenges, such as natural disasters?

The decision to focus on future-proofing our modes of governance reflected the fact that governments and communities will confront many significant challenges and risks over the coming decades—be they economic, social, political, environmental, technological, geological or meteorological (see Howell 2013). There is thus a need for appropriate foresight, planning and preparedness. Serious risks that threaten public health and safety or the capacity of governments to maintain public order must be properly identified and mitigated (at least to the extent that this is feasible and cost-effective); and governments need to develop the capability and tools to address such challenges as and when they arise.

For those immersed in emergency management, such tasks are part and parcel of the job. The relevant policy frameworks and language may differ somewhat between countries, but the basic roles and demands are similar. For instance, in New Zealand, emergency management focuses on the so-called four 'rs' relating to disasters: reduction, readiness, response and recovery. The Australian equivalents are prevention, preparedness, response and recovery. Of course, whatever the precise labels, the basic objectives are closely related and interconnected. Thus, for instance, any sensible recovery effort in the wake of a major disaster needs to give appropriate attention to prevention and preparedness—that is, for the next disaster. Moreover, the *recovery* process is not merely about the reconstruction of physical infrastructure, but it is also—more fundamentally—about the restoration of the afflicted communities (assuming this is feasible and sensible). It is thus concerned with all aspects of human wellbeing—social, economic, environmental, psychological and physical.

Yet future-proofing the state goes well beyond emergency management, as is highlighted by many of the contributions to this volume. It is not simply about preparing for, or responding to, disasters of one kind or another. The challenge is far broader. Indeed, so large is the potential canvas, so demanding the task, it might reasonably be asked whether future-proofing the state is a meaningful, realistic or sensible objective. After all, future-proofing may simply be too difficult. For instance, the future may be considered too unpredictable and uncertain, and/or the potential risks too severe, and/or the complexity and gravity of the challenges too great and/or the policy tools, resources and capacities of governments too limited. Yet while such impediments might render the goal of future-proofing immensely demanding, and while complete future-proofing is certainly a forlorn hope, this does not mean that no effort should be made. There is no case for giving up in despair. Realistically, we cannot turn our back to the future; nor would it be ethically justified to turn a blind eye in the face of well-established and serious risks. Individually and collectively we have a moral responsibility to take seriously the challenges that confront us on the horizon and prepare as best we can for whatever the future may hold. Equally, we owe it to future generations to consider carefully how our actions today will impact on their wellbeing—and, wherever possible, minimise the potential harms and maximise the projected benefits.

In all such matters it will be essential for governments to take the lead. Only the state has the means to undertake the necessary horizon scanning, risk identification and assessments, and the required strategising and planning. Only the state has the coordinating capacity, legitimacy and coercive powers to determine the appropriate actions, channel the required resources and incentivise the desired behaviours. Unavoidably, therefore, citizens look to their governments for leadership—to understand what is going on, to prepare and plan, to mitigate risks and to respond when crises occur. Inevitably, too, citizens are quick to blame governments that fail to exercise proper foresight or tolerate unacceptable levels of risk. This immediately raises several difficulties. What constitutes an acceptable level of risk varies over time. Citizens tend to be much more risk-averse immediately after a disaster or crisis than before such events.

Equally important, the incentives in democratic political systems are for decision-makers to focus on contemporary ills rather than future threats and opportunities. Likewise, there are short-term electoral incentives for politicians to engage in 'bias arbitrage'—that is, to focus on issues for which the public exaggerates the risks and to downplay or ignore those issues for which the public underestimates the risks (for example, climate change). This structuring of political incentives generates a constant and enduring challenge to ensure that the state invests adequately in the task of governing for the future and protecting humanity's long-term interests. Fundamentally, of course, this is a governance issue: it is about the quality of leadership; it is about resource allocation and priority setting; and it is about ensuring that narrow, short-term considerations and powerful vested interests do not override the wider public interest.

With these broad considerations in mind, this chapter has three main purposes. First, it identifies the major long-term challenges and risks facing humanity, including some of those specific to the Australasian and South Pacific regions. Second, it briefly examines the respective roles of governments and other stakeholders in preparing to meet these challenges and risks. Third, it explores what is meant by 'future-proofing the state' and discusses some of the specific issues raised by this task. These include, among other things, how to increase the incentives for governments to give proper weight to long-term policy issues; how governments might enhance the resilience of public institutions and critical subsystems and hence improve their capacity to cope with shocks; and how, in responding to various stresses and crises, it might be possible to maintain, if not enhance, public trust in governmental institutions. Where appropriate, I will refer briefly to other contributions to this volume.

The Challenges Facing Humanity

What are the critical long-term challenges, risks and potential shocks that humanity faces? Plainly, there are many: some we know about or can be readily foreseen; others are as yet unknown (see Howell 2013; Lee et al. 2012; Smil 2006; Upton 2012; and Chapter 3, this volume). Those we know about differ significantly in their nature, complexity, probable impact and likely duration. They can also be grouped in many different ways. For instance, a risk analysis prepared for the 2013 World Economic Forum (Howell 2013) classifies the most important current global risks under five general headings: economic, environmental, geopolitical, societal and technological. Ten specific risks are then identified and assessed under each heading, giving 50 risks in all. These are set out in Table 1.1.

Table 1.1 Global Risk Landscape by Categories

General category		Type of risk	Description
Economic	1	Chronic fiscal imbalances	Failure to redress excessive government debt obligations
	2	Chronic labour market imbalances	A sustained high level of underemployment and unemployment that is structural rather than cyclical in nature
	3	Extreme volatility in energy and agricultural prices	Severe price fluctuations make critical commodities unaffordable, slow growth, provoke public protest and increase geopolitical tension
	4	Hard landing of emerging economies	The abrupt slowing of a critical emerging economy
	5	Major systemic financial failure	A financial institution or currency regime of systematic importance collapses with implications throughout the global financial system
	6	Prolonged infrastructure neglect	Chronic failure to adequately invest in, upgrade and secure infrastructure networks
	7	Recurring liquidity crises	Recurring shortages of financial resources from banks and capital markets
	8	Severe income disparity	Widening gaps between the richest and the poorest citizens
	9	Unforeseen negative consequences of regulation	Regulations that do not achieve the desired effect, and instead negatively impact industry structures, capital flows and market competition
	10	Unmanageable inflation or deflation	Failure to redress extreme rise or fall in the value of money relative to prices and wages

General category		Type of risk	Description
Environmental	1	Antibiotic-resistant bacteria	Growing resistance of deadly bacteria to known antibiotics
	2	Failure of climate change adaptation	Governments and business fail to enforce or enact effective measures to protect populations and transition businesses impacted by climate change
	3	Irremediable pollution	Air, water or land permanently contaminated to a degree that threatens ecosystems, social stability, health outcomes and economic development
	4	Land and waterway use mismanagement	Deforestation, waterway diversion, mineral extraction and other environment-modifying projects with devastating impacts on ecosystems and associated industries
	5	Mismanaged urbanisation	Poorly planned cities, urban sprawl and associated infrastructure that amplify drivers of environmental degradation and cope ineffectively with rural exodus
	6	Persistent extreme weather	Increasing damage linked to greater concentration of property in risk zones, urbanisation or increased frequency of extreme weather events
	7	Rising greenhouse gas emissions	Governments, businesses and consumers fail to reduce greenhouse gas emissions and expand carbon sinks
	8	Species overexploitation	Threat of irreversible biodiversity loss through species extinction or ecosystem collapse
	9	Unprecedented geophysical destruction	Existing precautions and preparedness measures fail in the face of geophysical disasters of unparalleled magnitude such as earthquakes, volcanic activity, landslides or tsunamis
	10	Vulnerability to geomagnetic storms	Critical communication and navigation systems disabled by effects from colossal solar flares
Geopolitical	1	Critical fragile states	A weak state of high economic importance that faces strong likelihood of collapse
	2	Diffusion of weapons of mass destruction	The availability of nuclear, chemical, biological and radiological technologies and materials leads to crises
	3	Entrenched organised crime	Highly organised and very agile global networks committing criminal offences
	4	Failure of diplomatic conflict resolution	The escalation of international disputes into armed conflicts
	5	Global governance failure	Weak or inadequate global institutions, agreements or networks, combined with competing national and political interests, impede attempts to cooperate on addressing global risks
	6	Militarisation of space	Targeting of commercial, civil and military space assets and related ground systems that can precipitate or escalate an armed conflict

General category		Type of risk	Description
	7	Pervasive entrenched corruption	The widespread and deep-rooted abuse of entrusted power for private gain
	8	Terrorism	Individuals or a non-state group successfully inflict large-scale human or material damage
	9	Unilateral resource nationalisation	Unilateral moves by states to ban exports of key commodities, stockpile reserves and expropriate natural resources
	10	Widespread illicit trade	Unchecked spread of illegal trafficking of goods and people throughout the global economy
Societal	1	Backlash against globalisation	Resistance to further increased cross-border mobility of labour, goods and capital
	2	Food shortage crises	Inadequate or unreliable access to appropriate quantities and quality of food and nutrition
	3	Ineffective illicit-drug policies	Continued support for policies that do not abate illegal drug use but do embolden criminal organisations, stigmatise drug users and exhaust public resources
	4	Mismanagement of population ageing	Failure to address both the rising costs and the social challenges associated with population ageing
	5	Rising rates of chronic disease	Increasing burden of illness and long-term costs of treatment threaten recent societal gains in life expectancy and quality
	6	Rising religious fanaticism	Uncompromising sectarian views that polarise societies and exacerbate regional tensions
	7	Unmanaged migration	Mass migration driven by resource scarcity, environmental degradation and lack of opportunity, security or social stability
	8	Unsustainable population growth	Unsustainably low or high population growth rates and sizes, creating intense and rising pressure on resources, public institutions and social stability
	9	Vulnerability to pandemics	Inadequate disease surveillance systems, failed international coordination and the lack of vaccine production capacity
	10	Water supply crises	Decline in the quality and quantity of fresh water combines with increased competition among resource-intensive systems, such as food and energy production
Technological	1	Critical systems failure	Single-point system vulnerabilities trigger cascading failures of critical information infrastructure and networks
	2	Cyber attacks	State-sponsored, state-affiliated, criminal or terrorist cyber attacks
	3	Failure of intellectual property regime	The loss of the international intellectual property regime as an effective system for stimulating innovation and investment

General category		Type of risk	Description
	4	Massive digital misinformation	Deliberately provocative, misleading or incomplete information disseminates rapidly and extensively with dangerous consequences
	5	Massive incident of data fraud/theft	Criminal or wrongful exploitation of private data on an unprecedented scale
	6	Mineral resource supply vulnerability	Growing dependence of industries on minerals that are not widely sourced with long extraction-to-market time lag for new sources
	7	Proliferation of orbital debris	Rapidly accumulating debris in high-traffic geocentric orbits jeopardises critical satellite infrastructure
	8	Unforeseen consequences of climate change mitigation	Attempts at geo-engineering or renewable energy development result in new complex challenges
	9	Unforeseen consequences of nanotechnology	The manipulation of matter on atomic and molecular levels raises concerns about nanomaterial toxicity
	10	Unforeseen consequences of new life-science technologies	Advances in genetics and synthetic biology produce unintended consequences, mishaps or are used as weapons

Source: Howell, L. (ed.) 2013. *Global Risks 2013*, 8th ed (Geneva: World Economic Forum).

Of these top-50 global risks, the five with the greatest likelihood (as assessed in late 2012 and early 2013 by the report's authors) were: severe income disparity; chronic fiscal imbalances; rising greenhouse gas emissions; water supply crises; and mismanagement of population ageing. The top-five risks in terms of impact were: major systemic financial failure; water supply crises; chronic fiscal imbalances; food shortage crises; and the diffusion of weapons of mass destruction. Interestingly, two risks appear in both lists: chronic fiscal imbalances and water supply crises. The emphasis placed on severe income disparity—that is, the widening gap between the richest and the poorest citizens in many states—is also intriguing. It suggests that the report's authors concluded that income inequality has reached such high levels in a sufficiently large number of states as to pose significant risks to political stability and social cohesion. Whether this assessment is correct, of course, is open to debate.

While the risk classification system adopted by Howell (2013) has merit, it is important to note that many of the 50 global risks cannot be readily confined to a single category. For instance, environmental risks, such as species overexploitation, poor water management and the development of antibiotic-resistant bacteria, may pose significant economic risks (or even geopolitical risks). Likewise, societal risks, such as rising religious fanaticism, may affect geopolitical stability, which in turn may have negative economic impacts. Moreover, many of the risks are closely interconnected. For instance, food shortage crises (listed under societal risks) are clearly linked to water supply crises, land and waterway mismanagement, persistent extreme weather and rising greenhouse gas emissions. In short, many of the 50 risks are linked in various ways and/or have multiple potential consequences for humanity.

For the purposes of this brief analysis, I have clustered the major challenges facing humanity over the coming decades into four broad categories: the pressures arising from population growth, demographic changes and migration; the environmental challenges arising from resource scarcity and the waste absorption limits of the biosphere; a range of other, largely human-induced challenges and risks; and the seemingly increased prevalence of natural disasters.

Population-Based and Demographic Changes

Looking forward over the next half-century, the global population is projected to expand—from around 7 billion in 2012 to around 9 billion by 2050, and possibly 10–12 billion by the close of the twenty-first century (Royal Society 2012). This growth is likely to exacerbate existing resource scarcities (for example, with respect to land, water and energy supplies), intensify the stresses on certain ecosystem services, increase migration pressures and generate new geopolitical tensions. The risks of food shortages and international tensions over water and energy resources are particularly concerning.

In the developed world, most countries, including Australia and New Zealand, will experience significant demographic shifts. Their populations will age and become more diverse. Migration—whether internal or external, inward or outward—may pose significant issues of adjustment, inclusion and social cohesion for national governments. These factors will also pose a range of economic (including fiscal) and political challenges. A notable migration issue over the longer term in the South Pacific region will be the inundation of certain low-lying micro-states, such as Kiribati and Tuvalu, as a result of sea-level rise, and the need to relocate entire peoples.

Environmental Challenges

Likewise, various global (and sub-global) biophysical constraints—including the scarcity of non-renewable resources (such as oil and gas) and conditionally renewable resources (such as water)—and increasing pressures on the planet's common-pool resources (for example, the atmosphere, oceans and biodiversity) will generate a range of economic and social stresses. Compounding this, climate change over the coming century is very likely to increase the frequency and/or severity of meteorological and hydrological disasters (see IPCC 2007, 2013). Human settlements will thus face a growing threat of damaging large-scale events (for example, severe droughts, floods, heatwaves and bushfires).

Other Human-Induced Challenges and Risks

Governments face many other types of difficulties (including largely self-inflicted wounds, such as the costly 'leaky-building disaster' in New Zealand or the failure of local councils to require fireproof housing in bushfire-prone areas in Australia), which need to be managed and responded to. These human-induced challenges and risks vary in their likely magnitude, impact and duration, and include

- global and regional economic shocks, such as the global financial crisis of 2008–09 and the related sovereign debt crisis of 2011
- major technological changes, with resultant impacts on the pattern and structure of employment
- civil unrest and disorder, perhaps triggered by high-profile, politically divisive events
- acts of terrorism, cyber attacks and the failure of critical systems
- entrenched inequalities in wealth, income and opportunities, including severe and persistent ethnic inequalities
- major health problems, including the rise of obesity and epidemics
- biological disasters resulting from specific bacteria or viruses (exacerbated in some agricultural subsectors by crop monocultures)
- changes in societal values, attitudes, expectations and family structures, with significant implications, amongst other things, for the delivery of various social services
- changes in the nature and pattern of social media and mass communication, with implications for democratic processes, the character of social movements and forms of protest
- the risks posed by the increasing complexity and interdependence (at various spatial levels) of multiple systems—social, technical and infrastructure.

Natural Disasters

In recent years many countries have witnessed highly destructive natural disasters, including major meteorological, hydrological and seismic events. In the case of Australia and New Zealand, these have included

- the Victorian and West Australian bushfires of 2009–11, the widespread bushfires of late 2012 and early 2013, and the NSW bushfires in October 2013
- the large-scale flooding in Queensland, New South Wales and Victoria during late 2010 and early 2011, with subsequent major flooding events during the summers of 2011–12 and 2012–13

- the Canterbury earthquakes, especially those of September 2010, February 2011, June 2011 and December 2011
- the Cook Strait earthquakes in July and August 2013, which did significant damage in the small settlement of Seddon, but fortunately only modest damage in Wellington
- damaging hailstorms in Sydney (19 April 1999), Melbourne (7 March 2010) and Perth (22 March 2010)
- major tropical cyclones, such as Larry (2006) and Yasi (2011)
- protracted and severe drought conditions in many parts of Australia during 2003–09.

Some of these events not merely caused large-scale damage to property and infrastructure (and related economic losses), but also resulted in significant loss of life.

Equally, within the wider Asia-Pacific region, there has been a string of devastating natural disasters in recent years—most notably: severe floods in Pakistan in mid 2010 and mid 2011, and in Thailand in late 2011; and large earthquakes and tsunamis in Indonesia in late December 2004, in the South Pacific islands in late March 2009, in Chile in late February 2010 and in Japan in mid March 2011. Epidemics, such as the Severe Acute Respiratory Syndrome (SARS) pandemic in 2002–03 and the H1N1 influenza (that is, swine flu) pandemic during 2009–10, have also posed challenges for many governments in the Asia-Pacific region. Other kinds of natural disasters remain constant possibilities, including volcanic eruptions, cyclones and solar flares.

Clearly, some of these risks and challenges could be isolated events; but many may impact to varying degrees on our societies simultaneously. Indeed, there is an increased risk of multiple disasters occurring within short periods, thus placing extreme pressures on the resources and capabilities of the state (at all levels) and the communities affected. In response terms, this implies that governments and communities will have to deal with inordinately complex and interrelated problems, many taking the guise of 'wicked' problems defying simple or immediate solutions. Unfortunately, some of these disasters may be 'unmanageable' in that governments will lack either the resources to cope or the capacity to intervene with any degree of effectiveness, and local communities will be left to fend for themselves for extended periods. But it is surely better to know about, prepare and plan for such eventualities ahead of time, even if our responses may be inadequate. The fact that we cannot anticipate and regulate all risks, let alone control the future, does not mean that governments should simply relax and sit on their hands.

Preparing for Long-Term Challenges and Future Risks

Governments, in short, will be confronted by a multiplicity of complex future risks, the scope, scale and severity of which may all increase over time—in some cases markedly. Of course, such risks will also affect many other important stakeholders, such as business, civil society organisations (for example, think tanks, research institutes, interest groups and professional bodies) and local communities. Together they will be expected to prepare for and help manage these eventualities. But such actors are not necessarily presently geared up to deal adequately with the many challenges on the horizon. And to act appropriately and effectively may require more sophisticated thinking than has hitherto been demonstrated, as well as new ways of approaching problems. In this context, some stakeholders are unlikely to have the required knowledge or research capabilities, the right staff and skills, the appropriate mindset and aptitudes, or even the authority or capacity to deal with future risks.

Moreover, given the nature, magnitude and range of the risks, many different tasks require attention. In no order of importance, these include

- the need for improved global and national governance of common-pool resources, including the capacity to take effective action to reduce long-term risks, such as human-induced climate change, resource scarcity, biodiversity loss and ocean acidification
- the need for heightened disaster preparedness and adaptive capacity
- the need for robust scientific evidence and a capacity to assess risks in a rigorous and independent manner
- the capacity to mobilise resources quickly and efficiently
- the capacity to maintain critical infrastructure, including essential services, social assistance programs and important supply chains, during protracted 'emergencies'
- the need to enhance coordination and cooperation at multiple levels: intergovernmental, inter-agency and across governmental and non-governmental organisations, including business and the not-for-profit sector
- the need to foster increased community resilience and forms of community self-reliance
- the need for improved investment in risk mitigation, including enhancing the resilience of critical infrastructure (for example, via greater built-in redundancy). This applies to water services, wastewater services, electricity networks, transport infrastructure, telecommunications infrastructure, and other essential services. Although public funds will be available to cover

some of the costs of such re-engineering, more creative funding instruments will also be needed, including shared funding, co-funding, public–private partnerships, levies and charging.

Governments do not, of course, 'own' this policy space; nor will they necessarily deal with future challenges solely by means of direct or in-house provision. It is a shared space and requires a shared commitment across all relevant stakeholders. It will also entail smarter policy responses, cultural changes, some normative reconceptualisation, and learning from empirical experiences of what works (whether locally or elsewhere).

The challenges and risks outlined above raise a variety of philosophical and practical questions. One of these concerns the respective roles and responsibilities of governments, business, civil society organisations, communities and individuals, including how risks should be shared and how the 'policy bounds' or ambits should be negotiated. But there are many related questions.

- To what extent can (and should) the state reduce the range and magnitude of the risks it is likely to face over the coming decades, and how should it prepare to manage the hazards, disasters and exogenous shocks (whether natural or human induced) that are bound to occur and over which governments have little or no control?

- Of the risks that societies face, which are the primary responsibility of governments, and how, in general, should the costs be shared and/or allocated?

- What weight should be placed on the precautionary principle, and what potential benefits and opportunities might we be willing to sacrifice in the interests of 'playing safe'?

- To what extent can (and should) the state enhance its resilience (for example, by increasing reserves and redundancy) and hence its capacity to withstand negative shocks, whether economic, social, ecological, geological or meteorological?

- What policy frameworks and approaches appear to offer governments the best prospects of coping with uncertainty, minimising the impacts of negative shocks and maximising the potential to seize new opportunities?

- How can governments, other stakeholders and communities best learn from their mistakes, avoid repeating the failures of the past, and minimise policy regress over time as the political salience of a major disaster recedes?

Future-Proofing the State

In broad terms, the notion of 'future-proofing' refers to the process of attempting to anticipate or predict future developments in order to: a) prevent, or at least mitigate, possible negative consequences by reducing vulnerability and enhancing resilience; and b) seize opportunities as and when they arise. It has been applied to various spheres of human activity including, for instance, the future-proofing of electronic data—where it means selecting data formats and physical media that will maximise the chances of enabling continued access to the original information.

Accordingly, future-proofing entails exercising foresight and implementing strategies that are likely to enhance sustainability and resilience (for example, institutional, fiscal, environmental, innovation, incentives, social capital and so on) and reduce potential hazards and threats. From the state's perspective, governments can influence, at least modestly or at the margins, the kind of futures that societies experience. At the same time, however, human societies and the natural world are dynamic. The extent to which any future-proofing can be effective will necessarily be limited, as underscored by Bridget Hutter in Chapter 9: there are many uncertainties; our predictive capacity is constrained; some risks cannot be foreseen and/or are difficult to assess; some risks are costly and/or politically inconvenient to mitigate; and other risks may be very difficult, if not impossible, to mitigate (for example, because they are globally driven or beyond the control of governments to influence).

Many areas of academic research are relevant to the issues surrounding 'future-proofing', including future studies, governance (including adaptive and lateral governance), strategic management, organisational learning, sustainability, social capital, complexity, transformational change, innovation, and so forth. There is also a vast body of work on risk identification, risk assessment and management, distinguishing between risks and uncertainty, risk sharing and financing, asymmetries of information, and how to realign incentives and avoid moral hazards.

The remainder of this chapter considers briefly five particular challenges that are crucial if progress is to be made towards the goal of future-proofing the state. Many of these are explored more fully in subsequent chapters

1. increasing the incentives for governments to consider important long-term policy issues

2. increasing the resilience of public institutions and critical subsystems and hence their capacity to cope with future shocks

3. maintaining and enhancing trust in public institutions

4.   improving emergency management and disaster recovery

5.   improving the capacity of governments to learn from their own failures.

Bringing Important Long-Term Issues into Short-Term Political Focus

A significant body of social science literature suggests that democracies are systematically biased towards the present. In short, it is argued that elected governments tend to focus on short-term issues at the expense of long-term issues, and typically give more weight to the interests of current voters over those of future generations. This 'presentist bias' or 'political myopia' is evident in many policy domains across the democratic world. Examples include underinvestment in major infrastructure, inadequate protection of biodiversity, an unwillingness to address the long-term fiscal costs of current policy settings (for example, with respect to retirement income policy, long-term welfare dependency, student finance and criminal justice policy), the poor management of natural capital (especially critical, non-substitutable resources), and inadequate measures to mitigate human-induced climate change. The long-term economic, fiscal, social and environmental consequences of such political myopia are potentially serious, both in scope and in scale.

In relation to possible solutions, it is important to consider the merits (or otherwise) of various institutional arrangements and policy measures that governments have already put in place in an endeavour to give more weight to the interests of future generations and/or ensure that policymakers take future risks (and opportunities) more seriously. Such arrangements include

*   statutory requirements for treasuries/finance ministries to produce periodic long-term fiscal forecasts and statements of the long-term fiscal position of the government (for example, in New Zealand the Treasury is required to produce annual 10-year fiscal forecasts and periodic 40-year forecasts)
*   statutory requirements for government departments/agencies to prepare and publish strategic plans or related documents that scan the horizon, identifying risks and developing possible policy responses
*   statutory requirements for local governments to undertake long-term planning and disaster management exercises on a regular basis
*   the creation within relevant agencies of specialist risk-management and contingency planning units
*   the establishment of independent institutions with specific mandates to consider long-term policy issues (for example, commissions for the future, planning councils, and so on)

- enhanced legislative oversight with respect to long-term policy issues (for example, Finland's Parliament has a Committee for the Future, which, among other things, undertakes research on futures-related issues)

- legislative provisions that require policymakers at various levels of government to take account of the precautionary principle in their decision-making processes

- constitutional requirements for policymakers to consider the interests of future generations (for example, as noted by Pierre-Alain Schieb in Chapter 3, Finnish prime ministers are required on taking office to outline in Parliament their vision for Finland 15 years ahead).

The relative merits of these and other policy instruments designed to bring long-term issues and considerations into short-term political focus need careful consideration.

Building Resilience to Cope with Future Stresses and Shocks

As previously highlighted, resilience is critical to the successful management and regulation of risks. In recent years the notion of resilience has been much in vogue and has generated a large literature, especially in relation to socio-ecological resilience. Many definitions and conceptualisations are on offer. As applied in engineering, for example, resilience has been associated with three main properties: the capacity to bounce back after a shock or stress; the capacity to endure greater stresses; and the capacity to be disturbed less by a given level of stress (Howell 2013:37). But while this particular understanding of resilience is relevant to objects or infrastructure, such as buildings, bridges and dams, it is less appropriate to people, institutions and systems. For instance, an institution or a system may demonstrate resilience 'not by returning exactly to its previous state, but instead by finding different ways to carry out essential functions; that is, by adapting' (Howell 2013:37). Accordingly, a broader understanding of resilience is required. In this regard, the Intergovernmental Panel on Climate Change (IPCC 2007:90) has defined the resilience of a social or ecological system as its ability 'to absorb disturbances while retaining the same basic structure and ways of functioning, the capacity for self-organization, and the capacity to adapt to stress and change'. A resilient system, therefore, is one that can maintain its basic functions when confronted with disturbances or stresses; it retains, as Jocelyne Bourgon argues in Chapter 4, the 'capacity to adapt, to evolve and to prosper in a turbulent world'.

Resilience is closely related to the notion of vulnerability, as Brian Walker notes in Chapter 11. Vulnerability refers to a community's or a system's susceptibility to, and ability (or lack thereof) to cope with, adverse impacts. The degree of vulnerability depends on the nature, magnitude and duration of the shocks that are experienced, the sensitivity of the community or system to these shocks, and their capacity to adapt. While some known risks can be reduced or even eliminated, other risks are either too costly or too difficult to reduce. Having the capacity to manage 'residual risk', as it is termed, is critical.

Building on such insights, at least three kinds of capabilities are essential if a country, and in particular its governmental institutions, is to be resilient: a) adaptability—able to respond and adapt to changing demands and circumstances; b) sturdiness or robustness—able to survive unexpected or sudden shocks, including systemic shocks; and c) resourcefulness and recoverability—able to re-establish a 'desired equilibrium' (whether this is close to the previous order of things or a new regime of some kind) while ensuring critical services and operations are maintained. If these capabilities are important at the national or governmental level, they are equally necessary at the sub-national, subsystem and sectoral levels. Indeed, the resilience of governmental institutions will be influenced by, and dependent upon, the capacity of the various subsystems to cope with the stresses to which they are subjected.

Such an analysis immediately raises two questions. First, how might the resilience of countries (and their respective subsystems) best be assessed? And second, how can the level of resilience be improved and, moreover, improved in the most cost-effective manner?

With regard to an assessment diagnostic, Howell (2013) proposes a framework for evaluating a nation's resilience involving five subsystems (economic, environmental, governance, infrastructure and social) and five components of resilience (robustness, redundancy, resourcefulness, response and recovery). For each of the five components, specific evaluative criteria or attributes are identified. For instance, 'robustness' is defined as 'the ability to absorb and withstand disturbances and crises' (Howell 2013:38). Ways of increasing robustness might include ensuring that there are adequate fail-safes and firewalls in a country's critical networks and infrastructure. Criteria for assessment might include specific tests of reliability, the capacity to contain the impact of unexpected shocks and the adaptive capacity of decision-making processes— or to take another example: redundancy. The concept of redundancy refers to 'having excess capacity and back-up systems' to help ensure core functions and critical systems can be maintained in the event of unexpected shocks, disturbances and volatility (Howell 2013:39). Without doubt, redundancy can be vital, as both Peter Ho and David Kirk emphasise in their contributions to this volume. Criteria for assessing whether the level of redundancy is adequate might include the capacity of backup systems to undertake a specified level of core functions and the extent to which risks are spread through the provision of diverse delivery systems.

It is one thing to develop a diagnostic tool to assess the level of resilience; it is quite another to apply this tool effectively and improve the level of resilience.

Increasing the degree of redundancy will almost certainly entail additional costs. In other cases, the level of resilience may not be readily amenable to policy interventions. For instance, having a robust level of social capital—including a strong network of civil society organisations, high levels of trust and social cohesion, and a tradition of social entrepreneurship—is undoubtedly important during the response and recovery phases of major disasters (as highlighted by recent natural disasters in Australia and New Zealand and emphasised by various contributors to this volume). But it is by no means self-evident how governments can enhance the level of social capital, let alone ensure that it is properly harnessed and deployed when disaster strikes. Having said this, governments can certainly facilitate or hinder the development of social capital. For instance, empowering local communities, implementing collaborative modes of governance (and lateral governance) and co-funding various local initiatives can help facilitate, but not guarantee, the accumulation of social capital.

Maintaining and Enhancing Trust in Public Institutions

There has been considerable concern in recent decades about the decline in the level of trust in public institutions in many long-established democracies. Various explanations for the loss of trust have been advanced, but whatever the causes, there is general agreement that low trust is politically, socially and economically damaging. Other things being equal, governments are likely to be less resilient and less able to cope with difficult challenges if citizens have little trust and confidence in those who hold public office and/or provide public services. Hence, rebuilding and maintaining adequate levels of trust in public institutions should be priorities. Possible ways of addressing the current 'trust deficits' are usefully explored by Murray Petrie in Chapter 8. As he indicates, transparency, participation and robust accountability mechanisms are critical.

Managing Natural Disasters: Recovery strategies, modalities, institutions and lessons

A considerable part of this volume is devoted to the topic of natural disasters, with various reflections on the multiple challenges and opportunities such events generate for governments. This includes the ways in which governments can best prepare for, respond to and help the recovery process after disasters; the opportunities disasters provide for policy innovation and experimentation by governmental agencies (and non-governmental organisations); the role of social capital in enabling communities to cope with and recover from disasters; and the challenges large-scale disasters can pose for the maintenance of decentralised governance systems and the integrity of the democratic process.

Different kinds of disasters, of course, require different responses and modes of recovery. Localised, one-off events, such as fires or hailstorms, specific acts of terrorism or short-lived riots, pose different recovery challenges to large-scale and protracted events, such as major floods, damaging earthquakes with numerous significant aftershocks, or substantial economic shocks, such as the Global Financial Crisis and the related sovereign debt crisis, particularly in Europe.

For good reasons, the 2012 ANZSOG conference gave particular attention to several of the major natural disasters that have afflicted Australia and New Zealand in recent years, in particular

- the Victorian bushfires in early February 2009
- the Queensland floods during late 2010 – early 2011
- the Canterbury earthquakes, especially those in September 2010 and February 2011.

In each case, these disasters caused substantial damage and generated significant stresses for the governments of the respective jurisdictions. Unsurprisingly, too, in each case the relevant governments established independent bodies to investigate aspects of each disaster and how well the response and recovery strategies worked in practice, although analysis of the latter has varied significantly, reflecting the particular circumstances and distinctive features of the disasters in question. Drawing on the reports of these independent bodies, Rachel Brookie and James Smart in their respective chapters outline and assess the recovery strategies adopted and highlight the lessons arising. Likewise, John Ombler and Sally Washington in Chapter 21 explore the opportunities created by the Canterbury earthquakes for policy innovation and, in particular, new ways of delivering public services, while in Chapter 22 Lyn Provost and her colleagues provide an audit perspective on the public sector's response to the earthquakes. Here, I briefly summarise some of the key features of the three particular disasters.

The Victorian Bushfires

The Victorian bushfires in late January and early February 2009 affected almost 80 townships, destroyed more than 2000 homes (and 3500 structures) and displaced about 7500 people; 173 people died, with more than 400 injured; there were also large forestry, agricultural and horticultural losses, with total costs estimated at more than A$4.4 billion. The Federal and Victorian governments established the Victorian Bushfire Reconstruction and Recovery Authority (as a joint initiative) several days after the main disaster on 7 February (Black Saturday). This was headed by Christine Nixon, the outgoing commissioner of Victoria Police. Its mandate was to oversee the rebuilding of the many communities affected by the fires. Subsequently, in April 2009, the Victorian Government established a royal commission, which was asked to examine the 'causes and circumstances of the bushfires', all aspects of the government's bushfire strategy and responses, and the issues arising (for example, with respect to preparation and planning for future bushfire threats, land-use planning and management, the fireproofing of buildings, emergency response, the quality and availability of public information, training and resourcing, and so on). The royal commission delivered its interim report on 17 August 2009 and its final report on 31 July 2010 (which contained 67 recommendations covering a diverse range of issues, including emergency and incident management, planning and building, land management, and so on).

The Queensland Floods

Large-scale flooding affected much of Queensland (and several other States) during December 2010 and early 2011 as a result of a series of storms and cyclones. At one point, three-quarters of the State of Queensland was declared a disaster zone. The floods forced the evacuation of many thousands of people; more than 30 people lost their lives; and there was significant and protracted disruption to business activity across much of the State. Insurance losses exceeded A$1 billion, and total economic losses may have exceeded A$10 billion (with some estimates as high as A$20–30 billion). A recovery taskforce, headed by Major General Michael Slater, was established to coordinate initial recovery efforts. Later the Queensland Reconstruction Authority was created (under legislation) to develop, coordinate, implement and manage the Statewide plan for rebuilding and reconnecting communities affected by the floods and cyclones. The authority's board is chaired by Major General Dick Wilson, and the chief executive is Graeme Newton, previously the State's Coordinator-General and Director-General of the Department of Infrastructure and Planning. The Queensland Government also established a commission of inquiry into the floods on 17 January 2011, with broad terms of reference, and the commission completed its interim report on 1 August 2011, with 175 recommendations. The Australian Government imposed a flood levy to fund reconstruction work.

The Canterbury Earthquakes

Earthquakes are very common in New Zealand, but few cause major damage. An unexpectedly large quake occurred in the vicinity of Christchurch on 4 September 2010; this was followed by three significant aftershocks—on 22 February 2011, 13 June 2011 and 23 December 2011—with numerous smaller aftershocks. The February quake resulted in the collapse of many buildings with the loss of 185 lives. The cumulative damage has thus far been substantial, with much of the central and eastern parts of the city severely affected. More than 30 000 houses are estimated to have sustained damage exceeding NZ$100 000, with the total fiscal costs estimated to exceed NZ$13 billion and insurance losses well in excess of NZ$20 billion.

In response to the quake in September 2010, the Government established the Canterbury Earthquake Recovery Commission under the *Canterbury Earthquake*

Response and Recovery Act, which was enacted on 14 September. The commission's role was to offer advice on prioritising resources and allocating funding and to help coordinate the efforts of central and local governments. Subsequently, following the February quake, the Government established the Canterbury Earthquake Recovery Authority (CERA) (also via legislation). CERA's mandate is to lead and coordinate the recovery effort, including business recovery, restoring local communities, and enabling effective and timely rebuilding. The Chief Executive of CERA is Roger Sutton. On 14 March 2011, the Government announced the establishment of the Canterbury Earthquakes Royal Commission to investigate a range of issues including building collapses and the consequent loss of life, damage to key buildings, and the adequacy of building standards and codes. An interim report was released in mid October 2011, and a final report (in seven volumes) was completed in stages during 2012. A separate technical investigation into a number of specific building collapses was commenced on 16 March 2011 by the Department of Building and Housing, and several reports have been released.

With these three major natural disasters in mind, it is important to step back and reflect on some of the broader policy issues to which they give rise. For instance, relevant questions include

- the merits or otherwise of the specific institutional arrangements that were established to investigate the disasters and coordinate the recovery process—including their design features, powers, capability, resourcing, administrative arrangements and consultative processes
- whether there was adequate leadership and competent governance, including effective intergovernmental and inter-agency coordination
- whether government agencies effectively coordinated and partnered with business, other non-governmental organisations and local communities
- whether there was adequate protection of democratic rights, including opportunities for citizen participation and consultation
- whether short-term political imperatives, such as the pressure for quick decisions on future land-use options, prevailed over long-term planning considerations and the wider public interest
- whether policymakers applied the lessons arising from previous disasters, both local and international (for example, Kobe and New Orleans), in their disaster response and recovery processes.

Quite apart from this, the large-scale disasters that have afflicted Australia and New Zealand in recent years have raised a raft of difficult policy issues that will no doubt be the subject of ongoing and vigorous debate. Such issues include: the cost of, and limits to, insurance (and reinsurance); the related question of how the losses arising from major disasters should be shared across the relevant communities (including taxpayers and ratepayers); the extent to which those faced with losing their land and/or various property rights (for example, due to damage, flood risk, fire risk, and so on) should be compensated; and the extent to which new, and potentially costly, building standards and planning procedures should be implemented and, if so, over what time frame. Such issues, needless to say, are all politically charged and require adroit management.

Responding to Human-Induced Disasters and Government Failure

Aside from natural disasters, governments are also confronted from time to time with human-induced disasters; this includes self-inflicted wounds or government failures. Such failures are inevitable. The many possible causes include poorly designed and/or badly implemented regulatory frameworks, weak governance, human error, poor conflict management and corrupt practices. Some of these failures have been, and will no doubt continue to be, extremely costly. In New Zealand, as discussed by Peter Mumford in Chapter 7, significant changes were made to the regulation of the building industry during the 1990s, with a move from relatively prescriptive building codes to performance-based regulation. Some years later it became apparent that many new residential and commercial buildings were leaking. Investigations revealed that this was due to poor construction, the use of inappropriate materials and bad design. In short, the new performance-based regulatory framework had failed (Mumford 2011). The cost of rectifying the so-called 'leaky building' problem has been estimated at more than NZ\$10 billion.

A central issue arising from cases of this nature is whether governments are prepared to invest adequately in policy learning—including rigorous, independent evaluations of what went wrong and why, and careful analyses of how similar self-inflicted wounds might be avoided, or at least minimised, in the future. If policy learning is not an integral part of the decision-making process then it is inevitable that similar costly failures will be repeated. Thankfully, the democratic process includes some automatic stabilisers: electors ultimately reject those who prefer not to learn.

Conclusion

In summary, governments face a daunting array of risks. For various reasons, as discussed earlier, both the complexity and the magnitude of these risks appear to be increasing. Moreover, unless the crucial environmental and resource-related challenges currently confronting the global community are effectively tackled, there will be a greater likelihood of major natural disasters (for example, arising from climate change) and heightened geopolitical tensions (for example, arising from resource constraints). The existing weakness of our global governance arrangements, especially for managing common-property resources, increases the probability that the required policy changes will not be made—or at least will not be made in time. Accordingly, the management of, and recovery from, disasters is likely to become an ever more demanding burden on governments, both national and sub-national.

Elected officials will have little choice but to respond. Citizens, after all, expect governments to manage and, if possible, mitigate severe and large-scale risks on their behalf. Indeed, this responsibility is arguably one of the state's defining or inherent functions. But it is no easy task. Nevertheless, while governments certainly cannot control the future and while the state can only be 'future-proofed' to a modest degree, there is a strong ethical imperative for governments to devote resources to addressing long-term policy challenges and enhancing the capacity of public institutions to withstand future shocks.

Politically, perhaps the most difficult challenge is the powerful electoral incentive for decision-makers to focus on today's problems at the expense of tomorrow's threats and hazards. As discussed in this chapter, there are various institutional mechanisms that can help rebalance the incentive structure in democracies so that governments give more attention to long-term risks and the interests of future generations. But realistically such mechanisms are likely to have only a modest impact.

Finally, resilient governments depend on resilient societies; the two are inextricably intertwined. Hence, future-proofing the state requires vigorous non-governmental institutions and secure reserves of social capital. If governments have only a limited capacity to ensure such outcomes, neither are they powerless. Above all, they need to use their resources prudently and intelligently.

References

Birkland, T. 2006. *Lessons of Disaster: Policy Change after Catastrophic Events* (Washington, DC: Georgetown University Press).

Birkland, T. 2007. *After Disaster: Agenda Setting, Public Policy and Focusing Events* (Washington, DC: Georgetown University Press).

Bourgon, J. 2009. New Governance and Public Administration: Towards a Dynamic Synthesis, Canberra, 24 February.

Bourgon, J. 2011. *A New Synthesis of Public Administration: Serving in the 21st Century* (Montreal: McGill-Queens University Press).

Council of Australian Governments (COAG). 2011. *National Strategy for Disaster Resilience*, February (Canberra: COAG).

Daniels, R., Kettl, D. and Kunreuther, H. (eds) 2006. *On Risk and Disaster: Lessons from Hurricane Katrina* (Philadelphia: University of Pennsylvania Press).

Gill, D., Pride, S., Gilbert, H., Norman, R. and Mladenovic, A. 2011. 'The Future State Project: Meeting the Challenges of the Twenty-first Century' in Bill Ryan and Derek Gill (eds), *Future State: Directions for Public Management Reform in New Zealand* (Wellington: Victoria University Press).

Handmer, J. and Dovers, S. 2007. *Handbook of Disaster and Emergency Policies and Institutions* (London: Earthscan).

Howell, L. (ed.) 2013. *Global Risks 2013*, Eighth edn (Geneva: World Economic Forum).

Hughes, P. and Smart, J. 2012. '"You Say You Want a Revolution" … The Next Stage of Public Sector Reform in New Zealand', *Policy Quarterly*, 8(1).

Intergovernmental Panel on Climate Change (IPCC). 2007. *Climate Change 2007: Impacts, Adaptation and Vulnerability. Working Group II Contribution to the Fourth Assessment Report, Summary for Policy Makers and Technical Summary* (Geneva: IPCC).

Intergovernmental Panel on Climate Change (IPCC). 2013. *Summary for Policymakers. Working Group I Contribution to the Fifth Assessment Report* (Geneva: IPCC).

Kumar, C. and Srivastava, D. 2006. *Tsunami and Disaster Management: Law and Governance* (Hong Kong: Sweet & Maxwell Asia).

Lee, B., Preston, F., Kooroshy, J., Bailey, R. and Lahn, G. 2012. *Resources Futures: A Chatham House Report*, December (London: Chatham House).

MacHale, D. 2002. *Wisdom* (London: Prion Books).

May, P. and Williams, W. 1986. *Disaster Policy Implementation: Managing Programs under Shared Governance* (New York: Plenum Press).

Mumford, P. 2011. *Enhancing Performance-Based Regulation: Lessons from New Zealand's Building Control System* (Wellington: Institute of Policy Studies).

Organisation for Economic Cooperation and Development (OECD). 2012. *OECD Environmental Outlook to 2050* (Paris: OECD).

Queensland Floods Commission of Inquiry. 2011. *Interim Report*, August (Brisbane: Queensland Floods Commission of Inquiry).

Queensland Reconstruction Authority. 2011. *Operation Queenslander: The State Community, Economic and Environmental Recovery and Reconstruction Plan 2011–13* (Brisbane: Queensland Reconstruction Authority).

Ronan, K. and Johnston, D. 2005. *Promoting Community Resilience in Disasters: The Role for Schools, Youth and Families* (New York: Springer).

Ryan, B. and Gill, D. (eds) 2011. *Future State: Directions for Public Management in New Zealand* (Wellington: Victoria University Press).

Royal Society. 2012. *People and the Planet*, The Royal Society Science Policy Centre Report 01/12 (London: The Royal Society).

Smil, V. 2006. *Global Catastrophes and Trends—The Next Fifty Years* (Boston: MIT Press).

Upton, S. 2012. Long term fiscal risks—New Zealand's case in the context of OECD countries, Paper prepared for Affording the Future Conference, Wellington.

2009 Victorian Bushfires Royal Commission. 2010. *Final Report: Summary* (Melbourne: State Government of Victoria).

2. The Role of Government in Future-Proofing Society

The Right Honourable John Key

My government has four priorities in its second term (2011–14). The first is to manage the Government's finances responsibly. New Zealand has faced a number of challenges over the past three-and-a-half years, from a recession to the Canterbury earthquakes. The Government has absorbed much of the cost of these events on its balance sheet, so we can cushion New Zealanders from the worst effects. But that money has to be paid back. So we have put a huge amount of effort into making savings and, in particular, into changing some of the long-term term drivers of government spending, so we can get back to surplus over the next few years and start getting our debt down again.

The public sector has played—and continues to play—a very important part in this approach. We have worked with the public sector to identify opportunities for savings, and indeed to identify opportunities for investment, too. We believe people who understand their own services are in the best position to make financial trade-offs and to introduce innovation that genuinely improves public services. As a result, chief executives and senior public servants have been focused on understanding how their organisations work, what drives their costs and how to measure service levels. That approach seems to be working.

Our second priority is to continue building a more competitive and productive economy. We have a very busy program of work going on in a number of areas, to make sure that our regulatory settings are right, that the infrastructure is there to support growth and that resources can flow to their most productive use.

Our third priority is to deliver better public services to New Zealanders within tight fiscal constraints. If you think about it, New Zealanders—and Australians for that matter—have two fundamental interests in their public services. On the one hand, as users they get the benefit of these services, and on the other they also pay for them. For the most part, they do not have much choice either way. They are required to pay through their taxes, and there is often little or no alternative in the provision of public services. So the key challenge facing the Government, and public servants, is to fashion a public sector that works for the people who use its services and is affordable for the taxpayers who fund it.

But the world has changed over the past few years. What seemed affordable, at a pinch, in 2006 or 2007 is now contributing to a structural deficit in the

Government's accounts. Spending is being reined in to match what the country can afford, but at the same time people's expectations of public services continue to grow. So over the next few years the Government needs good advice and new thinking from the public sector. In fact there has never been a better opportunity for experienced and committed public servants at all levels to contribute to constructive change. It will not be easy but it will be rewarding.

Our fourth and final priority is to support the rebuilding of greater Christchurch, our second-largest city. This will be the biggest economic project ever undertaken in New Zealand. There have already been big implications for the New Zealand Public Service, and that will continue over the course of the rebuild. I will have more to say about Christchurch shortly.

First, I would like to begin with a few brief reflections from the perspective I have on the ninth floor of the Beehive in Wellington. The first is that public policy is hard. So is public management. They are challenging tasks, and much more difficult than commentators, businesspeople, newspaper column writers and the public often think. To my mind, the intellectual and practical challenges of the public service are what attract so many capable and motivated New Zealanders to work in it.

Public policy and management are also hugely important tasks. Governments always need good advice, they need a sound system of financial management, they need skilled people to run what are often large organisations, and they need to know how their decisions will affect society and the economy.

As prime minister, I find the most difficult, hard-to-tackle issues of public policy inevitably end up passing across my desk. In working through those issues, I rely heavily on the advice and judgment of public servants. It is crucial that ministers know all the sides of a particular issue, have all the relevant information and fully understand the implications of different courses of action. Since becoming prime minister in late 2008, I have been impressed by the professionalism and competence of public servants in my own departments and across the public sector as a whole. The approach of my government has been to respect people's professional skills and to back public servants who want to get on and make New Zealand a better place.

As just one example, we have reintroduced the practice of having officials regularly attend cabinet committee meetings. That is for two reasons. We want to get advice from the people who have the greatest knowledge of particular issues. And we actually think it is good for officials to see where ministers agree and disagree, what they feel comfortable with and what drives their consideration of a particular issue.

We also respect the neutrality of the public sector. It is one of the great strengths of the New Zealand public management system. But while it is important for governments of all stripes to respect the political neutrality of the public sector, it is equally important for public servants to respect the political mandate of the Government. So the first thing I would say to you is that advice from the public service is highly valued and it is always considered carefully.

Yet that advice can only go so far, for government is not a technocratic exercise. In the end, the biggest, most fundamental decisions governments are called on to make cannot be calculated in a spreadsheet. And in a lot of areas, the most thorough policy analysis does not lead to an inevitable conclusion; it simply highlights the fundamental judgments that have to be made around concepts like fairness, opportunity and the balance between individual and social responsibility. That is why we have an elected government—so that politicians make those sorts of judgments and are accountable to the people of New Zealand, or of Australia, for doing so.

Governments also have to bring things to a head. The public and the media can debate issues forever but, in the end, the government has to cut through them and make a decision, which will invariably please some people and disappoint others. In some cases that decision is to do something and in other cases it is to *not* do something. Either way, a decision has been made. In making those decisions, my government has been very pragmatic.

We are guided by the values and principles of the party we represent in Parliament, but we are also focused on what is sensible and what is possible. Partly, that is the nature of the political system in New Zealand. It is sometimes said that politics is about convincing 50 per cent of the population plus one, and that has never been truer than under our multimember proportional electoral (MMP) system. But, in any event, government is a practical business. You do not start with a blank sheet of paper; you start with the country as it is. And by making a series of sensible decisions, which build on each other and which are signalled well in advance, and by taking more people with you as you go, you can effect real and durable change. That has certainly been our experience in New Zealand.

I also believe in keeping my word with the electorate. One of the characteristics of this government has been that we have been consistent and upfront with New Zealanders about what we are doing and why. We campaigned openly on a very clear program and that is what we are implementing. At each election we have sought a mandate for new policies we want to put in place. And we have made clear assurances about the policies we will maintain.

Trust is fundamental to the relationship between politicians and voters, just as it is fundamental to the relationship between politicians and public servants. Some governments have really surprised people on coming into office but that has never worked out very well. So whether people like us or not, they know what to expect from us.

Looking ahead, good public sector management will be critical in the years to come. Around the world, governments are facing persistent budget deficits and a growing debt burden they will be struggling with for years. Yet their citizens are rightly expecting the sort of twenty-first-century services they get from private sector industries competing aggressively for their business, like banks and airlines. The combination of these two forces will place governments and public servants around the world under constant pressure to deliver better services for less money.

New Zealand is no different. We are in a new environment that will persist for at least the next decade. The mid 2000s were characterised by the idea that big increases in government spending, dispensed across a whole range of areas and in a relatively untargeted way, could transform society. According to this view, the sheer weight of spending would eventually prevail; however, that particular experiment ran out of money in 2008 with little genuinely transformational to show for it.

Public management in the foreseeable future will be focused on determining which public services and income-support measures are the most effective, and working out how to provide those within a tightly constrained budget. It will be focused on presenting a service that is far more coordinated than it is now. New Zealanders do not live in government departments and they do not always understand the demarcations between different arms of government. To them, the government is one big organisation that should be able to help them when they need it. And they are right—it should.

Technology will make that goal more achievable. It is important that new technology is not just tacked onto current business practices. Rather, it should facilitate change in those business practices. And public management will be focused on getting results.

We have been very clear with the public service about what we want it to focus on. In March 2012, I announced a set of results I want to see achieved over the next five years. They are not everything the Government is doing, or everything the Government thinks is important. But they are results for which I want to see real progress. They involve tackling some of the longstanding, difficult issues we have in this country. And they tend to fall between or across the responsibilities of individual government departments, which is part of the reason they are difficult to tackle. Many readers, especially New Zealanders, will be familiar with these 10 results and with the targets attached to each of them. The targets are quite ambitious. Some of them are, for example

- to reduce by 30 per cent the number of people on a working-age benefit for more than 12 months
- to reduce the incidence of rheumatic fever by two-thirds
- to reduce the violent crime rate by 20 per cent.

I make no apologies for having high expectations. I do not want targets that are easy to reach. I want people to have to stretch, and feel uncomfortable, and change the way they have always done things, in order to reach the targets. And the Government will back them in doing that.

I have appointed a minister to lead each of the 10 results and a public service chief executive has been made accountable for demonstrating real progress against his or her result. We are giving the public sector the flexibility, the encouragement and the mandate to make real change.

I certainly do not underestimate the challenges involved in this new approach. The targets are difficult, and to reach them means changing the way the public sector functions. In the past it has almost operated as a loose federation of separate agencies. In the future it will have to operate much more as an integrated system. I am delighted to say the leadership of the public service has been very supportive of this new approach. At times during the process of developing the results program they were at least as ambitious as ministers were. That is a great sign that things needed to change and that in fact they will change.

I would like now to discuss the Canterbury earthquakes, our response to them and the lessons we have learnt from that response. Governments on both sides of the Tasman have been tested by disasters quite frequently in recent years. Australia has experienced the Victorian bushfires and the Queensland floods. In New Zealand, we have had earthquakes.

The first Canterbury earthquake struck in the early hours of Saturday, 4 September 2010. Damage and liquefaction were widespread. But when we look back at that event with the benefit of hindsight, it's clear that in many ways we were lucky. We were lucky the earthquake happened at 4 am, when most people were not out and about. We were lucky that while people were injured, no-one lost their life. And we were lucky for another reason that we could not have known at the time: that we would be practised and ready when a far more destructive earthquake struck a few months later.

On 22 February 2011, 185 people were killed in one of this country's worst natural disasters. It is the kind of event governments spend years preparing for, but in truth you never really know you are ready until the day comes. In Canterbury, we saw the benefits of good preparation and planning. The immediate response was well coordinated, with clear leadership structures that were widely understood. People knew what their roles were and set about getting things done.

Beyond the initial emergency response, the Government faced a huge number of challenges. There were accommodation needs; questions over whether employers could keep their businesses open; and major infrastructure needs like water, wastewater, electricity and roads. On the ground, the public sector was forced to find new ways to deliver services. I am pleased to say that in adversity, the public sector really stepped up to the plate. A healthy amount of freedom was given to frontline staff to get things done—and they did.

The Government also moved rapidly to address the many policy issues we faced. For example, we had a support package for employers and employees, including subsidies, available less than a week after the earthquake. It was crucial to keep the lines of communication open between employers and employees in order to preserve jobs, so we designed the package quickly and erred on the side of generosity rather than having stringent rules.

Another example was the Government's residential red zone offer to property owners. This involved the Government offering to purchase properties on the worst affected land at their current rating valuation. The scheme enabled homeowners to move on with their lives quickly. There were many other policies developed in those conditions and sometimes we pushed people very hard. It will not surprise you that there were some robust conversations at times— because, to some people, it appeared things could not be done as rapidly as we wished. But we got there. We got there because people were innovative and flexible.

It is now 17 months since the destructive earthquake on 22 February and as a government we have been examining the lessons we can take from it, particularly around how the public sector operates. The kind of innovation we saw is what we would like to see from the public sector in ordinary times—not just in times of disaster. Collaboration *between* agencies was a feature, and this extended to involving the private sector, non-governmental organisations (NGOs) and representatives of the public alongside government. There was greater sharing of information between agencies, and more sharing of resources. People were agile and showed initiative. They came up with solutions that focused firmly on what the people of Canterbury actually needed. The challenge now is to take that innovative approach and apply it to the public sector when we are not in a time of crisis—and I think the public sector is open to that.

The final point I would like to make about Canterbury is that the earthquake response has taken us into new territory as a government. We have learned some valuable lessons from overseas disaster recoveries, but have very much taken decisions that fit the New Zealand context. Our response has included appointing a minister, Gerry Brownlee, to specifically oversee the recovery. We have passed legislation to give additional powers to central government and we set up a new government agency, the Canterbury Earthquake Recovery Authority, or CERA, to provide leadership and coordination. CERA has wide powers, which were the source of some contention when we passed the necessary legislation. We were conscious to strike the right balance between getting things done and having adequate checks and balances around the organisation.

I believe we got that balance right. There is still a lot to be done in Canterbury but we are making good progress.

3. Foreseeable Shocks and the Critical Challenges Facing Humanity in the Twenty-First Century

Pierre-Alain Schieb

My contribution to this volume is about the notion of foreseeable shocks and what their consequences or implications are for risk governance. But I have expanded the title to its current form because the chapter is also a discerning conversation about a new class of global risk, the likes of which we have not seen before—at least over the course of the postwar generation.

For the past 18 years, I have belonged to the International Futures Programme (IFP) of the Organisation for Economic Cooperation and Development (OECD), which is a slightly different animal to, say, the community structure of the OECD or the working parties in the OECD. In contrast to these institutions, the IFP has a number of degrees of freedom to select themes and to invite international organisations, NGOs and members of the private sector to collaborate with us. We are also to a large extent a self-funded program, with 95 per cent of our budget coming from voluntary contributions.

Unlike other OECD institutions, however, we don't need all 34 member countries to be aligned about priorities. Consequently, we can have six, seven or 10 countries help decide what should be our next pioneering or pilot project. I insist on this point because if you think about future-proofing the state, the first lesson is that one way or the other governments in member countries have to have some kind of foresight strategy or foresight unit. It could be embedded at the prime ministerial level of cabinet; it could be in different departments or outside the government altogether, as with the case of think tanks in the United States.

Several models are available to try to make sure that the future is to a certain extent taken into account. And yet, the only country we know of having something related to the long-term future embedded into the constitutional by-laws is Finland. Every new Finnish prime minister coming into power has to deliver a speech to Parliament about his or her 15-year vision for Finland, and also serves on a permanent commission of the future in the Parliament.

Finland's institutional arrangements to facilitate long-term planning are exceptional in the world and raise an interesting question: how do we incentivise the political system to give more weight to the long run in a context in which all the political incentives typically lead to planning that only extends the length of an electoral cycle? This is particularly difficult—and pressing—in the current global context, where we are faced with short-term economic difficulties.

So what mechanisms, institutional arrangements or processes would I recommend at the political and national governmental levels to encourage long-term thinking? That is a difficult question, because 'one size fits all' will never work. Finland's approach may be exceptional, but there are other approaches to long-term planning around the world. In other cases, the notions of consultation and inquisitiveness—rather than a constitutional requirement as in Finland—also result in a longer-term approach to planning.

Take Sweden. When they were faced with the long-term problem of what to do with nuclear waste, the institutions in charge of the problem selected three spots on the coast of Sweden. What they then did was supply funding to local communities to ensure they had access to the expertise of independent scientists. This is an example of addressing long-term potential challenges, albeit by a different mechanism.

Probably the first deficiency we have in the government structure of OECD countries is that not all of them have the same quality of research about the policies relating to emerging issues—something we reported on in July 2011 (OECD 2011). In so doing we were trying to establish a set of policy options (everything we do is aimed at delivering policy options for governments). We also know we have to have a positive attitude to shocks, because shocks can be positive—they can be a disruptive technology, change the market structure or have other positive impacts. In this chapter, however, I will explore the kind of damaging shocks that may happen, especially the global ones.

Twelve years ago the IFP launched its first project on emerging risk, and since then we have recognised several trends: growing interdependence in the economic, environmental and social spheres; increased interconnectedness and also complexity of systems; and an increased concentration of assets and population.

Two notes on this: first, even if you do not consider climate change or any change in the occurrence of important share-damaging hazards, the trend is leading to a high concentration of population and assets. This trend is growing even in OECD countries and is creating a lot of potential damage and casualties. So to a certain extent, you could split up the debate and say that even if we take constant probabilities of occurrence into account, there is still greater potential damage from any kind of event like that.

The second note is that, as you may remember in 2007, just when the subprime mortgage crisis was supposed to stop, we had a new economic factor due to globalisation, which was that economists were starting to recognise a notion of synchronisation of economies on a global scale. And I am reminded of this with the current debt crisis many countries are facing, because a possible consequence of this high level of debt is that we could again see a kind of synchronisation of microeconomic trends—but this time in the declining trend. This would be very harmful, and is something I will explore later in this chapter, because there is a big difference between what you usually call a large-scale disaster and a global shock.

What constitutes a global shock? First, you need a vector, itself characterised by the notion of mobility—whether it be the mobility of people, the mobility of money, the mobility of information, the mobility of viruses or the mobility of goods. Often a high level of mobility occurs because many of the potentially damaging global shocks are local shocks drifting or cascading into other continents or countries.

Returning to the notion of population concentration, even in OECD member states people are continuing to migrate from the country to the city (currently 78 per cent of OECD members' populations live in cities; within 10 or 15 years that figure will be above 80 per cent). Moreover, migratory trends within these countries cannot be characterised just by urbanisation: within many OECD countries there is also a trend of transmigration to coastal areas—particularly among retirees. Population concentration increases your vulnerability to shocks.

Let me now move on to an example of future-proofing—in this case, concerning aviation safety. Single European Sky ATM Research (SESAR) is the codename for Europe, and NextGen is the codename for the United States. The only thing you have to understand about these new air traffic-control systems is that they are examples of conversion technology. They represent a new level of complexity, whereby assistance is given but a pilot is not needed. (I am a pilot myself and I have learned that now I have become a mission manager, I will just run computers—something that is perhaps not so pleasing for both the passenger and myself.)

Despite my personal reservations with these developments, they are obviously highly beneficial because they are leading to safer travel with fewer collisions; the aim is a shorter separation time when you land or take off at an airport. Although this is a good aim, it also leaves the regulators with a more difficult task, because the systems won't be fully operational for 15 years; until that time there will be two systems in place. So although the new technology will eventually be beneficial, its rollout is potentially causing problems for the regulators.

The Future Global Shocks Project

The process we had for this OECD project was to have a steering group of delegates from 15 governments, with the additional input of five or six multinational companies. In this way we like to always have a blend of academics, research institutes, private sector representatives and governments to make recommendations, and to make our analytical component as robust as possible. To this end the steering group decided to go with five case studies. These five studies are not necessarily of the most important or even most damaging events, but rather represent an important sample of global trends.

To select the case studies we first consulted the World Economic Forum, which every year produces a risk map on a global scale. This provided an easy starting point to select our five case studies. When consulting the risk map, we were particularly interested in cases that illustrated the propagation of local to global shocks and rapid-onset shocks, and also complexity theory agent-based models, which look for tipping points.

Of 25–35 potential threats, we selected the following five case studies: pandemics, financial crises, cyber security, solar storms and social unrest. Of course, pandemics are a good example of special propagation, because they usually start in one place and then become a kind of global shock. When it reaches this stage, we know that part of the response is dealing with quarantine, and closing airports, schools and so on. So it's an example of spatial, geographical propagation.

Solar storms are an interesting case, with a range of possibly damaging consequences. These fall into three categories: spacecraft effects; ionospheric effects (concerning the atmosphere between the stratosphere and the exosphere); and ground effects. Spacecraft effects include things like astronaut radiation, solar cell damage and solar flare radiation; ionospheric effects include enhanced ionospheric currents and disturbances, aircraft crew and passenger radiation and navigation problems; ground effects include geomagnetically induced currents in power systems, signal scintillation, HF radio wave disturbance, pipeline corrosion and disturbed reception. In the worst-case scenario, a solar storm could lead to the collapse of 400 000-volt transformers and with them the entire power system.

NASA and the US National Academy of Sciences have predicted that in such an event it would take four hours for the first effects to assert themselves; within a month there would be a complete collapse of the economy and society. Recovery from such an event could take years. Moreover, we simply do not have a stockpile of quality transformers anywhere, so you cannot simply replace them. There are ways of shielding transformers, but this can be extremely costly.

There have already been examples in history of this type of disaster occurring. The Carrington Event of 1859 was a geomagnetic storm that produced the largest known solar flare. At the time there were no powerlines, computers or airlines, but there was extensive damage to the telegraph system in Europe and North America. We have seen recent geomagnetic storms cause damage in Sweden, Canada and parts of the United States, but nothing compared with the scale of the Carrington Event. In fact, these recent storms are estimated to be one-quarter as powerful as the Carrington Event. Another storm on the scale of the Carrington Event would lead to extensive damage.

The ash cloud over Europe in 2010 caused by the eruption of the Icelandic volcano Eyjafjallajökull was a good example of the danger of having just one disaster-prediction model—in this case, based in the United Kingdom. The principal problem was that neighbouring countries affected by the ash cloud had no access to the model so had no way of observing where the cloud was moving, the size of the ash particles, how they would affect aeroplane engines and so on.

This created a difficult situation for many countries, and is probably why most of Western and Central Europe chose to close their airports. The havoc Eyjafjallajökull wreaked on Europe's air traffic was a good example of what happens when you lack resources on a global or even multilateral scale, especially during the crisis itself.

Still on the subject of aviation safety, the United Kingdom recently published a Chatham House report concerning everything that relies on airfreight transport. The report concluded that if we were to face another volcanic eruption that produced a cloud that stayed for months rather than weeks, there would be all kinds of implications for the economic system.

I will now move to cyber security. Cyber security was the subject of a recent report by our team in the United Kingdom. They reached the same conclusion as our counterparts in the United States and France: there is no case for global shocks on the basis of a cyber security attack, at least in the next 10 years or so.

When this UK report was published in January 2011, we had more than 100 quick reactions all over the world. They were mainly comments made by journalists or experts who believed we had underestimated the risk of cyber attacks, and that they could lead to global shocks. They were confused by the fact you can have a strong attack on Australia or perhaps a strong attack targeting a particular company without it being classed as a global shock. But even though these events can be devastating for the victims, it is not a global shock if it doesn't have worldwide economic ramifications. After we received these criticisms, we put more in our report about what the difference is between a large-scale disaster and a long-term global shock.

Global Shocks: Lessons to learn

This brings us to the first of my concluding points: a global shock is quite different from a large-scale disaster. The second lesson we need to learn is that while we think there are increased opportunities for global shocks to occur in the twenty-first century, society at large is now quite resilient. Even if the preconditions for a global crisis as I have stated earlier in this chapter are met, there is now a high premium on international cooperation.

But we cannot take this for granted. First, there needs to be a greater level of international cooperation in terms of scientific mechanisms to meet potential threats. This also means more monitoring of potential threats. Second, to effectively combat potential threats there needs to be a continuation of projects; it doesn't work to discontinue projects every few years. Instead, governments need to be consistent over time—and climate change is a pertinent reminder of this.

Third, diversity is crucial: you don't want to put all your eggs in one basket. Because if, for example, you have software that is in 85 per cent of global computers, we think that's a big risk. In such situations the system should be dismantled so as to avoid a global engineering failure. We don't want that kind of monopoly.

Another recommendation is the stockpiling of supplies in case of a crisis—be it of food or whatever. Undoubtedly this would be very costly, but it probably could be done on a regional basis. The success of such a scheme would depend on having a very accurate real-time system to know where those resources are and what is in them.

But building reserves and building redundancy, of course, run contrary to all the trends in the public and private sectors over the past 30 years. In a time of economic constraint, convincing people to do this can be difficult.

So it's a combination of having real physical reserves and tracking where those reserves are and what is in them. But who will pay for them? During a global shock you cannot rely on your nice neighbour to provide potable water, generators and spare parts; perhaps the private sector could help foot the bill. This goes even further for vaccines and rare resources; we know that when it comes to pandemics, the countries that are home to the larger drug companies feel they are quite safe.

If you don't have a drug company in your own country, however, you start to question who will have priority for the delivery of vaccines. These are the things countries and regions must start thinking about, because when a crisis strikes, you can't rely on others to help you sustain your population's needs.

Getting back to the issue of global science mechanisms, one of the big questions is: who will monitor them? It should be done affordably, so international cooperation is critical—because if you share the cost you have no redundancy; no country is in the mood to do it themselves.

We need, then, to inject more science during crises to better understand what is happening and to invest in real-time models to evaluate the location of resources or evacuation plans and other aspects of preparedness. So you have a range of questions about this, and, as I said, if you have more diversity you need less redundancy, and you are not competing for the same resources as your neighbours.

The same goes for the private sector. In the private sector the key factor will be sharing data; the sector needs to get over its current preoccupation with confidentiality and trade secrets. One way we can start to make this happen is to ask the private sector to release some of the duties regarding deregulation, and to provide greater access to their transactions: perhaps transactions of their system or environmental transactions. It could be a trade-off: we give the private sector more freedom in certain areas if they give us more access to their data.

Reference

Organisation for Economic Cooperation and Development (OECD). 2011. *Future Global Shocks: Improving Risk Governance* (Paris: OECD). Available from: <http://www.oecd.org/governance/48329024.pdf>.

4. Governments Fit for the Future: Lessons in building resilience

The Honourable Jocelyne Bourgon

In this chapter I will explore the topic of building more resilient communities and public institutions, drawn from the lessons of the 'New Synthesis Project' (Bourgon 2011). The theme of resilience is very much related to the theme of the social context or landscape within which governments are called upon to serve, the increasing complexity of the issues they have to deal with, and the increasing volatility of the environment within which they have to make policy decisions and take action.

For some, the concept of resilience brings to mind images of catastrophic failures, natural disasters and pandemic diseases, because resilience is on such strong display in those circumstances. But I prefer to explore the concept of resilience in a softer way. Yes, it is strongly on display when you say a society is able to weather a crisis and emerge from it stronger than before. I would argue, however, that resilience is also on display when countries and public institutions show they are able to adapt, evolve and transform themselves in response to changing circumstances—and are able to do it in a manner that *avoids* crises and *reduces* the risk of failure, in particular when the costs of these failures will be borne by society as a whole.

The first point to make about resilience is that it is built gradually over a long period. This is what is needed if it is going to be in abundant supply when countries need it most. Resilience is found in self-reliant individuals who are able to take charge of their lives and find solutions to the problems they are facing; it is found in the bonds and the relationships of trust between individuals, families, communities and public institutions. And it is found in public institutions which are able to adapt to changing circumstances and coevolve with society.

I believe that focusing on resilience can help us shed a different light on the role of government in society, and the relationship between government, citizens and society. In the course of this chapter, I will draw freely from a project conducted over a couple of years that has explored a new synthesis of public administration. Called the New Synthesis Project, it involved senior practitioners and academics from six countries working as partners. By bringing together a representative sample of national public administrations, we were able to benefit from the richness of diversity of socioeconomic circumstances, history, ideology, culture, language and so on.

Countries were selected to give a truly global spread: there are two from the Americas (Canada and Brazil); two from Europe (The Netherlands and the United Kingdom); and two from the Asia-Pacific region (Singapore and Australia). But there is also a huge degree of diversity in this matrix, reflected in the vastly different geographies, demographics, democratic histories and economic situations that these six countries have. And this diversity was the starting point of our research project about governance in the twenty-first century: are those differences significant enough to change our practices, and if so, what do these different approaches entail?

Building on Strong Foundations for Resilient Capacities

We live in a world which is increasingly complex, volatile and prone to global cascading failure. As a consequence, governments today are called upon not simply to do what is predictable (to do it with increasing productivity, performance and efficiency), but they are also expected to effectively address those issues that are beyond what can be predicted, and to do this in a way that improves the capacity of society to absorb shock and disturbances, and to prosper in all circumstances.

I would argue that the task of those who are in government today is more challenging than ever before. There is now a long list of potential crises a government can face—some predictable and preventable, others not. Governments today must accept and recognise that there is every reason to believe that the frequency and the scale of shock from crises and disturbances will continue to increase.

When it comes to building resilience, there is no doubt there are many people across the globe who have invested years of effort in conducting relevant public service reform and exploring why we are not better prepared and equipped to anticipate and prevent crises. These people strive to steer their respective countries in a way so that they can prosper and adapt to changing circumstances. They have adopted business principles to improve productivity; centred many policies on citizens, with greater focus on user satisfaction; and they have eliminated sizeable government deficits (although post GFC many other nations have to relearn how to balance their books).

No-one is disputing the commitment of the men and women around the world who have been leading ambitious public sector reforms aimed at increasing the resilience of their states; but we need to delve into this issue more deeply. The reformers have given us solid foundations but these are insufficient to address some of the complex problems we are now facing. Their reforms did not prepare government for the problems that stem from living in a post-industrial world. So, in spite of all these reformist efforts, in spite of all this energy and courage, we need to ask ourselves: is there a systemic reason that explains why it is still so difficult to depart from the traditional ways of governing our societies?

To address this question, it is valuable to consider where the governance system in our respective countries comes from. In most cases, the system of public administration in place has evolved over hundreds of years, taking its modern shape from the late nineteenth century and early twentieth century. This period was characterised by a process of change related to industrialisation and democratisation. Looking at the systems of public administration that are deeply entrenched across the OECD, you find fundamental institutions and conventions that have served their countries well and have given them strong foundations. But these systems also beg the question: what is the ongoing contribution of these institutions and conventions to governing in the future? From the 'industrial age' we inherited a system of public administration premised on a political system governed by the rule of law. Together these systems value due process and a delegated authority that are the bases for control, accountability and performance management; they became systems ideally suited to the mass production of public services.

At the same time, a particular strength in some circumstances can become a weakness in others. While traditional systems of public administration may be ideally suited to the mass production of public services, they have found difficulty in anticipating what is needed for a society to adapt to that which is not foreseen and not predicted. Hence, our starting point in the New Synthesis Project was to recognise that traditional approaches of public administration leave governments in a reactive position when it comes to unpredictable shocks and crises. Therefore, we needed to improve our capacities to anticipate, to introduce proactive interventions and course corrections, and to build capacities to absorb shocks and disturbances.

There is more to the role of our public services than the programs they administer and the services they provide. They serve a broader public purpose, and whatever they do has wider ramifications beyond the authority and responsibility they operate within—in particular, they contribute to system-wide results reflected in societal results. To achieve these public results, we build self-reliant individuals and resilient communities; we develop a sense of civic spirit that is conducive to collective actions and a sense of working together to achieve better results at a lower overall cost. A country with these attributes is better positioned not only in predictable and favourable circumstances, but also in unpredictable and chaotic circumstances.

Yet many problems in society exceed the capacity of government when working alone. Their traditional powers, such as the authority to legislate and to enforce laws or powers to tax and spend, are not sufficient to be effective on their own. Governments need to work with and through others to achieve public results. All the instruments of state have to be used to lever greater collective capacity in society to achieve better results and allow the entire society to make contributions to the value-adding chain. This opens up an expanding space of possibilities as governments contemplate the complex decisions necessary to achieve improved societal results.

Improving Institutional Capacities

In order to focus on these broader possibilities, we need to improve our institutional capacities—the very institutions that govern society that evolved over a long period. We need to strengthen the organisational capacity of our public sector organisations so they are not only efficient but also contributing to future societal benefits. We want them to have the capacity to work collaboratively with each other (multi-institutional) and to engage across the community and private sectors.

We also need a society and government able to innovate, shape so-called 'emergent solutions', and to find and address the complex problems we are facing. Moreover, no matter how smart governments are, they need to develop a very strong adaptive capacity because there will be unpredictable shocks and crises. If they are successful in escaping the traditional triangular definition of public administration (based on the rule of law, the separation of politics from administration, and a merit-based career public service characterised by political neutrality and anonymity), they will have something that is much closer to a dynamic and adaptive system, where government transforms society and must be transformed by society, and where the government adapts to changing circumstances on an ongoing basis.

Institutions, then, are not necessarily fit for the challenges they confront or face ahead. I will cite two examples briefly. The European Union is in trouble because the institutions that have been created are not commensurate to the problems they are facing. There is an increasing gap between the aspirations, the challenges at hand and the capacity of the collective institutions that have been created. The United States is also facing a crisis of authority, because the institutions they have created to introduce checks and balances to serve the collective interests have lost sight of this purpose. The strength of 'blocking' interest groups is now greater than the collective instrument that should give effect to the will of the majority.

In short, no institutional arrangement is appropriate for all time: it needs to be able to adapt to changing circumstances. That is part of the challenge for people in government—not only to deal with the immediate policy issue or firefighting crisis of the day, but also to make sure that as the guardian of public institutions, we bring in the capacity to adapt on an ongoing basis. I would venture a hypothesis: the developed countries that have been the most successful with the previous concept of governance may find it more difficult to adapt than those which are inventing and creating a different model of governance.

Framing an Adaptive System of Governance

The conclusion to this point is that different times require different ways of thinking, different mental maps and forms of openness to different ways of doing things. I believe we need a new analytical framework to create a government fit for the future, and we need to work out the interconnections between the four essential functions of governance: *compliance*, *performance*, *emergence* and *resilience* (as shown in Figures 4.1 and 4.2, spanning the continuum between predictability and unpredictability). We need a compliance function that we know well; we also need a performance function to deliver outputs, an emergence function to anticipate likely scenarios and a resilience function to build enduring capacity. These four functions must work together to produce an adaptive government (Figure 4.2), and in the rest of this chapter I will explore some of the innovative practices that are emerging as powerful connectors of these four functions: anticipatory abilities and adaptability through co-creation and co-production. These connectors increase the adaptive capacity of government, and contribute to the government's resilience.

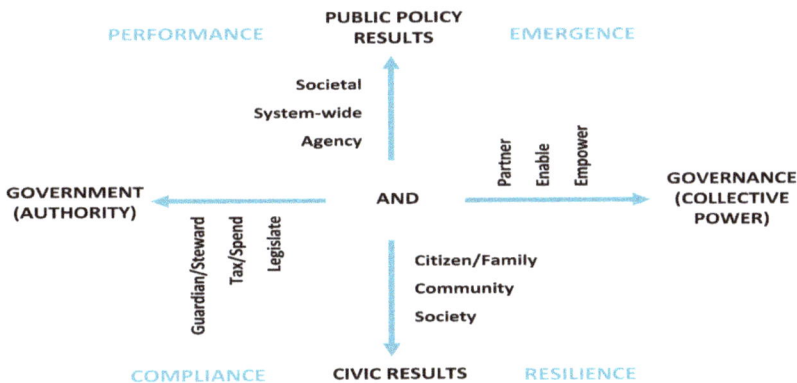

Figure 4.1 Functions of government

Source: ANZSOG, after Bourgon 2011.

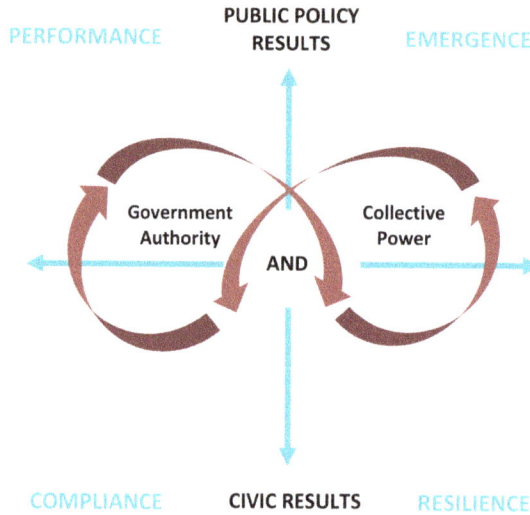

Figure 4.2 An Adaptive System of Government

Source: ANZSOG, after Bourgon 2011.

We need an emergence function to be able to anticipate and to introduce course correction and to do it before time. In particular, when the cost of failure will be borne by society as a whole, we need to be able to shape solutions in a more organic way than we have been able to do in the past. We need constantly to be aware of this insight and conserve energy; we need the stability and predictability provided by institutions so we can cope with the volatility that is out there. We need to be able to work across and we need to be able to adapt. So what are the important connectors that link these four essential functions?

First, anticipation is a key quality if we want to prevent crises, and crisis prevention is far less costly than crisis recovery. I do not think our recent track record on crisis prevention has been as good as it could be. Singapore has a long tradition of looking far into the future and of long-term strategic planning. They developed the Risk Assessment and Horizon Scanning (RAHS) program and set up the Centre for Strategic Futures, both in 2009. These anticipatory ventures, perhaps the most sophisticated of their type in the world, enable Singapore to combine the strength of scanning and scenario planning with a strong focus on experimentation and innovation. Singapore's ability to detect emergent signals gives them an advantage to initiate proactive intervention.

Other countries are undertaking similar futures exercises and foresight scenario planning initiatives. Finland has adopted a more political process involving an all-party parliamentary committee looking ahead 25 to 50 years. It is a public process and they engage civil society in a conversation about the future of their country. These initiatives give a country the advantage of better anticipation; however, countries which are investing in these practices over a long period derive more benefit than just the capacity to anticipate. They develop a high level of public understanding of the challenges faced in the country, the consequences of various choices and the trade-offs. That awareness facilitates consensus building, it improves the capacity to align leaders from the public, private and civil sectors, and improves the likelihood of success for an ambitious collective agenda.

By improving the capacity to focus on the future, we produce a long chain of interrelated results that improves the government's adaptive capacity more generally. In particular, we improve the government's capacity to blend short-term considerations with long-term actions, and also society's capacity to develop an awareness of what might be a preferable future. So we have created a process of dynamic change, transforming government and society. This process builds resilience including the capacity to adapt to changing circumstances.

Second, co-creation is another important form of connection linking the four functions. Co-creation is the coming together of end users, beneficiaries, interested parties and service providers for the purpose of shaping, testing and experimenting with policy response in practice. It would be a mistake to prescribe co-creation in all circumstances as there will always be situations where governments are best positioned to act on their own. Governments are best positioned to act on their own when they can define the issue, when they have the necessary tools and can enact reform with confidence.

Let me provide an example of co-creation from Denmark. Denmark has a range of laws and programs supporting people with disabilities, but the Government faced a traditional dilemma: unlimited or growing demand, and limited or declining resources. In the traditional space policymakers have few options: they can explore how to do more with less; they can provide fewer services or make a case to inject more resources. The range of possible solutions in the traditional space is narrower than it needs to be; however, if governments explore the possibilities of co-creation then many more options are possible. In the Danish case, the first step was to map out each process or stage step undertaken by potential users—those trying to qualify for the services. The mapping report found major problems and paradoxically argued that a citizen would have to be healthy to go through all the hoops that are required in order to qualify for a program that is aimed at supporting disabled people. It also found public servants themselves had to go through many loops to provide the services for people with disabilities.

Having done the client-mapping exercise and provided that to the stakeholder group, it was not hard to come up with better ways of doing things—a case of co-creation in practice. They tested various ideas and improvements and established they were working before they rolled them out nationally. They have evaluated the results from the first year, demonstrating that they have achieved better results with lower costs—an impressive achievement for a government operating under fiscal constraints. What is more impressive is that they have dramatically improved the satisfaction levels of their users. The Danes were prepared to test their ideas even if they could not establish direct causality between their proposals and the outcomes. They were prepared to experiment and explore co-creation because they believed they could come up with a better policy response.

Hence, public agencies have to be able to operate as experimentation platforms, which many of our agencies and departments have not been designed to do. They have neither the policies nor the infrastructure to facilitate that end. They are imbued in traditional ways of doing policy: undertaking research, devising policy options based on the best available knowledge, mapping out which options to take, and finally taking the option to a minister for a decision. These agencies generally do not have a safe space where policy workers can go and test ideas in practice or transform delivery processes, such as the Danish 'MindLab' initiative provides.

Good policy formulation depends on monitoring the implementation stages to examine whether the policy is achieving the intended result and/or becoming aware of unintended consequences. Hence, it is a more experimental and long-term process. We need to capture the implementation knowledge from stakeholders so we continue to improve the policy response—this gives policymakers a stronger adaptive capacity but also builds resilience. It builds resilience because it involves all stakeholders in a manner whereby they share responsibility for the result. And it develops a much more active relationship between government, users and beneficiaries.

Another possible connector is co-production. Co-creation of a solution by a group of diverse actors does not necessarily mean that government is obliged afterwards to co-produce the service with them. Co-creation and co-production could occur a long time apart and could involve different groups. In Bourgon (2011), there are many examples of co-production. Some are major undertakings and others are relatively minor. In Singapore a prison manager used co-production to improve the successful reintegration of inmates. The manager reconceptualised the role of the prison, going from a focus on the agency's narrow results (the safekeeping of the inmates), to asking where does the prison add value in system-wide or societal terms? Once the prison authorities began to consider how systemic and societal factors and a range of outside actors affected results, they were better able to cooperate with these actors. In this case, mapping out individual prisoner's circumstances prompted prison authorities and stakeholders to conclude that they had to change public opinion about the benefits of facilitating more effective reintegration of inmates into the community. This new approach made it possible for employers to feel comfortable in offering jobs to former inmates, which in turn increased the confidence of inmates, who believed they had gained a second chance and a way to gain skills and support themselves once released. It also made the families of inmates more confident in supporting the inmate while they were still incarcerated. Ultimately, this process created a long chain of shared responsibilities. It produced a collective effort to achieve the intended results, which no single actor could do on their own (not the prison system, the families, employers or the community). This example is now supported by evidence from 10 years of data. Much progress has been achieved over the 10 years in the successful reintegration of ex-offenders, and the reduction of recidivism.

The second example concerns the transfer of welfare payments to the 50 million poorest families in Brazil, many living in remote communities. Traditional programs alleviating poverty were run out of individual departments, which addressed various aspects of the problem such as education, family and health problems. All of these departments ran good programs, but were effectively siloed in their approaches. Each program addressed one aspect or one consequence of poverty: poor children not going to school because they are put in the labour force, high child mortality because of poor health, and lack of attention to women during pregnancy, among others. Each program had a long list of factors that contributed to their success. They were well managed, complied with all the requirements of central agencies in a traditional way, and reported back to Parliament. The only problem was that poverty was not decreasing. It is the irony of public administration that officials can sometimes comply with every legal and political requirement and miss the mark of a program's intended purpose, which in this case was to reduce poverty. In Brazil's case, program redesign involved integrating all the services, removing virtually all the conditionality of the programs, and empowering the head of the family to receive the money and use it in the manner felt to be most appropriate—a huge act of faith. The head of the family would become an active co-producer in the achievement of results.

Media coverage of the policy change was ferociously hostile: it portrayed considerable sums of money being given to people who ostensibly could not be trusted; it suggested the money would be used for alcohol, drugs and other antisocial purposes. It took the strength of President Lula da Silva to proclaim that the Government refused to design a program based on distrust, and his administration would fix any problems whenever they found them along the way. Three program evaluations have now been completed: one by the United Nations, one internal program review and another by the World Bank/

International Monetary Fund (IMF). The program is now a source of inspiration to others in Latin America, even though it was challenged politically when it started. Furthermore, during the last election, every major Brazilian party publicly supported this as the best program they had to reduce poverty.

A third example involves the city of Charlotte in the US State of North Carolina, which reveals the potential for technology to enable self-organisation and to contribute to the adaptive capacity of society and build its resilience. Charlotte has a large, and therefore expensive, energy consumption footprint. The traditional approaches to manage energy usage by governments and their bureaucratic administrations involve taxation powers and pricing, legislation and regulation. Instead of adopting such traditional approaches, the Charlotte City Council forged an agreement with the owners of commercial buildings in the central part of the city to install large television screens in the foyers of these buildings that displayed to residents or workers up-to-the-minute information about the amount of energy being consumed by each building. Generally, these screens showed the energy consumption from the previous day and the previous week, and projected the present day's energy consumption as a way of showing users of the building how their behaviour was changing energy usage. Based on the initial phases of this initiative, the managers of the project expect a 20 per cent reduction of energy consumption within the first year.

A similar, smaller example of the benefits of co-production using technology occurred in downtown London over attempts to reduce the number of accidents involving cyclists in the area. Instead of adopting a traditional policy route to identify the problem—that is, creating a committee, commissioning a study, submitting to a parliamentary committee, taking the recommendations and then shaping policy based on the final report—what the City of London council did was simply to issue regular public data about the location of cycling accidents downtown. The local cycling association did the rest. They created an app that provided up-to-the-minute advice to cyclists about dangerous routes, congestion, what to avoid and how to navigate. The results were remarkable and the number of cycling accidents has been reduced. In both of these examples, no law was created or changed, no subsidy was given, no new tax was imposed; yet noticeable results were achieved. Public administration was used intelligently to encourage people to pursue their individual interest in a manner that also enhanced the collective interest.

What has emerged from these examples is that co-production starts from the fundamental notion not only that a user or a beneficiary of a government service should be considered a 'cost' to government in the short-term, but also that in the longer term, with proper investment in co-produced programs, users can become real assets. Moreover, if these assets are put to productive use in society, the results of social programs demonstrably improve and end up costing society less overall. A third finding from these processes has been the realisation that no country is rich enough *not* to put to productive use all available assets. Our experience with co-production processes has transformed our concept of service delivery: the responsibility for creating and achieving public results is not just a matter for government; it is a shared responsibility and requires a collective effort.

Significantly, new technologies have the potential to achieve an array of results in self-organisation and self-reliance. We have perhaps only just begun to explore the full potential of technology-enabled self-organisation. Governments could use these technologies to assist them to become 'fit for the future'. Technology is potentially more powerful and more cost-effective than creating a new funded program. It can be more efficient and more instrumental in changing behaviour than legislating, without the burden of compliance and enforcement that legislated approaches entail.

Conclusion

So, to conclude, resilience is ultimately a test of our capacity to adapt, to evolve and to prosper in a turbulent world. As I said at the beginning, resilience is not found in one place or in one format; indeed, paradoxically, the more despair and crises occur the better because resilience only develops through experience and learning. It is found in self-reliant individuals able to take charge of their future and solve problems. It is found in an innovative society able to shape emergent solutions to the complex problems of our time. It is found in relationships of trust and the social capital we accumulate over a long period. And it is in public institutions which are able to adapt to changing circumstances, because they are not fit for all time.

So, to paraphrase a famous quote, we cannot solve the problems we ourselves have created using the same thinking that was used when we created them. In this contribution, I tried to address the issue of what are the capacities of government administrations worldwide to give themselves different mental maps of our collective capacity, which in turn encourages more collective responsibility and inventive solutions to the constantly changing challenges of our complex post-industrial world.

Reference

Bourgon, J. 2011. *A New Synthesis of Public Administration: Serving in the 21st Century* (Montreal: McGill-Queen's University Press).

5. Governing for the Future: What governments can do

Peter Ho (Hak Ean)

On 25 February 2003, the Severe Acute Respiratory Syndrome (SARS) virus entered Singapore through three women who had returned from Hong Kong with symptoms of atypical pneumonia. The virus then spread with frightening speed through the hospital system. It confounded our medical authorities in the beginning. They did not know how the virus spread and why it spread so aggressively. The fatality rate was shocking. By the time the SARS crisis was declared over in Singapore, 33 people had died of the 238 who had been infected.

'Black Swans'

SARS was an unexpected 'black swan' for Singapore. Nassim Nicholas Taleb (2008) described a 'black swan' as a hard-to-predict event with a large impact. Indeed, it was a frightening time for Singapore. Overnight, visitor arrivals plunged and the entire tourism industry came to a grinding halt. SARS severely disrupted the Singaporean economy, leading to a contraction and a quarter-long recession that year. There are many lessons to be learnt from the SARS crisis of 2003, but I would like to highlight one, in order to set the context for my contribution to this volume of essays. It is that other 'black swans' will surprise us, time and again, as much if not more than SARS.

In recent years the world seems to have been beset by a succession of strategic shocks including the destruction of the World Trade Centre on 11 September 2001, the financial and economic turbulence of 2008–09, the 2011 Japanese tsunami and nuclear meltdowns and the Eurozone crisis. I imagine the Christchurch earthquake of February 2011 was a 'black swan' for New Zealand. Furthermore, the frequency of such shocks seems to be increasing, and the amplitude of their impact appears to be growing. The question is why?

The Great Acceleration

From the middle of the twentieth century—a period sometimes called the 'Great Acceleration'—change has accelerated at a pace on a global scale that is unprecedented in history. Population growth has surged. Combined with rapid urbanisation, it has generated enormous consumer demand. The effort to meet this demand through industrialisation and mass production has had a huge but unpredictable impact on the Earth's ecosystem. Globalisation resulting from and combined with technological innovation has in turn accelerated change on all fronts—political, economic and social. Much of this change has followed unpredictable trajectories. The reason for this is 'complexity'.

Complexity

Complex is not the same as complicated. It is something very different. The natural world is complex. An engineering system like a machine or an aeroplane or a telecommunications satellite is merely complicated. Its inner workings may be hard for a layman to understand, but it is designed to perform certain predetermined functions that are repeatable. It embodies the Newtonian characteristics of predictable cause and effect.

In contrast, a complex system will not necessarily behave in a repeatable and predetermined manner. Cities are complex systems, as are human societies. The Earth's ecology is also a complex system. Political systems are complex. Countries are complex. The world as a whole is complex and unordered. In all likelihood, a complicated world has not existed for a very long time—if it ever did.

The Great Acceleration has seen huge leaps forward in technology—in telecommunications, the Internet and transportation—leading to vastly increased trade and the movement of people around the world. But the connections and feedback loops resulting from the Great Acceleration have greatly increased complexity at the global level.

The ancient Chinese philosopher Lao Tzu instinctively grasped the complex nature of the world we live in when he wrote in the *Tao Te Ching* (or *The Way*) that 'everything is connected, and everything relates to each other'. But connections and interactions within a complex system are extremely difficult to detect, are inexplicable and emergent. Efforts to model complex systems, such as the Club of Rome's famous model of economic and population growth, have not proved very useful. Unlike in a complicated system, the components of a complex system interact in ways that defy a deterministic, linear analysis. As a result, we are constantly surprised and shocked by 'black swans' and other unknown unknowns.

Wicked Problems

Unfortunately, complexity not only generates 'black swans', but also gives rise to what the political scientist Horst Rittel (Rittel and Webber 1973) called 'wicked problems'. Wicked problems have no immediate or obvious solutions. They are large and intractable issues. They have causes and influencing factors that are not easily determined *ex ante*. They are highly complex problems because they contain many agents interacting with each other in often mystifying ways. They have many stakeholders who not only have different perspectives on the wicked problem, but also do not necessarily share the same goals.

Tackling one part of a wicked problem is more likely than not going to lead to new issues in other parts. Satisfying one stakeholder could well make the rest unhappy. A key challenge for governments is to move the many stakeholders towards a broad alignment of perspectives and goals; but this requires patience and a lot of skill in stakeholder engagement and consensus building.

Climate change is an example of a wicked problem at a global level. Pandemics are another. So are ageing populations in the developed world. Sustainable economic development, which is not unconnected to the triangular problem of food, water and energy security, is an enormous wicked problem.

In our increasingly interconnected and globalised world, such wicked problems do not manifest in a singular fashion. Their impact can and will be felt around the world, in many forms, and in many fields such as politics and economics, and in social and many other dimensions.

Retrospective Coherence

Complexity theory includes the concept of 'retrospective coherence'. The current state of affairs always makes sense when we look backwards. The current problem is logical. But this is more than saying that there is wisdom in hindsight. It is only one of many patterns that could have formed, any one of which would have been equally logical. Simply because we can explain why the current state of affairs has arisen does not mean that we are operating in a complicated and knowable world.

While what we are today is the result of many decisions taken along the way, retrospective coherence says that in a complex system, even if we were to start again and make the same decisions, there is no certainty we would end up in the same situation. This is another way of saying that applying the lessons of history is not enough to guide us down the right path into the future.

Governments which do not understand retrospective coherence will often assume that the operating environment is merely complicated, not complex—one in which cause and effect are linked such that the output can be determined from the input, in which one step leads predictably to the next. This is of course a dangerous assumption if the operating environment is complex.

Governments and Complexity

When governments ignore the complexity of their operating environment, they are at risk of assuming that policies that succeeded in the past will continue to work well in the future. They will deal with wicked problems as if they are amenable to simple and deterministic policy prescriptions. The temptation to take this approach is understandable. It is easier, requires less resources and may actually lead to positive outcomes—but only in the short term; however, government policies that do not take complexity into account can, and often do, lead to unintended consequences, with a real danger of national failure in the long run.

Unfortunately, the evidence suggests that many governments will opt to take this path, out of political expediency, because of cognitive failures or simply because they lack understanding and the tools to deal with complexity. Governments which learn to manage complexity, and how to govern in a complex operating environment, will gain a competitive advantage over those which do not. But to manage complexity requires fundamental changes to the mindset, capabilities and organisation of government.

In his book *Making Things Work: Solving Complex Problems in a Complex World*, Yaneer Bar-Yam writes that 'the most basic issue for organisational success is correctly matching the system's complexity to its environment'. This is another way of saying that the complexity of the government developing the policy should match the complexity of the system that will be affected by the policy.

Fighting a Network with a Network

Let me illustrate this with an example. On 7 December 2001, the Singaporean authorities announced the detention of several Singaporeans who were members of a previously unknown network of Islamic extremists, the pan-South-East Asian Jemaah Islamiyah (JI). JI had been plotting acts of mass terror against several targets in Singapore. Singaporeans were preparing to kill fellow Singaporeans in pursuit of demented ideological goals.

This was the 'black swan' for Singapore that literally overnight produced a wicked problem for the Government: how to deal with the threat posed by extremists who were part of a larger South-East Asian network, and who lived and worked within the community, like ordinary Singaporeans.

Someone told me in those uncertain days that you needed a network to fight a network. It was a profound observation that implicitly acknowledged that JI, as a sprawling, multilayered network, was a complex organisation.

Our response, in terms of both organisation and policy, had to match JI's complexity. It was not possible to destroy the JI network by just hunting down the leadership and decapitating it. To do so would be to deny JI's essentially complex nature.

Singapore took a whole-of-government—perhaps even a whole-of-nation—approach to the threat posed by JI. The traditional approach—of delineating the boundaries between agencies, so each would be responsible for a particular area—clearly would not work. No government agency had the full range of competencies or capabilities to deal completely with this complex threat.

Rather than go the American way by creating our own Department of Homeland Security, we decided a better way would be to strengthen coordination and integration among government agencies. We leveraged on the diverse strengths of existing agencies. This meant coordinating the counterterrorism efforts of line agencies and ministries at the operational level, while integrating strategy and policy at the whole-of-government level. This approach meant we would only have a small but active centre, the National Security Coordination Secretariat, with the capacity to drive the strategic national agenda in counterterrorism, but which would not interfere with the accountabilities of each agency.

So, many agencies were included at different levels from the security, economic and social sectors. Community groups and leaders were activated to manage potential frictions and manage communal sensitivities. In the beginning, it was a real challenge. The non-security agencies felt that this was a matter to be dealt with by the security agencies. The security agencies in turn felt that their turf was being trampled on.

Whole-of-Government

Now, looking back, this whole-of-government approach had a compelling logic. A complex and multilayered network of government agencies and non-governmental organisations had been created. The policies that were implemented were complex—both defensive and offensive, employing both hard and soft powers. We established a complex system to deal with a complex situation. It is an approach the Singaporean Government has since applied to other wicked problems like population and climate change.

Governments will need to consider how they should be organised to deal with black swans, unknown unknowns and the wicked problems that complexity generates. Creating new departments to deal with new wicked problems can be wasteful and ultimately ineffective if these creations do not contain enough organisational complexity.

Developing policies and plans to deal with such wicked problems requires the integration of diverse insights, experience and expertise. People from different organisations, both from *within* and *outside* government, have to come together to pool their knowledge in order to discover potential solutions. Cooperative mechanisms need to be set up to enable the sharing of information and to strengthen collective action.

The whole-of-government approach injects diversity and complexity into the policy process. It recognises that in complex situations, and when dealing with wicked problems, insight and good ideas are not the monopoly of single agencies or of government acting alone. It strikes a balance between the strength and stability of the formal vertical government structure and the diversity of forms of different perspectives and solutions derived from a larger and more varied horizontal network of government and national resources.

While the whole-of-government approach may be an imperative, it is not easily achieved. Governments, like any large hierarchical organisation, tend to optimise at the departmental level rather than at the whole-of-government level.

In a hierarchy, the leader at the top receives all the information and makes the decisions; but, under stress, hierarchies can be unresponsive—even dangerously dysfunctional—because in reality decision-making bottlenecks exist at the top.

Complexity stresses hierarchies. The world that governments operate in today is too complex and too fast changing for the people at the top to have the full expertise and all the answers to call all the shots. Therefore, vertical silos need to be broken down, so information can flow horizontally to reach other departments. It is not 'need to know' but knowing enough so that each component of the larger organisation can respond to issues and challenges as they arise. An environment that encourages the spontaneous horizontal flow of information will enlarge and enrich the world view of all departments. This in turn improves the chances that connections hidden by complexity, as well as emergent challenges and opportunities, are discovered early.

'Auftragstaktik' (Mission Command Tactics)

The German military adopted with great success (at least at the operational level) a concept of military command called *auftragstaktik* ('mission-type tactics'). It was a philosophy of command that acknowledged the complexity and the chaos of war.

In *auftragstaktik*, even the most junior officers were empowered to make decisions on the spot, because they had a better and more direct feel for the situation on the ground. It meant that down the line, every officer had to understand not just the orders, but also the intent of the mission. In turn he was empowered to make decisions to adjust to the situation as he judged it, in order to better fulfil the intent of the mission.

Whole-of-government implicitly contains the central idea of *auftragstaktik*, which is that in complexity it is not possible for everything to be centrally directed. Not unlike *auftragstaktik*, whole-of-government depends critically on people at all levels understanding how their roles fit in with the larger national aims and objectives. Agencies must have a strong sense and a shared understanding of the challenges the nation faces, and the underlying principles to guide responses. Then it depends on the good sense of each agency to ensure its own plans and policies are aligned with the national imperatives, to the point that they instinctively react to threats and opportunities as they arise, knowing that what they do will advance the larger national, rather than departmental, interests.

Whole-of-government is a holy grail. In countries like Singapore, it remains very much a work in progress. It requires emphasis, support and constant attention from the top.

Dealing with Cognitive Biases

There is another challenge to governments in complex situations, as was evident in the April 2010 eruption of the Icelandic volcano Eyjafjallajökull. When a huge cloud of volcanic dust started to spread over Europe, air-traffic authorities grounded thousands of aircraft as a safety precaution. Europe was almost paralysed. It caused travel chaos around the world and disrupted global supply chains for weeks.

We know volcanoes erupt from time to time. We also know it is risky to fly through volcanic ash clouds. Yet why, despite this knowledge, was the world so surprised by and unprepared for the impact of this eruption?

First, although the risk of eruption is known, it is very difficult to assess its probability of occurrence. Behavioural economists point out that we underrate the probability of an event when it has not happened recently and overrate the probability of an event when it has. As a result of this cognitive bias, the risk of an eruption was underrated in this case, as Eyjafjallajökull had been quiescent for a long time.

Second, the effect of the eruption on aircraft flights was the result of complex interconnectivities and was therefore highly unpredictable. When the volcano erupted, aviation authorities depended on the predictions of analytical models and reacted with caution by shutting down all flights. But as the commercial impact grew, the industry began to question the reliability of these models and proposed doing experimental flights to probe whether it was safe to fly. In the event, the experimental flights proved to be a better indicator for action than reliance on the models. This is a clear demonstration of the value of exploration and experimentation when we are confronted with complex phenomena instead of depending only on the predictions of analytical models.

Cognitive bias and the extreme difficulty of estimating the cumulative effects of complex events make preparing for unforeseen situations an exercise fraught with difficulty. It also adds to the challenges of governments operating in complex situations.

Managing Complexity

In such a complex operating environment, governments should be adaptive and able to navigate situations characterised by emergence, multi-causality and ambiguity, as they were during the eruption of the Icelandic volcano.

Governments often have to make big decisions, and develop plans and policies, under conditions of incomplete information and uncertain outcomes. It is not possible to prepare exhaustively for every contingency. Instead, a 'search and discover' approach should be adopted. The deployment of experimental flights to check out the real risk of flying into a cloud of volcanic ash exemplifies this approach. The military calls this approach the 'OODA' (observe, orientate, decide, act) loop, which is a recurring cycle of decision-making that acknowledges and exploits the uncertainty and complexity of the battlefield.

Scenario planning is a linear method of carrying out the OODA loop, in the sense that it projects futures based on our understanding of the operating environment today. Used intelligently, it can be a very important tool for planning, and can help overcome cognitive biases by challenging our mental models. But it is insufficient in a complex, unordered environment.

Nonlinear methods should be part of the government complexity toolbox. They include back-casting, policy gaming (which is akin to military war-gaming, but applied to the civilian policy context to condition policymakers to complex and uncertain situations, and to help them confront their cognitive biases) and horizon scanning (which is the process of detecting emerging trends, threats and opportunities).

Governments must also be able to manage the risk that is a natural result of operating in complexity. There will always be threats to national outcomes, policies and plans, because no amount of analysis and forward planning will eliminate the volatility and uncertainty that exist in a complex world. These threats constitute strategic risk.

There is, however, little by way of best practice to address systematically or ameliorate the threats to national goals that these risks pose. In Singapore, the Government is developing a unique Whole-of-Government Integrated Risk Management (WOG-IRM) framework—a governance chain that begins with risk identification and assessment at the strategic level to monitor risk indicators and, finally, to resource mobilisation and behavioural changes to prepare for each anticipated risk. WOG-IRM also plays an imperfect but important role in discovering the interconnections among risk factors. This in turn helps to reduce some of the complexity. The WOG-IRM framework is a work in progress, and we have started using it for strategic conversations on risks that occur at the whole-of-government level.

Organising in Complexity

The WOG-IRM framework is also critical to building resilience, which is the ability to cope with strategic shock by adapting to, or even transforming with, rapid and turbulent change. Resilience ought to be a key characteristic of governments that operate effectively in a complex environment.

Resilient governments must go beyond an emphasis on efficiency. Lean systems that focus exclusively on efficiency are unlikely to have sufficient resources to deal with unexpected shocks and volatility, while also having the bandwidth to make plans for an uncertain future filled with wicked problems.

This is not an argument for establishing bloated and sluggish bureaucracies; but it is important for resilient governments to have a small but dedicated group of people to think about the future. The skill sets needed are different from those required to deal with short-term volatility and crisis. Both are important. But those charged with thinking about the future systematically should be allocated the bandwidth to focus on the long term without becoming bogged down in day-to-day routine. They will become repositories of patterns that can be used to facilitate decision-making, to prepare for unknown unknowns, and perhaps to conduct policy experiments through policy gaming or other simulations.

To this end, the Singaporean Government set up the Centre for Strategic Futures (CSF) a couple of years ago. It is a think tank which promotes a whole-of-government approach to strategic planning and decision-making. It works on leading-edge concepts like WOG-IRM and resilience. It promotes fresh approaches like policy gaming for dealing with complexity. It encourages experiments with new computer-based tools and sense-making methods to improve horizon scanning. Although a small outfit, the CSF is a catalyst for strategic change in the government and its agencies.

Conclusion

The future promises ever more complexity, carrying in its train more black swans and unknown unknowns. Governments must learn how to operate and even thrive in this complexity, and to deal confidently with strategic shocks when they occur. The first step is to acknowledge the inherent complexity of the operating environment. Then they should consider the imperative of a whole-of-government approach, and the adoption of new nonlinear tools for managing complexity and strategic risk. These will not eliminate shocks. But by improving the ability to anticipate such shocks, governments might actually reduce their frequency and impact. In turn this will help make governments and nations more resilient as their leaders govern for the future.

References

Bar-Yam, Y. 2004. *Making Things Work: Solving Complex Problems in a Complex World* (Cambridge, Mass.: Necsi Knowledge Press).

Rittel, H. and Webber, M. 1973. 'Dilemmas in a General Theory of Planning', *Policy Sciences*, 4(155).

Taleb, N. N. 2008. *The Black Swan: The Impact of the Highly Improbable* (London: Penguin).

6. Do Governments Suffer from Political Myopia: What is the problem and what can be done about it?

Robyn Kruk and the Honourable Sir Michael Cullen

Robyn Kruk

The former US President Bill Clinton was fond of saying that he was always an optimistic, 'glass half-full' person, because he took pessimism to be an excuse for inaction. And while I occasionally express cynicism about governments and ministers, I am generally positive about ongoing change and the need for change, but also realistic about the challenge of the task.

I speculate that I was probably asked to address this topic because I have run the NSW health agency (Australia's largest) and both the State and national environment agencies. In the health agency, State treasury officials too often considered me the cause of their deficit problems and said if I could only get the budget in order there would be no problems across the rest of the State budget. Alternatively, when I was an environment head it was the 'green tape' introduced by the agency that was allegedly responsible for the poor state of accounts of the country. So both agencies always considered themselves very much the 'Nigel no-friends' of the Government. Ironically enough, the tenures of CEOs in my position are usually among the shortest in government. The average length of tenure of a health CEO is approximately 18 months. The only tenure shorter is that of health ministers. In the five years I was the CEO of NSW Health I worked with three ministers and all were convinced or had suspicions that their appointments were the result of a plot within their own party to knock them over. It was a similar story in the environment area.

So, my starting point for this chapter is: to what extent is political myopia a systemic problem and what can be done about it? I wish to begin by questioning the suggestion that political myopia is something new and has arisen only because of the Global Financial Crisis, and that the myopia problem and lack of foresight are linked only to the public sector. I would contend that both of these are misconceptions.

The policy sectors of health and environment are interesting because they tend to have boom and bust cycles. Both are areas that people care about significantly and are among the top issues that come up as being matters of public concern; certainly health comes up normally in the top two or three, while the environment ranks normally in the top six, although that can vary depending on economic circumstances. They are also policy sectors where political parties tend to seek to differentiate their product. Both may rely on great technical complexity for their arguments. Both are areas that attract very broad interest and have been subject to deliberate media campaigns that seek to sway public opinion. Whether it is a story about what damage has been done in the health system or an environmental issue, both are very prominent in media circles.

Environment budgets have been taking an absolute battering in recent times, even in Canada and Australia, which have had relatively robust balance sheets. Both health and the environment tend to vacillate, with periods of cuts and austerity followed by systemic failures, scandals and inquiries, which then subsequently lead to injections of significant capital.

So, is political myopia a problem? Yes it is. Is it unique to government? I believe strongly it is not. Is it a new phenomenon? Again, no. And it is not solely the fault or responsibility of politicians. Foresightedness is difficult to achieve; so I want to mention some of the experiences that have worked for me in my various roles in government.

When studying public policy it is often said that if people do not care about an issue then politicians do not need to care either. But I have already argued people care for both health and the environment and there are plenty of quantitative studies to support that contention—so why do we find political myopia in these instances and how can we seek to future-proof their budgetary requests? Clearly the public's expectations are high in these policy areas and I would say that certain forms of myopia have developed precisely because those expectations have not been successfully dampened.

For instance, I recall a former NSW treasurer who used to open the budget committee every time the health minister and I appeared, by saying, 'I'm short, fat, bald and ugly and what's the government going to do about it? Oh, here are the health officials.' That statement concisely encapsulated a whole range of challenging health budget issues, including expectations about a nanny state or the very deliberate promulgation of the latest medical advances and latest medical technology. It included the belief that one can live forever, one can look forever youthful, that there is a silver bullet for every disease or malady. Those expectations have not been dampened. In fact they are actively promulgated in commercial and social media. So is there a form of myopia attributable to those expectations? Yes, I believe so, but we probably all share in those expectations and help create them.

The related issue to address is the question of what assists to perpetuate those expectations. One of the things that troubled me most as health CEO was that despite the fact that health was one of the few agencies to receive additional monies, the growth in demand meant it was still operating in a structural deficit at any point in time. But the expectation created in the community was that health was getting new money and additional services would be provided, and there would be no cutbacks in services. Hence, one of the key issues in expectation management was that many budget announcements and political processes actually stoked the expectation that there was additional money. That, in effect, fed what we used to call in the health area the 'a-ort-a syndrome': 'they (the government) ought to do something about that.'

That was probably the biggest issue that beset us most frequently in the media. And it was hardest to counter if there had been massive build-up of expectation because new monies were apparently being provided. Accordingly, I would suggest first that it is easier in many ways to initiate reform, lead service configuration changes and lead policy changes where there is an overwhelming perception that there is a climate of austerity and the facts support the view. The most difficult situations I have had in terms of future-proofing budgets and making them sustainable are where changes are made without knowing the impact or giving any consideration to the likely impact. Across-the-board budget saving targets are illustrative.

The second issue that perpetuates some of the difficulty in future-proofing a budget is where policy proposals are devised and initially introduced to the community in the form of green or white papers. These are all too often silent on the proposed source of funds. Yet, if word gets out, it is normally reported in the media that the initiative is already being introduced, whereas in reality it has merely been floated as an idea in the traditional Westminster bidding mode of cabinet. The process, in effect, increases the risk of a 'run on the bank'; it increases the public's expectations, and thereby makes a long-sighted approach far more difficult.

The third issue is that when treasurers make budget announcements, the tendency has increasingly been to announce only the *increases* in expenditure—which may in fact most often be funded by offsets or redirected monies or reinvestments from other areas. Yet in making those new funding announcements, treasurers neglect to announce the areas from whence the funds are being redirected. So people again are given the expectation that there is additional money.

The final point—one I notice is shared with Canadian and British colleagues—is that there is supposedly a move to provide greater flexibility to directors-general. Yet directors-general (or CEOs or departmental secretaries, whatever the title) are provided with fiscal discipline targets accompanied normally with some quite stringent and counterintuitive directives such as: 'There will be no loss of frontline staff; there will be no closure of services; there will be no bad media in my patch. If you get some negative media in my colleagues' patches, that is a bonus.' Some tight strictures are issued in terms of how the cuts may actually be manifested. These are the types of issues that I would describe as the challenges I faced in future-proofing budgets, and I am sure many others have faced similar ones.

Health has traditionally been somewhat quarantined from cuts because there have regularly been some additional monies provided, but to future-proof health the equation arguably needs to be changed. Some funding mechanisms or payment regimes can have the perverse effect of driving demand. For example, a 'fee for service' focus rather than an 'episode of care' focus has fundamental impacts for future health budgets and health outcomes more generally. We need to ask how the incentives and funding regimes for new activity are to be structured, whether through direct government funding (including transfers between the Commonwealth and the States), through co-payments from patients to physicians or on the achievement of health outcomes—or to challenge expectations that we can all live beautifully forever.

In my health budgets only 2 per cent was directed towards preventative health measures while 98 per cent was directed towards chronic and acute services—a major imbalance and a poor long-term investment scenario. If we want to ensure health expenditures are sustainable and future-proof the policy sector then we need to divert money from the acute machinery into the preventative area. Is this a feasible long-term strategy? I would argue that it is but readily acknowledge that it is not without significant political challenges. I will suggest five things that will help make these long-term changes.

First, we need to institutionalise foresighted reporting. In Australia, Ken Henry, the former treasury secretary, released a series of seminal intergenerational reports that actually encouraged long-term thinking and debate. They put risks and opportunities on the policy agenda and have become a major resource for the public sector, for industry and also for the media.

Second, transparent reporting is needed. In my areas of work, some of the most incredibly powerful, well-orchestrated interest groups in the climate change area and in the health technology area are well cashed to push a particular argument to make life quite difficult for ministers or governments.

In the health sector, the move that made the most significant changes in my experience was the creation of a statutorily based, transparently focused and independent reporting function—one that is separate from the health administration system. The issues need to be reported on independently, regularly and accessibly and be less vulnerable to mistranslation or a bipartisan presentation. Such reporting needs to be robust throughout government. We take for granted that the Australian Bureau of Statistics reports on the economic wellbeing of the country, including social and mental wellbeing. While it is sensible to have the accounts of the country pick up the people issues and look at the effects on resource use and exploitation, such reporting needs to be hardwired into government to make them the backdrop to discussions.

Third, in terms of the quality and integrity of health services, most health systems have now moved to transparent reporting of so-called avoidable events that impact on patient safety; however, this was not always the case. The most difficult issues that the health minister faced day-by-day were often perpetuated by a pattern of not releasing quality and safety data. By totally shifting our focus and instituting an independent, regular reporting structure on how many people were damaged, injured or subjected to avoidable, adverse events the game changed significantly and the information provided was considered to be more reliable. That is not to say that this transparency did not put considerable pressure on the health minister. I remember after the first such report I said to him, 'You have to go out tomorrow and say, "This number of people have died or been seriously injured in the health system", but then you have to say "We've also underestimated that number".' The minister said, 'You have to be joking!' The issue was that this reporting introduced a transparency in the health system and totally changed the nature of the debate in the media. It provided an insight into health care that was more complex than an argument about dollars, which always suggests a simple, short-term fix or solution is possible.

In relation to the media some political circles are lagging behind the population. The next generation of voters does not read newspapers, but politicians still respond to the *Daily Telegraph* as if it presents the facts. Actually, the NSW Bureau of Crime Statistics and Research, which is part of the NSW Attorney-General's Department, is considered one of the most credible and accepted resources in relation to true crime statistics, yet, because it is not a newspaper, its data remain unread, unknown and largely ignored. So it is necessary to hardwire some of the hard research data into the policy backdrop.

Furthermore, citizens show no greater trust of bureaucrats than they do of politicians. There is suspicion of officials and their motivations. For instance, I could have far more influence in the health debates and in the media by getting some clinicians in white coats to present an argument than I ever could by making a statement. Pick the right people to proffer your debates. A minister fronting the media in relation to a patient safety event immediately politicised the issue and guaranteed ongoing and ill-informed press. If a doctor addressed the issue and acknowledged 'this is terrible, I can relate to it personally, it is not acceptable', the issue would die quickly in the 24-hour media cycle. So it is also a matter of being a bit more responsive in the bureaucracy to looking at an active role in 'issues management' as opposed to having politicians always fronting up and then being surprised when they basically roll over.

Fourth, recognise that the bureaucracy has a significant role and one highly dependent on both political and public trust. Hilary Mantel's 2009 book *Wolf Hall* presents an interesting insight into the historical relationship between the government and the bureaucracy and I encourage you to read it. It concerns the relationship between Henry VIII and Sir Thomas Cromwell. It looks at the politics of the royal court, but an underpinning sentiment is the importance of trust in the relationship with the bureaucracy.

Members of the bureaucracy have devoted their careers to understanding some of the most complex matters and putting forth proposals to future-proof the department. It is important always to be aware of what is within the department's control and what can be done to promulgate a change in the public debate and the potential impact on political capital for the minister or government. Westminster bureaucrats too often think it is for the minister alone to promulgate the case for change and to play the so-called long game at the cost of short-term gains. If I relied on a minister to promulgate the case for change it would not have occurred in many instances. Future-proofing budgets is ultimately a shared responsibility. Similarly, it would be naive to expect a minister to risk sacrificing their career on the basis of bureaucratic advice alone without an appreciation of the potential support or criticism for a less myopic view. The issue of trust in this situation is quite significant.

The final thing that will reduce myopia is that the line between so-called political research and public sector policy research has become greyer—particularly in relation to social research. This is not necessarily a bad thing. The investigatory work we did in both health and the environment to get a better understanding of the fundamental issues that concerned the community, and to use it as a proper basis for engagement with the community, was significant in introducing some long-sighted strategies the health area needed. Now, those policy challenges do not disappear. They are qualitatively different from instantaneous political polling of opinions, but it meant that we had to maintain a capacity with health to undertake matters that were separate from managing the issue of the day. This allowed the department to separate the fact that people needed to have long-sighted strategies as their primary focus and that managers needed to make decisions about the priority of those people over and above some strictly organisational functions.

In summing up, the whole narrative of austerity makes future-proofing budgets a lot easier largely because of the potential impact on public expectations. Governments and bureaucracies have developed a holistic focus, and share a common language and a level of understanding and awareness about some of the difficulties we face; however, transparency and independent reporting are critical even though the organisations that do them may become the subject of cuts, too. In the United Kingdom there were reported cuts to their Office for National Statistics and to their Office for Budget Responsibility. Areas that were clearly given the task of reporting honestly on the situation were in many instances having to report bad news. It shows inversely the critical importance of those agencies.

The Honourable Sir Michael Cullen

One of my former Labour colleagues, Mike Moore, would sometimes pose a question when we were getting carried away, saying rhetorically, 'What's posterity done for me?' That's a question politicians can ask themselves in many respects. It is a question that may suggest why we descend into a kind of myopia about what governments can be expected to deliver. But it also implies that the core problem is simply related to 'elected governments' when the root problem probably lies much deeper than that. By that I mean the case can be made that politics and governments tend to deal in the short term and struggle to come to grips with the long term, but that phenomenon is not confined to, or even most evident among, politicians. In fact, politicians who try to deal with long-term issues nearly always find themselves in conflict with pressure groups which benefit from the status quo and with a largely uninterested public—especially if there are more immediate pressures vying for attention, such as economic ones. And when don't such pressures loom large for the ordinary person?

I would like to make two preliminary points. Above all, politicians now face a media whose interest barely extends beyond the immediate news cycle, which is roughly one hour. Media comment is seldom around the inherent *value* of policies. In many cases it is often hard to find out what the policy *is* from media coverage because its comment is usually about how the policy is going to be received by the public, not about what it is and to what extent it has neutered the opposition.

The media's underlying assumption with any long-term announcement is that it is intended to be a diversion from immediate issues; and in any case those making the announcement cannot be made accountable for the outcome because they will not be there when the outcome occurs or does not occur. Those are the attitudes found among the quality end of the media; but there is also a world called 'talkback radio', which cynically trivialises everything or demands instant gratification.

In other words, it is a little unreasonable in a world of instant comments and pervasive cynicism to expect that politicians will be the one group focused on the long term—and that they should do what is considered right, take the electoral consequences and disappear into the holy glow of a grateful future. This ignores reality. All too often what that actually means is their political opponents are elected, they then overturn the policies, and, worst of all, your own former colleagues abandon these same policy principles because it makes them unelectable. That is what is likely to happen over carbon taxation at the 2013 Australian election.

The other preliminary point to make is: I question the assumption that democratic governments *are* particularly prone to systematic 'short-termism'. I see not the slightest evidence of that in relation to the big questions such as climate change, demographic transformation, ecological diversity, indigenous rights, economic sustainability or any other planet-saving issue. It would be very hard to argue that non-democracies are generally doing better than democratic societies in that regard. Rather the evidence tends to point in the opposite direction. China is now the largest emitter of carbon dioxide in the world and, no doubt, India will soon follow behind. In so far as democracies tend to be more polluting societies, that is simply because they are richer societies.

In democracies there is some evidence that where the electorate's attitudes are based more on rational principles and display greater international awareness they also tend to be more open to policies that help future-proofing. And that may just be a rather ponderous tautology. The real knotty problem about democracy and the prospects for future-proofing is that there is often an inherent contradiction between the two. Let me illustrate that with a vivid example, which you may appreciate more than some of the audiences ever did in my previous job as New Zealand's finance minister.

For much of the past 30 years New Zealand's purist classical liberals and their political associates have been trying to use legislation to prevent a social-democratic government adopting fiscal policies consistent with its principles. And that was pretty much the stated purpose of the author of New Zealand's *Fiscal Responsibility Act of 1994*: it was meant to lock in the conservative policies of the then minister of finance in New Zealand for the long term.

Treasury prevented such an outrage against democracy by ensuring that once the rhetoric was stripped away, the Act was in fact basically about more openness in fiscal intentions. As such it has proved very useful and I was able to incorporate it into the *Public Finance Act* with some amendments.

The fact is that in democracies the people must be allowed to decide and get it right or wrong, or there is no democracy. Obviously, New Zealand Labour believes the people got it wrong in 2008 at the election that removed the Clark Government but there was no appeal against that judgment.

Such statements about parliamentary sovereignty need qualification in a number of ways, not least in relation to fundamental human rights. There are things that should not be subject to temporary passing majorities. The search for legislative or judicial bulwarks against bad judgment is not just a futile but also a profoundly elitist agenda and one for which the left is just as culpable as the right on occasions.

Let me not be misunderstood. I am not arguing for a passive acceptance of the failure to address the kinds of issues to which I have referred. The current weakness of international action on climate change is a clear case of collective pusillanimity in the face of a real common danger where defined and obvious solutions are conceivable and available. Not quite as bad is the fact that, so far, international finance capitalism has emerged from the Global Financial Crisis practically unscathed, having successfully socialised the cost of its failures, greed and incompetence, at a terrible cost to present and future generations; and indeed some are now trying to find ways to blame governments for the problem rather than the real authors of it.

So it will be no surprise that my argument is that what can be done that is both effective and consistent with democratic processes is relatively limited and may be far from sufficient to achieve a refocusing on the long-term big issues. And that refocusing will only come about when there is a sufficient groundswell of public support for it. The challenge is how best to assist in framing public understanding in a way that may generate that support. That is the real challenge to be faced.

The first part of the answer is to do better what we do already. Following up on one of Robyn Kruk's points, that means, for example, continuing to increase the level of openness about what the government has decided, how they did it and why they did it, and extending that to what the government is doing at present. It means generating more open and informed debate about the underlying principles and realities. In other words, increasing public understanding of what the relevant factors are in decision-making may assist in support for better decision-making. The one caveat to bear in mind, however, is that unfortunately the media tends to sensationalise any discussion about options. That tends to lead to foreclosing the options immediately as politicians run to the corner of safety, saying: 'No, we've ruled that out because of course if we don't all hell is going to break loose.' I get quite amused, I must say, when I read the rewriting of history on New Zealand's *Foreshore and Seabed Act*, which completely misses the way the media reaction to the court decision constrained almost entirely the options open to the government of the day in dealing with that issue. We have now arrived at a happier place in that regard.

Alongside that greater openness runs a stronger emphasis on articulating the long-term fiscal framework and pressures. New Zealand has already been in the forefront, having pioneered some of these exercises already. At present Treasury is working with a number of us towards the new long-term fiscal framework commencing probably next year. But here again we need a more responsible approach by the media in not sensationalising the outcomes of such information provision; otherwise it becomes counterproductive.

The third way of framing public understanding to strengthen support for longer-term issues in public policy is to adopt a range of measures of social and economic performance that encourage long-term thinking. It is now well established that the primary measure we use, gross domestic product (GDP), encourages resource depletion rather than sustainability and encourages energy production and consumption rather than efficiency and conservation. It would be fascinating using such different measures to compare Australia's GDP with New Zealand's GDP, given the degree to which Australia depends upon resource depletion. A broader national accounting system may give quite a different picture about the comparison of the two countries and the trends over the past 20 or 30 years. Helping people understand that we are consuming our future at an unsustainable rate may assist in support for the kind of paradigm shift the world needs.

The fourth is to create, or recreate in New Zealand's case, an institution with power to engage in long-term future thinking across the board and to collaborate with like-minded institutions in this area. And rather than sitting in splendid but weak isolation, and therefore likely to be staffed by people favourable to whatever the current government's general philosophy is, such a body should be hosted in one or more of our universities. In particular, it would be a useful counter to the number of bodies which push short-term growth agendas with no sustainable long-term considerations. There is no countervailing influence, certainly in New Zealand, at the present time, in that regard.

As a final suggestion, I would argue we are well overdue for a full review of commercial legislation, accounting principles and the like to see how the current regimes favour 'short-termism' and how they could be changed to provide a better focus upon the long term. It is not just a matter of detail—for example, we are now required to have quarterly profit reporting in the public sector, which sees agencies focus upon every quarter's profit rather than a longer-term picture. But the whole mindset that underlies the way we approach these issues in the commercial sector suggests you will probably find at least as much short-term thinking as you will find in the political sector in societies such as ours.

Recently, I had a debate with Treasury. The standard measure of labour productivity calculates the output per worker employed. That sounds sensible. The problem is that if you have a strongly growing economy, where unemployment is dropping, average labour productivity falls. It looks as though you are doing worse economically. Logically, in an economy where workers are laid off and mass unemployment is rising, labour productivity numbers will go up as a consequence. So in fact if you were to measure labour productivity by the output per person in *the whole workforce*, as opposed to merely those in employment, you might get a better statistic on which to base decisions. If you have to make a choice between 100 per cent being employed with, say, a 90 per cent productivity rate and a 90 per cent employment and 100 per cent productivity rate, the only reason we would choose the latter rate is because Australia, with its higher wages, is sitting opposite us and takes our people. On any rational grounds you would choose the 100 per cent employment option. Socially it is a far better outcome than having 10 per cent unemployment. It is not a stupid example because many European countries were stuck before the Global Financial Crisis with high levels of unemployment, but apparently high productivity levels. That is not a socially desirable outcome.

That brings it back, then, to my earlier point: 'short-termism' is not a unique feature confined to politics and is not even at its worst amongst politicians. Politicians are doing what they are meant to do. They are responding to public demand and to the rewards that are available to them in that regard. If there is no reward for thinking long term then politicians are much less likely to do so. I know it comes as a terrible shock to some people, but when you are actually in government you want to get re-elected to government. Politicians do not see their role in life as being to hand over to opponents on some sort of rotating-turn principle of who should be actually governing the country.

'Short-termism', however, is also evident among the general population in many countries. I do not know how many long-term issues most people can grasp at once and deal with, because when they start adding them up they become overwhelming. People say, 'We're going to get old; we won't be able to afford health care; we can't afford the pension; and in any case if you live less than two metres above sea level you will be in deep trouble if you're going to live more than another 10 years', and so on. And for resigned escapists who decry the real world, they think: 'Well, so what?' People quickly retreat into a kind of short-term nihilism if they are faced with too many protracted long-term issues presented in a way in which there are no simple solutions. The terrible thing is that in most of these areas there are actually relatively simple solutions if we can get the debate framed in an intelligent fashion.

At heart I believe the real challenge is to convince a sufficiently large number of people that our patterns of behaviour must change. But do not confuse this with the notion that I am preaching a gospel of 'sackcloth and ashes' and making people feel guilty about the relatively modest affluence most enjoy in our societies at present. All too often radical green groups in particular fail to realise the need for an approach that is people-friendly and prosperity-friendly. Selling the idea to people that we are going to become worse off, or that a shrinking pie will be more equally divided up, is a heroic political enterprise that is not capable of fulfilment in a democratic society. Behavioural change is the most important challenge to be met but we have barely begun the task of doing so at present.

7. Policy Disasters Waiting to Happen: When predictable disasters flow from government decisions

Peter Mumford

I must confess that on reflection I did wonder whether, as a practising New Zealand public servant, it was a career-limiting move to accept an invitation to make a presentation on government decisions as the cause of policy failure. Being a public policy advisor, I probably contributed to a number of suboptimum regulatory regimes—those that have failed to deliver as expected. So perhaps reviewing these failures is a case of me looking in the mirror and seeing who is actually looking back. For public servants it is an occupational hazard: you can be associated sometimes with the success, but also sometimes with the failure, of the policies you have been working on and promoting.

The policy issue I have chosen to analyse concerns the challenge of creating resilient regulatory regimes. My study is informed by a recent case of regulatory failure in New Zealand resulting in the so-called 'leaky building crisis', but also work that Treasury has undertaken on best regulatory practice. The insights presented of regulatory failure resulting in the leaky building crisis were informed by my own research in this area, which has now been published by the Institute of Policy Studies (Mumford 2011).

Two Lenses: The human face and the policy opportunity

I would like to make clear from the outset that for many affected people, New Zealand's leaky building crisis is intensely personal. Their stories—which we read in the newspapers quite often—illustrate how people's lives can be affected when the state gets it wrong. If your units of analysis are individuals, families and communities, events like the leaky building crisis have a significant and dramatic effect, and we need to acknowledge that. For most of us in the public policy world, however, failures present a challenge: what went wrong? Why did it happen; and how can we ensure it never happens again? How can we learn from the mistakes of the past to create a better future? That is the public policy challenge that many of us face today.

The Broader Problem

Turning to the regulatory failure that led to the leaky building crisis, I know there will be differences of opinion regarding the villain in the piece. Some will put the crisis down to poor workmanship on the job, and some people clearly attribute it to poor-quality builders more generally. Others will argue that it arose because the state retreated from its core function of keeping people safe, relying instead on market disciplines. Both factors are probably relevant. In my view, however, the leaky building crisis was first and foremost a failure of performance-based regulation as it was implemented in New Zealand. By studying the leaky building crisis, we can certainly learn something about building regulation, but more importantly we can learn a lot about this novel regulatory approach that promised so much but ultimately did not live up to expectations.

Essentially, the leaky building crisis was a symptom of a broader problem. This problem (and its solution) can be found in the goal-based, non-prescriptive regulatory approaches that were adopted in the 1980s and 1990s in the building industry, the occupational health and safety area, and in environmental management. Many of these same regulatory approaches continue to be promoted around the world today; however, in light of experience their effectiveness needs to be evaluated. Accordingly, this chapter is not so much about the leaky building crisis per se or even about building regulation generally, but rather it is in effect about creating resilient and effective regulatory regimes.

This chapter is structured around three themes: why do regulatory regimes fail in general? Why did New Zealand's performance-based regulatory control regime fail? And what can we learn from this failure to create more resilient regimes in the future? The main message from this presentation is that some novel regulatory regimes can be quite experimental in nature. As experiments, they should be carefully monitored, with a particular focus first on what they are expected to deliver to society, and second, on the risks to delivery that arise out of the specific vulnerabilities of particular regulatory approaches. All regulatory approaches are different; they have their strengths and weaknesses. We need to know what they are and we need to be aware of their vulnerabilities.

Why do Regulatory Policies Fail?

At the outset, we should clarify what is meant by regulatory success and regulatory failure. I take a pragmatic approach: regulatory regimes are deemed to fail when the promises that were initially made when the regime was put in place are not met and, as a consequence, Parliament decides there are sufficient grounds to replace the existing regime with a new one.

By taking this approach, I am making a distinction between regulatory failure and regulatory improvement. Regulatory failure is a systemic failure of the regulatory regime. Regulatory improvement results from ideas and analysis that point to a better way, but it is not precipitated by a complete loss of confidence in the existing regime.

Much has been written on the sources of regulatory failure—including John Braithwaite's list produced for the OECD on why businesses do not comply with the law (*Improving Regulatory Compliance*, 1993). Braithwaite identified the following sources of non-compliance: failure of business to understand the law; a lack of commitment by business to the objectives that lie behind the law or the rules chosen to secure these objectives (or both); a perception by business that regulatory procedures are unjust; high cost of regulation; and enforcement including failure of deterrents, incapacitation and persuasion.

Of course, non-compliance with the law by itself does not inevitably result in regulatory failure. It is a matter of degree. For example, if some businesses fail to understand the law, this suggests the need for a more effective educational or enforcement strategy. If, however, *most* businesses do not know what they must do to meet their obligations under the law, not only will the law fail to achieve its objectives, but also the whole regulatory approach is called into question.

Why did this Particular Regulatory Policy Fail?

Parliament adopted a new law in 1991 that introduced a novel approach to the regulation of buildings. It was in part a reaction to what was described as a building industry that was over-regulated and controlled, and in part a response to the newly popular idea that regulatory requirements should be couched in terms of aims and performance rather than prescription and detailed rules.

Prior to 1991 the regulatory regime governing buildings in New Zealand was highly prescriptive. If you were a builder you would have to go and get the manual off the shelf, or perhaps you wouldn't even need to, because you would have been trained in a particular conservative style of building in New Zealand. It was a traditional industry with traditional designs and materials, which were reflected in numerous and complex local government by-laws. When the 1991 Act was created, it replaced somewhere between 300 and 400 local government by-laws with a single performance statute and performance-based building code. So the regime went from highly prescriptive to highly performance-based.

The idea of performance-based regulation was promoted as a general response to the high cost and inflexible nature of prescriptive regulation. In the 1980s and 1990s these approaches were pervasive and adopted not just in the building area, but also in the regulation of occupational safety and health, environmental planning, hazardous substances, and electricity and gas safety. Here, I cannot describe in detail how performance-based regulatory regimes are structured in all their many manifestations because all of the regimes in New Zealand are a little bit different, but suffice to say they all share one characteristic: the requirements that regulated entities must meet (and for that matter that regulators must enforce) are couched as high-level goals.

I can best illustrate this with reference to the requirement in the New Zealand *Building Code* relating to water ingress. The code requirement is that buildings must be constructed to provide adequate resistance to penetration by, and accumulation of, moisture from the outside. Prior to 1991, homeowners and the building industry together with government regulators did not need to worry about what was adequate. They could rely on prescriptive building standards often based on traditional construction methods, which in turn were embedded in the training of designers and builders. After 1991 prescriptive standards could still be used to inform practice but now they became what was known as 'acceptable solutions'. Designers and builders, however, now had a choice: they could seek approval for new designs and construction methods known as alternative solutions. The approval bodies—the territorial authorities—were required to decide whether these design and construction methods met the *Building Code* requirements for adequacy based on reasonable grounds.

From the mid 1990s, territorial authorities approved building designs that involved monolithic cladding, a construction method that didn't require a cavity between the cladding and the wall. In addition, joints were secured using sealants. Kiln-dried timber, itself an innovation, was typically used rather than traditional treated timber framing, and building designs did not include eaves. This was a response to market demands for larger houses on smaller sections or blocks, as it allowed houses to be built closer to boundary lines. This combination of modern design features and building technologies ultimately failed. The absence of eaves meant that more rain soaked the cladding. The cladding system did not provide adequate resistance to penetration by moisture from the outside. Water that penetrated the cladding accumulated because there was no cavity to allow it to drain away or dry out. The kiln-dried timber framing rotted when the moisture content reached and stayed at a certain level.

In total, since 1991, at least 42 000 buildings have been affected, and the consensus view is that the costs are in excess of NZ$11 billion. The real cost is eventually likely to be even higher than that. All of those who had a role to play in the building-control regime failed to predict how this particular combination of building technologies would perform in practice. The extent to which the cladding system would keep out New Zealand's wind-driven rain, the susceptibility of kiln-dried timber to rotting, the very high standard of workmanship required, and the need for ongoing maintenance were not taken into account in decisions to purchase, design, approve, build and maintain houses. What was deemed adequate by regulators when this combination of designs and building technologies was approved later proved to be demonstrably *in*adequate in practice. So, was this a case of intentional non-compliance with the requirements of the *Building Code*? While on the margin there were no doubt examples of poor workmanship, on the whole there was no intention to defeat the purpose of the law. This was an example of involuntary non-compliance.

Performance-Based Regulation and Regulatory Failure

I wish now to explore the role performance-based regulation played in this housing crisis, and associate it with the sources of regulatory failure. The New Zealand *Building Code* is performance-based. It sets goals but does not prescribe what must be done to achieve those goals. In effect the prime legal requirement was clearly stated: buildings must provide adequate resistance to penetration by and the accumulation of moisture from the outside.

While the goal was clearly stated, the law nonetheless created uncertainty, as it required judgments to be made about *what was adequate*, and did not provide guidance on who was best placed to exercise this judgment or how this judgment should be exercised. This is a defining feature of performance-based regulatory regimes. They rely on judgment (and for the most part, expert judgment) in situations where there are no precedents and often commercial pressures. The level of expertise must be commensurate with the complexity of the decision that is being taken. The more complex the judgment, the higher is the skill level required.

Returning to Braithwaite's six reasons for business's non-compliance with the law, which at the extreme will result in regulatory failure, I can find two that are potentially relevant to the performance and possible failure of performance-based regulatory regimes. The first is a failure of business to understand the law. In performance-based regulatory regimes, this can be more sharply defined as a failure by regulated entities to understand what is required to meet high-level performance requirements in situations where there are no precedents. The second is enforcement failure, including the failure of deterrents, incapacitation and persuasion. In performance-based regulatory regimes I would describe this as a failure by enforcement agencies to evaluate the efficacy of new technologies against high-level performance requirements in situations where there are no precedents.

'This Must Never Happen Again': Creating resilient regulatory systems

Since the crisis, we often hear it said that 'this must never happen again'. This is a mantra often repeated in the press and in royal commission reports. What can we learn from the failure of the building-control system to help us create more resilient regulatory regimes in the future? How do we resolve the problems of performance-based regulation, which might be described as dependence on expert judgment in complex decision-making contexts?

There are four possible solutions. One is to create more specific and measurable performance requirements. Colleagues in the building regulator division of the Ministry of Business, Innovation and Employment are taking this approach, and perhaps the term 'adequate' will not be as prevalent in the *Building Code* in the fullness of time.

A second solution is to ensure these problems do not arise by relying on safe precedents. This is the most conservative strategy. In the regulatory jargon it would involve reverting to prescriptive regulatory regimes. Research undertaken by the New Zealand Treasury indicates that some regulators are adopting this approach; effectively, our regulatory regimes and regulators are becoming much more conservative across the board; however, while prescription may provide certainty, it may also reduce flexibility, constrain innovation, impose excessive costs, and in some situations result in a level of regulatory complexity over time that either creates a disincentive to comply or focuses compliance on the wrong things. In other words, there is a risk—perhaps small, but a risk nonetheless— we could end up with the worst of both worlds. We may unintentionally produce high-cost regulatory regimes that do not achieve the state's primary objectives, be they related to health, safety, environmental protection or consumer and investor protection.

A third solution is to improve the quality of decision-making in situations where there are no precedents. We know some people or groups of people are better able to predict how novel technologies such as new building systems and products will perform in practice. They are described as experts and we rely on their professional judgment. Again, research undertaken within the New Zealand Treasury indicates that some regulators are adopting this approach, and in fact some regulatory regimes—traditional ones—have always been based on this approach. Relying on experts is, however, not as foolproof as it might first appear. What constitutes an expert has been studied at some length, and in some contexts, such as predicting the performance of complex and unproven technologies, a particular quality of expert is required. If we create regulatory regimes that are reliant on experts, we must be confident that experts are in fact available.

A fourth, more innovative solution is to treat novel technologies as experiments. From the outset, we must accept that we do not know how novel technologies will perform in all circumstances of their use. If we had treated a few monolithic clad buildings as site experiments, we would have been able to discover early on that they had deficiencies and might fail in certain circumstances. We could have monitored how they actually performed in the field, and against the inclement weather, and in the course of doing so we might have detected a problem in a timely manner. A few hundred vulnerable buildings could have been built before the serious problems were identified, and we could have avoided the tens of thousands of defective buildings that were ultimately built.

All of these are each plausible strategies. They might be employed either individually or in combination to resolve what we now know about the inherent weaknesses of performance-based regulation, but each of these strategies is itself subject to some uncertainty. How will they work in practice?

The Importance of Monitoring and Best Practice

This takes me to my final point: we must not assume a 'set and forget' approach to the design and implementation of regulatory regimes. At one level we must treat regulatory regimes as experiments, and indeed novel regimes such as the 1991 Performance-Based Building Control Regime was highly experimental. As experiments, regulatory regimes must be monitored and evaluated, and corrective action should be taken if required. The risk of not monitoring and evaluating is that we are surprised when regulatory regimes do not perform as expected and occasionally fail. More importantly, the consequences of failure can range from unpleasant to catastrophic, as we have found in the building area.

Avoiding failures completely is the ultimate objective, but minimising the risk and impact is also an important goal. If we accept the importance of monitoring and evaluating, the question becomes: what do we actually monitor? Health, safety and environmental outcomes, or indeed building quality outcomes, are important indicators of the performance of regimes. They tend to be after the event.

We also require measures of the health of regulatory regimes that allow us to make an assessment along the way. The New Zealand Treasury has developed a set of best regulatory practice principles and performance indicators, and assessed some 60 regulatory regimes against these.[1] The Treasury view is that

---

1 The full best-practice regulatory principles paper can be found at: <http://www.treasury.govt.nz/economy/regulation/bestpractice>.

regular monitoring against these principles, having regard to the indicators, is one important way of tracking the performance of regulatory regimes and identifying areas of risk that might require further review. The principles and indicators can also act as targets for continuous improvement and design criteria for new regimes.

The best-practice regulatory principles are

- growth-supporting—economic objectives are given an appropriate weighting relative to other specified objectives
- proportional—the burden of rules and their enforcement should be proportional to the benefits that are expected to result
- flexible—regulated entities should have scope to adopt least-cost and innovative approaches to meeting legal requirements
- durable—the regulatory system has the capacity to evolve to respond to changing circumstances
- certain and predictable—regulated entities have certainty as to their legal obligations, and the regulatory regime provides predictability over time
- transparent and accountable—rules development, implementation and enforcement should be transparent
- capable regulators—the regulator has the people and systems to operate an efficient and effective regulatory regime.

Each of the principles is associated with a set of performance indicators.

My ex-post assessment of the 1991 Building Control Regime indicated that it failed against a number of these principles and performance indicators. Hindsight of course is a wonderful thing, but our judgment is that if the assessment had been made in the 1990s, it would have revealed some latent weaknesses in the regime. We would have discovered major misgivings in relation to proportionality. We would have uncovered evidence of poor durability. And, third, we would have questioned the capability of the regulators to exercise expert judgments on novel building technologies. Would such an assessment have reduced the risk of building failures? Probably, but we will never know because the assessment was never done.

Reference

Mumford, P. 2011. *Enhancing Performance-Based Regulation: Lessons from New Zealand's Building Control System* (Wellington: Institute of Policy Studies).

8. Building and Maintaining Trust in Public Institutions: Is this possible?

Murray Petrie

Discussions of trust, integrity and social norms are a very important part of future-proofing the state. In this contribution I will assess New Zealand as a high-trust, high-integrity society, and identify some risks to trust and integrity. I will also discuss transparency, participation and accountability. The focus on transparency and participation has become increasingly prominent both internationally and domestically. The initial focus for most governments was on facilitating the disclosure of information. Now, it is more focused on active public participation in the design and implementation of public policies. I will also mention some specific areas for action in New Zealand, and some issues for discussion. I believe the case study of New Zealand will have some general lessons to be observed by Australia and other related countries.

A number of available indicators show that New Zealand is rated very highly in international measures of transparency and accountability. There is Transparency International's Corruption Perception Index. New Zealand has never ranked below fourth on that index, and for half of the time the index has been calculated, New Zealand has ranked first or equal first. Similarly, New Zealand ranks highly against indicators of open government and regulatory enforcement. On the Open Budget Index, New Zealand is second of 94 countries. In the area of freedom of the press, New Zealand is ranked sixteenth. These indicators present a general picture of New Zealand as a country of high-integrity and high-quality governance.

Now, what does the rest of the world look like? This map below is a visualisation of international Corruption Perception Index (CPI) scores. Those parts of the world that are in red or dark red are areas where corruption is perceived to be widespread or endemic. As indicated, corruption infects a large part of the rest of the world, including many countries that we trade with very actively, and increasingly so in Asia.

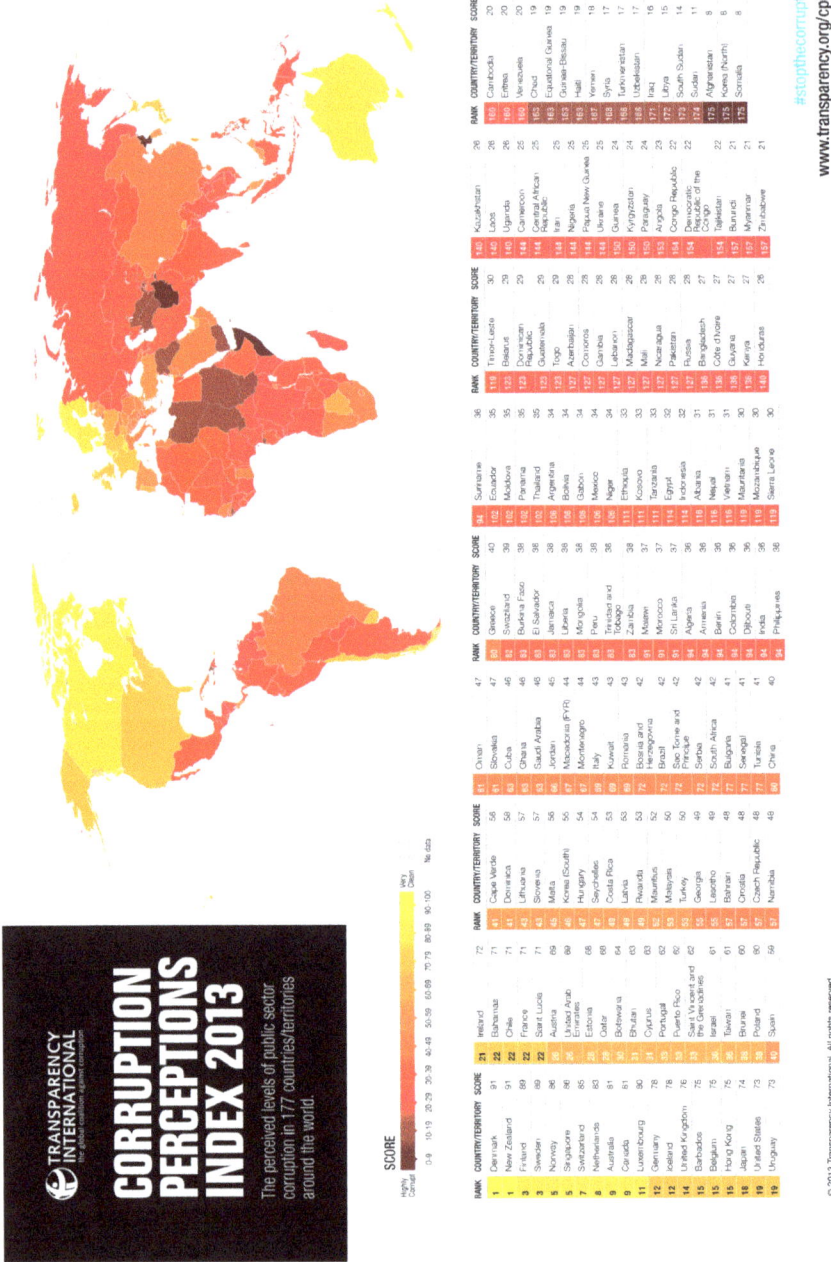

Figure 8.1 Corruption Perception Index, 2013

Source: Transparency International.

Australia is in a similar situation to New Zealand on the CPI. It lies in the second decile of the index. It operates a high-trust, high-integrity society in a world where corruption is essentially the norm. The relevance of the Australian and New Zealand examples is that both countries are designing mechanisms from which the rest of the world can learn.

It is important to understand why there is a lack of corruption in New Zealand. A large part of the reason for this is that the country has established and strong democratic institutions: an independent judiciary, a well-functioning parliament and watchdog institutions. It is also underpinned by stable social norms in a relatively small and cohesive society. It is, however, probably less cohesive than it has been in the past. The other countries that score very highly on the index are similarly small, advanced democracies, such as Denmark and Sweden. It is interesting, though, that Singapore has entered the top 10 on the CPI, having improved drastically in recent decades.

Let me explain why the issue of trust is such an important one. Trust is not a maudlin concept; it is not only a personal issue; rather, it is well known that societies with higher levels of trust achieve greater social, democratic and economic progress. One trend was evident when I returned to New Zealand after the Canterbury earthquakes after working overseas in countries where corruption is the norm. I attended a session at the Institute of Policy Studies on the Canterbury earthquake, during which presentations addressed questions such as how New Zealand's building standards affected the magnitude of destruction from the earthquake, and whether New Zealand needed to revisit its building standards. What struck me, coming from working overseas, was that in the whole discussion there was no single reference to whether or not the standards had been enforced; it was merely presumed they had been. The system had integrity. Moreover, there was no reference to the possibility that there was any corruption at any stage that exacerbated the damage caused by the earthquake. This is a good example of the social and economic value of a high-trust, high-integrity society. If one compares the different levels of death and damage caused by the Chilean and the Haitian earthquakes, the outcomes are staggering. Chile is a serious player, having a high quality of governance, while Haiti does not; and when both experienced a similar-sized earthquake the devastation was mild in Chile and catastrophic in Haiti. These two cases provide very dramatic illustrations of the consequences for societies of building or neglecting trust and integrity.

Our various social norms inform the rules of the game about what is desirable, permissible or tolerated. They are part of a wider set of mechanisms of social control, laws, incentives, information provision, nudging, and so on. They should be seen as part of that framework because the formal laws of the state, at the end of the day, require supporting social norms. And again, we see that in the examples from other countries: they have nice-looking legal frameworks that actually have very little impact and make very little difference on the ground because they are not supported by social norms. Voluntary compliance of the tax system is a very important example of a social norm that we in New Zealand may well take for granted.

There is also a range of social norms that underpins the operation of public institutions and the state, such as the constitutional convention of 'free and frank' advice that civil servants should provide to elected officials or the willingness to report wrongdoing. So if we consider this concept of trust and the related concept of legitimacy, three different forms of trust are often identified. *Contractual trust* relates to whether people adhere to their agreements. *Competence trust* refers to the faith citizens place in the competence of public officials and institutions; and *goodwill trust* describes the willingness to go beyond the minimum prescribed requirements of convention or law.

These are related to the two main dimensions of legitimacy. One is representative legitimacy, examples of which are how representative are our parliaments and whether we as citizens have the ability to access decision-makers. The second kind of legitimacy is performance legitimacy. This is an important element of effective public institutions that deliver public services—for example, maintaining the rule of law gives them a higher degree of perceived legitimacy.

Trust breeds more trust. The more one interacts with other people, the more they will begin to trust each other in economic relationships and personal relationships across the community. Only a relatively small number of countries, including New Zealand, experience this level of trust. Much of the rest of the world is trapped in a state where everybody assumes that everybody is out for themselves: why would someone pay taxes if they know no-one else is going to? Why would someone trust another person if it is likely they will be swindled? Those situations are hard to break out of because people refrain from the types of social interactions that might allow them to adjust their opinions. An interesting question for societies like New Zealand is whether our apparently high level of trust could unravel in the future? And if so, how, and how would we know? How might we detect what might be some quite subtle changes in the level of trust?

Cass Sunstein (1996), a US legal scholar who later entered the Obama administration as Administrator of the Office of Information and Regulatory Affairs, has argued that social norms can be surprisingly fragile. There can be large discrepancies between people's private judgments and their behaviour to conform to the norm. So, while they conform to the norm, privately they are questioning why they are doing so and asking if there is a way to change societal expectations about these norms. Sunstein (1996) points to changing norms around smoking as an example.

So what are some of the reasons why we might worry about the state of trust and integrity in New Zealand? What are some of the risks of corruption in New Zealand? These risks may include globalisation, increased cross-border linkages with countries where corruption is the norm, and trade—both export and import. One anecdote that illustrates this is where New Zealand exports to high-corruption countries. Siemens, the large German electronics and engineering company, appointed their star export manager as chief executive. He had been operating overseas. A couple of years later, the board was horrified to find he had started paying bribes in Germany. Siemens had to fire him, which was immediately damaging to the corporate image of the company. As such, there was a realistic risk that behaviours that are seen as normal overseas might become internalised through exports, through inward and outward investment, and through increasing immigration from countries where corruption is the norm. People have different views about whether it is legitimate or not to pay or to accept a bribe.

Money-laundering is another threat to building trust in public institutions. Front companies and shell companies have been recently common in New Zealand: it is very easy to set up a company in New Zealand, and perhaps monitoring mechanisms for impropriety are too lax. Organised crime is an increasing problem in New Zealand as it is globally. Professor Bob Gregory, at Victoria University, and two colleagues have published an interesting article on corruption in New Zealand that asks whether the rapid increase in income inequality in New Zealand could change prevailing attitudes around trust, integrity and legitimacy in a way that might cause some people to become more likely to commit fraud or corruption.

Another point relates to the rebuilding process following the Christchurch earthquakes. The earthquakes in Christchurch were a major shock to the economy and to New Zealand society. How this relates to the global trends of corruption during the rebuilding that follows natural disasters is interesting. Transparency International (TI) has done a lot of work in post-disaster situations around the world, and found that corruption often increases in these situations. Normal procurement practices are often changed because of the perceived need to respond rapidly to the size of the natural disaster. Insurance fraud can easily increase. So we should be vigilant about this risk in the rebuilding process in Christchurch.

The academic Robert Klitgaard (1988) has conceived a definition of corruption that is useful when thinking about which specific parts of the public sector are particularly prone to corruption and fraud. He says 'corruption is the coincidence of monopoly and discretion, minus accountability'. That points generally to the importance of competition and contestability. It is imperative to remove the level of monopoly discretion in the hands of public servants with strong regulations. The police, globally, are the public institution to which people pay the most bribes. This is verified by Transparency International's global corruption barometer. We are lucky in New Zealand to have a less corrupt police force, but it is nevertheless an institution about which the public sector should remain vigilant. New Zealand has experienced cases of corruption in a wide range of government departments, including the Immigration Department, the Customs Department and the Corrections Department. The judiciary, however, which is typically a corrupt institution around the world, ranks low on the list of corruption in New Zealand.

I consider we are naive about corruption in New Zealand. The country is transparent and honest in its domestic and international dealings; this increases the possibility for some to take advantage of New Zealand, which is why we should support the international conventions that criminalise the payment of bribes by private business. It is in our narrow and broader interests to support those initiatives. We are probably not very good at identifying corruption compared with others who have been doing it for a very long time.

At times, New Zealanders seem oblivious to conflicts of interest. Public lawyer Mai Chen, who is a member of Transparency International New Zealand, has described how she is at times astounded at how experienced executives are oblivious to a conflict of interest. Being a small country is often seen as an advantage in terms of trust and social norms and lack of corruption. It can also be a problem if we are not alert enough to the fact that we often know the people we are dealing with on the other side of a transaction.

There are also some latent weaknesses in our high CPI rating. First, the Corruption Perception Index measures only *perceptions*, not actuality. Moreover, these are the perceptions of some experts and businesspeople. Hence, the CPI is really attuned to focusing on the interface between the business sector and public officials, and whether bribes are expected to be paid to receive government services such as getting goods off the wharf, a regulatory approval and so on. Apparently, two of the six surveys that make up New Zealand's score on the CPI are by just one expert. This obviously raises the risk of bias. Perhaps more importantly, the focus of the CPI is on bribery, not on other forms of corruption, such as nepotism or political corruption. Indeed, some New Zealanders do admit to paying bribes. In a survey conducted in 2010, 3.6 per cent of respondents claimed that they or a member of their household had paid a bribe to an official of a public institution in the previous 12 months. This figure surprised a number of us. Has corruption in New Zealand increased in the past three years?

Seventy-three per cent said 'yes'. These figures are consistent with some other survey evidence. For instance, the State Services Commission has conducted an Integrity and Conduct Survey of more than 8000 respondents. Fifteen per cent of respondents reported observing illegal conduct in the previous year. Four per cent observed giving or accepting inappropriate payments or perks. Five per cent observed inappropriate alteration of documents.

The Office of the Auditor-General should be commended for taking the initiative and conducting a public sector fraud survey in 2011. Generally, the results were pleasing; however, one surprising and worrying statistic was that 23 per cent of the respondents said they had seen internal fraud in the past two years. Also worrying is the small number of people reporting wrongdoing under the *Protected Disclosures Act*. Simply put, there may be more corruption occurring than is being reported. The lack of reporting occurs despite a number of surveys showing that New Zealanders express willingness to report unethical behaviour. One interesting speculation made in the aforementioned article by Bob Gregory and colleagues is that the increase in reporting of corruption might, in some way, desensitise people to the undesirability of committing fraud and corruption.

Another area of concern is that there is a diverse range of norms in New Zealand. The 1998 New Zealand study of values, which is a bit dated, nonetheless reveals some interesting statistics. The survey focused on the ethnicity of respondents as a way of understanding differences in their attitudes to norms and values. Once respondents were asked to self-identify their ethnicity, a question posed was whether it was unjustifiable to accept a bribe. Ninety-one per cent of Europeans said 'yes', but only 72 per cent of Maori said 'yes'. On the question of whether claiming unentitled benefits was unjustifiable, 83 per cent of New Zealanders said 'yes', while less than 50 per cent of Pacific peoples said 'yes'. To the question of whether democracy in New Zealand was ineffective due to poor decision-making, most New Zealanders said 'no'; however, 44 per cent of those who had only a primary level of education said 'yes'. So the perceived effectiveness of our democracy remained low for certain strata of our society. When asked whether the *Treaty of Waitangi* should be abolished, 47 per cent of people in the lowest income bracket said 'yes'.

The Global Corruption Barometer has measured *which* institutions in New Zealand are perceived as being most corrupt. It is interesting that political parties and the national Parliament enjoy widespread cynicism and fairly high levels of perceived corruption. This is true at the global level as well. It is also true in Australia. The major difference between New Zealand and Australia here is the police force. New Zealand's police force has been measured as being low on the global corruption scale. In Australia, conversely, the police are up the top of the scale and are seen as being as corrupt as political parties and the national Parliament. The major prescriptive issue for New Zealand is to consider what actions it should now take to (re)build trust and integrity and to reduce risks. The Government has to be more proactive in fostering positive social norms. To combat the increased and often more sensational media coverage of corruption, public institutions need to do more to reinforce the fact that most people observe the law and that corruption is generally rare in New Zealand.

Some interesting UK evidence reports on the levels of compliance with their provisional tax system. The United Kingdom conducted a randomised control trial in which they mailed 140 000 letters to provisional taxpayers who had failed to make their first payment on time. One reminder letter notified the recipient that they had to pay their tax within six weeks or face punishment. The alternative letter in this trial included data on levels of voluntary compliance with the provisional tax system. Those receiving the second letter, which gave data on voluntary compliance in their immediate locality, recorded an increase of 15 percentage points in the number of people who paid before the six-week deadline. This is an impressive result and it raises the possibility that we need to be thinking more about using positive framing and positive reinforcement to offset the negative perceptions generated by the increased publicity of illegal behaviour.

Increased public participation is an important way of building greater trust in public institutions. In advanced democracies this is done frequently, but the international norms are starting to move beyond disclosure to focus very much on concrete, active, direct participation by citizens, in between elections, in policy design and implementation. One relevant example comes from the Global Initiative for Fiscal Transparency (GIFT). GIFT is a new, multi-stakeholder initiative that aims to promote greater transparency, participation and accountability. Its stakeholders are the International Monetary Fund (IMF), the World Bank, some global NGOs, plus some governments. A major principle of the GIFT initiative is that citizens and all non-state actors should have the right to participate directly in public debate over the design and implementation of fiscal policies.

Increasing public participation includes practices of informing, which is basically disclosure, consulting, involving, collaborating and, finally, empowering. One example of a measure taken to increase public participation is social auditing. This is becoming popular globally, but particularly in developing and middle-income countries in which civil society is increasingly involved in monitoring the implementation of a government investment project. Civil society could be monitoring the delivery of public services by using mobile phone technology, since the cost of new communication technologies has radically reduced in recent years. Hence, social audits are something we should think about as part of the social verification mechanisms in New Zealand.

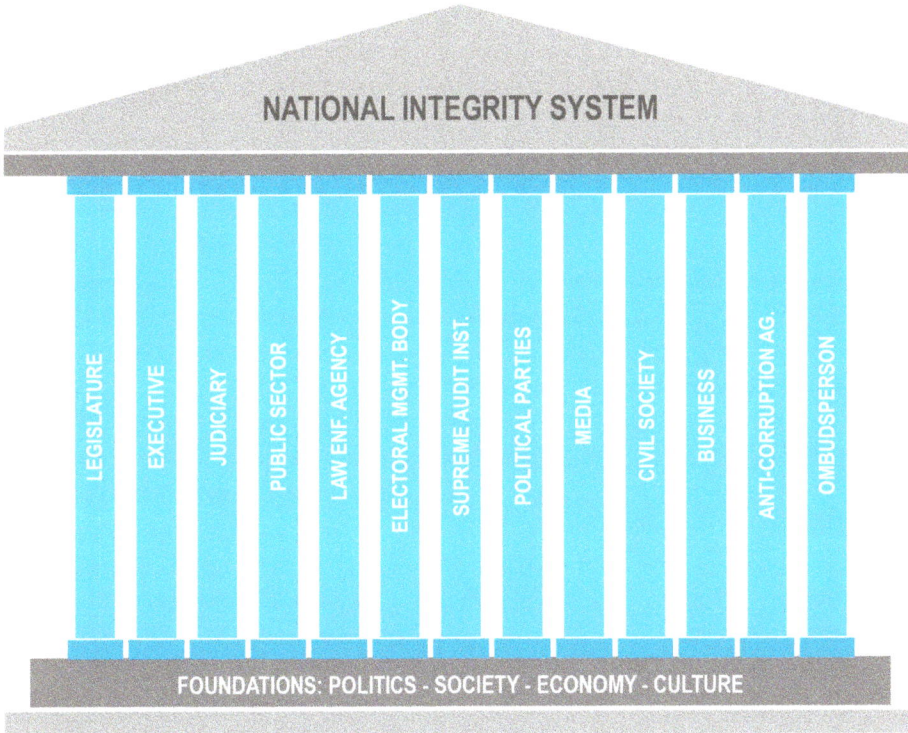

NATIONAL INTEGRITY SYSTEM

LEGISLATURE · EXECUTIVE · JUDICIARY · PUBLIC SECTOR · LAW ENF. AGENCY · ELECTORAL MGMT. BODY · SUPREME AUDIT INST. · POLITICAL PARTIES · MEDIA · CIVIL SOCIETY · BUSINESS · ANTI-CORRUPTION AG. · OMBUDSPERSON

FOUNDATIONS: POLITICS - SOCIETY - ECONOMY - CULTURE

Figure 8.2 Pillars of the National Integrity System

Source: Transparency International.

A further example of initiatives to increase public participation is participatory budgeting. The Swiss have been doing it for a very long time. Now, however, this trend is increasingly occurring at sub-national and local government levels around the world, albeit from a low base. In some countries this has allowed for the possibility of actually putting together packages of tax increases along with specific spending proposals, and, as they are doing in some countries such as Brazil, putting aside a small amount of money for citizen decision on how it is to be spent.

The creation of independent fiscal councils is another measure to be considered. Recent discussion about establishing one of these in New Zealand has become more noticeable. We have some real problems around the level of public participation in the setting of macro fiscal policy, and how much the public debt and the deficit should be and how we should be spending our money in a sectoral sense. An independent fiscal council would stand in stark contrast with and be a major improvement to New Zealand's current fiscal review process. At the moment, the only monitoring of fiscal policy in the country occurs in the single chamber of Parliament and the finance and expenditure committee, which is chaired by a member of the governing party. That committee has a budget to access independent advice, but it has never used it to retain advice on fiscal policy. Moreover, last year, the finance and expenditure committee received just two public submissions on the Government's budget policy statement; the Government does not respond to these submissions.

Citizen co-production offers a compelling avenue for increasing public participation. Again, an anecdote serves to illustrate the benefits of this process. There was a retired fireman sitting in a cafe in his home city in California when suddenly an ambulance pulled up next door. The paramedics rushed in to a restaurant and a group of people followed them in. The retired fireman asked the paramedics what had happened, and they told him that a man had just died from a heart attack. The fireman is rueful when he is told this, as he had been sitting in this cafe next door to the restaurant and he was trained in delivering cardiopulmonary resuscitation (CPR) that could have saved that man's life. In the aftermath of this event, the retired fireman submitted a proposal to his local council, which has now been adopted. The council has put together a register of everybody in the city who is trained in CPR. They compiled their mobile phone numbers. Now, when there is an emergency where it will take the ambulance some time to arrive at the scene, the council sends a text message to everybody on that list to see if there is anyone in the area who can give CPR. This is a good example of the kind of new public participation and co-production that is enabled by new technology.

The previous diagram (Figure 8.2) depicts an analytical framework developed by Jeremy Pope of Transparency International Berlin for a National Integrity System. Pope, the current Human Rights Commissioner, is strongly associated with this framework because he was the founding managing director of TI. The idea is that the state of integrity and transparency, and trust and effectiveness of government, is associated with how the different pillars in the national integrity system function. This includes the legislature, the executive, the judiciary, key watchdog institutions such as the auditor-general and the ombudsman, business, civil society, the media, political parties and so on. This is a framework that is a very useful way to think about assessing the state of integrity and governance.

TI New Zealand is about to commence a new systemic study. It will have been nearly 10 years since we did the last one. The study will assess New Zealand against international best practices in transparency, participation and accountability, and anticorruption. The project has received financial support from the Office of the Auditor-General and the State Services Commission, and we are approaching other agencies. The Department of Prime Minister and Cabinet is supportive. The release of the new study is intended to coincide with the centenary of the *Public Service Act*, which was passed in 1912 and implemented in April 1913. So it is a salient time to launch a new focus on transparency and accountability in New Zealand. The approach will be collaborative and consultative. The objective is

to test New Zealand's perception of itself, as a country with high
standards of transparency and accountability, free of and at low risk of
corruption, and to identify areas where action is needed to strengthen
transparency, accountability, and participation, and to kick-start the
necessary changes. (Transparency International 2013).

So what do I think are some specific areas for action? Well, we need to invest
more resources in diagnosis. The national integrity study is an important
example; however, there need to be more public surveys about attitudes towards
compliance and voluntary compliance, as well as towards norms of trust and
norms against bribery. We need to probe New Zealand's high rating. New
Zealand should inquire more deeply about whether it faces risks of corruption
and fraud.

I would argue that another important feature that is lacking in New Zealand is
an ethics code for MPs. This would improve the legitimacy of Parliament. New
Zealand needs more transparency in lobbying. The transparency of political
parties is also important. I think of financing issues that have been brought to
the fore in the past five years, but are still not properly settled. The boundary
between political parties and the public purse needs far more transparency. This
is partly related to the *Official Information Act*, which does not apply to the
administration of Parliament. There needs to be more focus on areas of highest
risk, utilising the framework of monopoly and discretion, and we need a more
results-focused public service.

The United Kingdom has been putting a huge amount of effort into this in
recent years. And again, while I generally do not think an anecdote constitutes
an argument, I believe this one is illustrative of some of the things we need
to be thinking about in New Zealand. In the United Kingdom, a leading heart
surgeon led an initiative, saying 'we need to publicise the mortality rate of
patients against individual heart surgeons'. That was agreed within the medical
profession and was put into place, I think, about two years ago. The mortality
rate has come down significantly in the United Kingdom since that happened.
Such initiatives have not been thought about much in New Zealand, and we
really do need to do that.

The destruction of the environment is a concern for the public. This stems
partly from what the Government does, and obviously, also what the private
sector does. This leads to the regulatory function. We need to think about triple
bottom-line reporting for government. This discussion has been brought up at
the global level. One of the principles of the GIFT initiative states: 'Governments
should strive to report the economic, financial and environmental impacts of
what they do' (GIFT 2012). We need to do a much better job of that in New
Zealand. We could, again, lead the world, if we take it seriously.

Our private sector seems remarkably complacent. Many people within the private sector do not know that since 2000 it is a crime to bribe a foreign public official. So, if you are offshore and you are an exporter, and you are trying to get your goods off the wharf, or whatever it might be, you are subject to New Zealand criminal law if you pay a bribe. Some New Zealanders working in overseas markets think they can avoid the legal punishments if they use an intermediary to pay the bribe; however, that is not the case: they are still breaking the law. It is important to conduct more training and raise awareness of the role of professional integrity. TI New Zealand is starting to work more closely with professional service firms and trying to engage them in raising awareness of corruption and bribery in New Zealand.

In the longer term, introducing mandatory civics education in schools is crucial to our objective. New Zealand urgently needs to educate its young people about the strong public and democratic institutions that we all take for granted. They should understand how our public system, our constitutional arrangements, our Parliament, our executive and our judiciary function and interact.

New Zealand should take more steps to abide by international law on corruption. In 2003, New Zealand signed the United Nations Convention against Corruption (UNCAC); however, it has still not ratified it. There are no defensible reasons for not doing so. Ratifying the convention would necessitate a small number of legal tweaks to New Zealand legislation. The ratification decision has been sitting in select committee for a couple of years, and we really do need to take that final step and ratify it. Ratifying it would require the Government to come up with a new national anticorruption strategy, and to do that in a widely consultative fashion.

Finally, New Zealand should join the Open Government Partnership. This is one of US President Barack Obama's foreign policy initiatives. The United States and Brazil have led this, and the United Kingdom is one of the founding members. It is a new club of countries which are committed to open government. There are a few low-level entry requirements: the main requirement for members is that they have to bring to the table and develop new initiatives that involve civil society and the private sector. New Zealand should seriously consider joining the Open Government Partnership to look at what is going on in other comparable countries such as the United Kingdom. It would be a way of signalling and cementing greater transparency and accountability in this and other areas.

References

Global Initiative for Fiscal Transparency (GIFT). 2012. *High-Level Principles on Fiscal Transparency*, 1 November. Available from: <http://fiscaltransparency. net/2012/11/high-level-principles-on-fiscal-transparency/>.

Klitgaard, R. 1988. *Controlling Corruption* (Berkeley: University of California Press).

Sunstein, C. 1996. 'Social Norms and Social Roles' *Columbia Law Review*, 96(4): 903–68.

Transparency International. 2013. 'Integrity Plus NIS Assessment: Taking High Trust to all Facets of New Zealand Society', *Transparency Times*, January. Available from: <http://www.transparency.org.nz/docs/2013/Transparency-Times-January-2013.pdf?PHPSESSID=08d6e857f537407d2cd9d8397ba0edb5>.

Part 2: Managing Risks and Building Resilence

9. Lessons for Government in Minimising Risk: What can the public service learn from the private sector?

Bridget Hutter

In my contribution to this collection of essays I will focus on risk regulation—my area of expertise. I will also touch upon contingency planning, because there is some overlap between these two subjects.

Managing risks and preventing disasters are increasingly at the centre of contemporary debates about governance. And as several contributors to this volume indicate, the potential for disaster is ever present. Each year, sadly, some of these potentials are realised. Not surprisingly, we have debates about nuclear safety in the wake of natural disasters—especially following the great East Japan earthquake and subsequent tsunami of 2011. Food scares are quite regular around the globe, particularly *E. coli* outbreaks. Germany suffered a particularly bad one in 2011. Then in this region, of course, there are natural disasters—be they floods and bushfires in Australia or earthquakes in New Zealand.

In each of these cases questions are asked about governments and about regulators—and in particular, about why they weren't better prepared. In other words, they are usually criticised. This is interesting at one level, because it underlines an expectation that we can govern the future and indicates a theme in social theory: we have a very modern preoccupation with risk and live in a world where risk-management approaches are increasingly advocated as a form of governance.

Social theorists argue that modern societies are characterised by new risk environments. These are associated at one level with substantive changes in society—for example, the growth of science and technology. Moreover, these risks are increasingly global in nature, often traversing national and organisational boundaries. Internet risks fall into that category, as do the threats of climate change. In addition, often these are what I call 'manufactured risks', meaning they are the unintended consequences of innovations, science and technology to which publics and the environment are involuntarily exposed.

Once they become such risks, governments have increasingly intervened to manage and regulate them. And in so doing, they have exemplified another feature of modern society: new ways of seeing the world that include both an orientation towards the future and a belief that we are able to anticipate, control and manage risk. This new approach has crucial consequences for governance.

From this perspective, then, regulation is one manifestation of a very modern belief that risk can be anticipated and controlled. Ulrich Beck (1992), a German sociologist, talks about a world in which we are increasingly occupied with debating, preventing and managing risk, to the point that he coined the phrase 'the risk society'. Similarly, Anthony Giddens (1999:3), a distinguished British sociologist and former director of the London School of Economics, argues that we have a growing preoccupation with the future, which he contrasts with former beliefs that were based much more in fate. The aspiration to control the future, Giddens argues, is a very modern perspective, so much so, he continues, that we also believe we are able to anticipate and do much more about natural disasters than we ever previously thought. So Beck (1992), again, writes that even natural hazards appear less random than they used to.

Social and organisational responses to expectations about anticipation and management of risk are considerable and can command enormous resources. Examples include the creation of specialist risk-management and contingency planning departments such as the United Kingdom's Civil Contingency Secretariat and the United States' Department of Homeland Security, both of which were established in the wake of 9/11. The latter commands particularly large resources.

Of course the private sector has its own equivalent departments: meta risk-management departments, compliance departments, and indeed an array of specialist staff, risk officers and compliance officers. All of these use a variety of formal risk tools and perspectives in a bid to avoid the repetition of previous risk events, and also to help identify and manage new risks. The expectations placed upon these departments and their personnel may be considerable.

One relevant example are the findings from the 9/11 Commission, which claimed that there had been a lack of institutional imagination on the part of the security services. The commission wrote that '[a]cross the government there were failures of imagination, policy capabilities and management. The most important failure was one of imagination. We don't believe the leaders understood the gravity of the threat' (National Commission on Terrorist Attacks Upon the United States 2004). This commission's emphasis on the need to have imagination is quite a hefty expectation, and underlines how great the expectations may have become.

Social commentators, for their part, tend to be sceptical about the expectation that we can anticipate and manage risk. They caution very much about some of the anticipatory expectations we place upon our governments and our organisations; Anthony Giddens (1999) talks about a plurality of future scenarios and the absence of certainty about which is the most accurate, referring, of course, to the generation of the multiple possible things that might go wrong, which we may model. Beck refers to the optimistic futility with which the highly developed institutions of modern society attempt to anticipate what cannot be anticipated.

And Charles Perrow, a sociologist from the United States, has spent a substantial part of his career writing about the ways in which organisations are imperfect and cannot provide complete security. In fact, one of his most famous books is entitled *Normal Accidents* (Perrow 1999) to underline the fact that in very complex systems it is inevitable that something will go wrong; we cannot get it right all of the time.

Given that my contribution to this volume was to address the limits of future-proofing the state, I will now explore somewhat why many social commentators are so gloomy about the best efforts of those engaged in future-proofing the state, and some of the expectations that are placed on them. I will use a number of examples. Overall, though, the headline message is that one reason for all the gloom is the recognition of the very complex social, political, economic and technical decision-making involved in future-proofing the state.

To start with, what constitutes a risk may not be clear. There may be debates and disagreement about what is risky. As Mary Douglas and Aaron Wildavsky wrote in *Risk and Culture* (1982), 'substantial disagreement remains over what is risky, how risky it is and what to do about it'. Though this book was written several decades ago, this was true then, is true today, and without doubt will be true in several decades. There is always debate about what constitutes a risk, how risky it is and what we should do about it. And what we increasingly know is that at a technical level, we often do not have the data to really tell us with any certainty what the risk may be.

One example that is increasingly discussed is climate change, where we know that the past may not be such a good indicator of what will happen in the future. This is particularly so because climate change may be increasing the incidence and patterns of natural disasters. So we cannot look at our historical data and think that that is going to be a good predictor of what is going to happen in future.

We also have another problem, other than the contestation of scientific knowledge: politics has become embroiled with science. Take the example of so-called 'Climategate', which involved a politically motivated challenge to the status of scientific evidence and knowledge about climate change.

The controversy began in November 2009 when a server was breached at the University of East Anglia's Climatic Research Unit, one of the research centres that constructs various global temperature and precipitation analyses. Two weeks before the Copenhagen Summit on Climate Change, 160 mb of data were copied from that server to various locations on the Internet: more than 1000 emails and 2000 documents, all relating to climate change research between 1996 and 2009. Most of the emails were rather technical and rather boring; but controversy focused on only a few of those.

A few emails, it was alleged by climate change sceptics, demonstrated that climate change scientists were manipulating data in order to claim that climate change was happening. These email correspondences, along with the other data, were used to suggest that dissenting scientific papers were not even being published—they were being rejected in order to promote the climate change cause. Despite the fact that successive inquiries refuted those claims, it was a very damaging episode at a time when international climate change talks were in progress.

A second example of a slightly different order is the Eyjafjallajökull volcanic ash episode, which Pierre-Alain Schieb alludes to in his contribution to this volume. As readers will remember, European air space was closed in April 2010 for just more than a week, and then intermittently thereafter during that European spring. That case was interesting because of the change in attitudes it caused. When the volcano first erupted, conventional precautionary advice was followed: aircraft should not mix with volcanic ash.

That was absolutely uncontentious in the first couple of days; but as Europe started to close more and more of its air space; as airlines started to lose vast sums of money—not just because their planes and staff were grounded, but also because of EU legislation that required them to pay the costs of stranded passengers—the knowledge base upon which the regulators were deciding that aircraft should not under any circumstances mix with volcanic ash began to be contested.

Consequently, airlines started pulling in different scientific experts who would challenge the effects and the levels at which aircraft engines were susceptible to volcanic ash. The meteorological evidence itself also began to be contested. So it was a very interesting case to look at because in a sense it was motivated by business interests that were being seriously damaged at the Easter holidays—an incredibly important time of year for them.

I raise it here because it is another example of how scientific evidence may be contested for other reasons, and sometimes political or indeed business reasons. It did result in a relaxation of the regulations quite soon after the event. I am currently doing research into how volcanic ash affects aeroplanes, and I have discovered that the safe level of ash in which a plane can fly is still contested.

In addition to those political and technical problems, future-proofing the state also involves some very complicated choices about social and economic costs and benefits and how they are distributed. Scarce resources have to be allocated—something that is particularly acute at a time such as this when there is a recession gripping much of the world. How those scarce resources are allocated will centre on very differing views about the role of the state in promoting very different interests, and very different conceptions of equality or inequality, or indeed freedom or restriction of trade.

What is the relative value you give to individual or collective goods? What is the relative value given to present as opposed to future generations? And what value do you place on the environment? Inevitably, there will be ambivalence about the answers to those questions. There may also be vested interests involved; the playing field is never level.

Competing interests also exist. Big organisations may be government stakeholders who have the power to shape the debate about what is taken to be risky and what is not, and how we respond. Consumers and potential victims may have less power, of course. What we do know is that all the different stakeholders and all the different players will have differing objectives at some point in the policy cycle. And these need to be dealt with.

My underlying point is therefore that the decisions being made about the future-proofing of the state are political and ethical as much as they are technical and 'objective'. Expectations that it is possible to govern the future can lead to strong moral and political imperatives. There are moral imperatives to protect publics, but also there are political imperatives to avoid blame; as Aaron Wildavsky wrote in his book *Searching for Safety* (1988:225), 'a strategy of anticipation is based on a fear of regret'. In some areas there are contentions that this is of growing importance. And we may actually be encouraged to be risk averse because of politicians' tendency to engage both in the blame game and in blame avoidance.

So there may be pressures to act as if we are in control—by producing elaborate planning documents, relying on complicated models and trusting in numbers when in fact sometimes we should not trust in those numbers if they do not have a strong evidence base. The danger, of course, is that it leads to the wrong policy choices. Aaron Wildavsky warned about this many years ago in *Searching for Safety*, where he argued for the need to balance anticipation and resilience.

Anticipation—both in regulation and in contingency planning—can, Wildavsky argued, lead to wasted resources because of the high volume of hypothesised risk, much of which may be exaggerated or false predictions. The focus must be rather on selecting appropriate strategies according to the evidence you have. I will dedicate the second half of this chapter to looking at regulation and, to some extent, disaster mitigation. When is it relevant to use regulation and when is it irrelevant? To answer these questions I will focus on natural disasters, but we also need to take on board other disasters for which we humans are responsible.

It must first be said, however, that expectations of anticipation and control are unusual when it comes to natural hazards. This is often in contrast with the literature on human-made disasters, for there is an acceptance that we cannot prevent what is going to go wrong, but expect that we might mitigate the consequences of natural disasters.

So how much we are able to mitigate, adapt and plan may be overestimated in terms of the expectations that are placed on governments and organisations. Of course there are various forms of mitigation that can prove useful; here I am focusing in particular on the ways in which risk regulation might be used to help mitigate the effects of future disasters; here I am not looking at the later stages.

From this perspective, the forms of mitigation that can prove useful include risk-avoidance strategies. These focus primarily on land-use policies (hazard zones, for example), and they focus in particular on delineating areas where settlements are regulated, ranging from hazard zones where no urban development or planning is permitted at all, through to development laws.

Many examples of these strategies are in use around the world. The State of California has legislation that requires a Natural Hazard Disclosure Statement to be provided by those selling property if it falls within a designated hazard zone. In Japan hazard zones have been created in areas related to disasters such as landslides, and since 2001, new building developments in hazard zones have been restricted. In Japan there have also been attempts to relocate people away from hazard areas, and to develop early warning systems.

In the United Kingdom, too, we have similar examples (such as areas where you need planning permission to build), though thankfully natural disasters are not common in that country, flooding probably being the exception. In fact, despite examples of floods that have been large by UK standards in recent years, I am still asked to sign petitions in my hometown from anti-planning planners lobbying for development in very well-known floodplains. This causes tensions.

Of course, some authors actually believe that the damage caused by natural and manufactured risks is exacerbated by social and special aspects of twenty-first-century living, over and beyond the planning laws. Perrow has recently written a powerful book (2007) in which he says we routinely allow heavy concentrations of economic power, hazards and populations in close proximity to each other, therefore enhancing the likelihood that a disaster, whether human-made or natural, will have a devastating effect. His example is the 2005 Hurricane

Katrina in Louisiana, where both the local population and industrial complexes were located in an area of high natural hazards. We saw its devastating effects. Around the world, however, we will see many examples where such co-location is ongoing and where we are not learning lessons.

Another well-known risk-reduction strategy is risk regulation. Perhaps the best-known examples are building codes—especially in earthquake and flood zones where the damage is primarily to buildings and infrastructure; devastating consequences of code breakdowns follow for populations. Those building controls embrace a variety of risk-regulation tools, design engineering and construction standards. New building codes are quite commonplace, and moreover, we know they are highly effective, especially where they incorporate learning from previous disasters.

Retrospective building upgrades are another example of risk regulation, which involves strengthening programs for existing buildings in areas of natural disasters. This approach is not common, and unsurprisingly so, for retrospective upgrades cost a lot of money. And yet, they do exist. Mexico City introduced a major program for retroactive strengthening following the 1985 earthquake there, as did California following the 1994 North Ridge earthquake. We know that where building codes do not exist, or where they exist but are not enforced, the loss of life is often considerably higher than in areas where those codes exist and are enforced. And I would underline strongly the importance of enforcement. There is no point having the code or a regulation if you decide not to enforce it.

Still on the topic of natural disasters, what happens when the disaster reaches the point where mass evacuations become a distinct possibility? If we look back to the March 2011 Fukushima nuclear meltdown, for instance, the Japanese Government actually considered evacuating Tokyo, a city of 30 million people. It didn't happen, obviously, and you would never wish for mass evacuations, but would it even have been possible? And should a government even attempt to do it?

I think a government should be prepared to do it—what is important is how to go about it. Sometimes the reaction is to put in place very detailed plans about what to do if X happens. The problem is that disasters rarely repeat themselves in precise ways. But we have to be prepared, which is why we emphasise resilience. We have to be prepared for the unexpected to happen and for things not to happen in the ways we expect. So we might have plans; but sometimes those plans are so detailed and they rest on so many assumptions that they may actually be quite dangerous. For this reason we need to think very carefully about what those plans look like, which is why the emphasis on resilience and de-centring and incorporating local populations is so important.

It is important not to rely on natural scientific evidence only, but also on social science evidence. And increasingly these two forms of evidence are being brought together. One example comes from a recent conference in Japan. An academic there had the most beautiful model about what would happen when a tsunami was going to hit Japan: there would be sensors out to sea that would alert people to the problem; alarms would also go off in the city, prompting affected citizens to move to higher ground. What was not in his model, however, was any understanding of how people behave when they hear an alarm: they don't calmly get out of their house and go to safer ground. They worry about their possessions, they worry more about their family, and they even worry about their pets. They don't move in ways in which you expect them to. And sometimes when these alarms go off they can cause panic.

In fact, one of the unintended positive consequences of the 2005 London underground bombing was that initially people thought this was not a terrorist attack, but a power failure. Consequently, people didn't panic; they thought, 'Oh, the underground electricity system must have broken down. We have to get people off the trains because a couple had crashed because of the electricity going.' And people left in a very orderly manner. If people had known or realised the truth, there might have been panic in evacuating that space.

Another crucial point I would like to underline is the importance of information. Governance decisions depend upon information: information about the likelihood of a disaster occurring, and about the probable damage that might occur. And the knowledge base upon which that policy is formulated is crucial. We need to be aware of the limitations of our data. Historical data, as I have already indicated with reference to the climate change example, may be insufficient. In this way, historical data may not be a good predictor of what is to come.

There may also be significantly less information available than we suppose. Sometimes policymakers—but especially the media and the general public—do expect that we are able to do things that we are in fact not able to predict. And it is important to take account of that. It really depends on the sort of risk and the sort of disaster you are involved in: there obviously will be some confidence in the location of a volcano, and we have a fair idea where flooding might happen, but it may be much more difficult to locate with very much certainty the location and occurrence of hurricanes and wildfires, for example.

Take the example of Hurricane Gustav in 2008. Its trajectory and force, which occurred in the same area as Katrina, proved very difficult to predict. Nearly two million people fled the Louisiana coastline in anticipation of a category three to four hurricane. By the time it reached Louisiana, however, it had been downgraded to category two. So those two million people need not have moved.

In hindsight, it raised questions about the policy decision to evacuate and how seriously the next hurricane warnings in Louisiana would be taken. There is a danger, of course, they might be ignored.

In the Australian context, similar difficulties have emerged with respect to bushfires and alarms for bushfires: you may have a risk of an alarm of a bushfire that doesn't then happen—something that can shake confidence. This point takes us to what is an important topic: the risks of risk governance, which may be quite considerable.

Gustav is an example of a false positive, but we also have false negatives. We have alarms or a failure to alarm that may shake public and policymaking confidence in both science and the scientific community. There are examples in the United Kingdom that also affect confidence in governments. It can also lead to the waste of valuable resources, which was one of Wildavsky's key arguments. It is worth noting here that when we talk about these issues, particularly around resources, with respect to developing nations, the sorts of decisions being made are sometimes much starker than we realise. When we in the developed world have a recession it's quite comfortable compared with many parts of the world. And when you discuss natural disasters with respect to some poor nations, the amount of investment you have to put into future-proofing the state imposes a much starker decision.

Of course, there may be unintended consequences of this risk anticipation. There may be risk aversion, fuelled by concerns about blame attribution. Sometimes measures designed to protect populations from natural disasters can become a source of danger in themselves. They may offer false reassurance, or they might fail, and in so doing, increase vulnerability. A case in point is the system of levees in Louisiana whose failure can cause unexpected and possibly larger flooding than would otherwise have occurred.

These strategies may also reduce the ability of organisations and societies to cope with the unexpected, which is why there is much discussion of resilience—meant to be a more flexible and evolved way of responding to disasters. There may also be value conflicts. The classic example here is of course security. Anybody who has recently visited Heathrow Airport will be aware of the incredible level of security travellers are subject to. They have to allow several hours in order to get through the airport—on a bad day, sometimes even longer. Those security measures are in place, of course, because of the threat of terrorist attacks.

And there are big debates about how worthwhile that security is and whether it may contravene human rights. In fact, at Heathrow's Terminal 5 the plans for security initially put in place were much more stringent than those that now exist because of protests and legal fights about the right to take passengers' fingerprints and photographs, let alone the added time en masse that it takes everyone to get through the airport. The fact is if that security was removed and something went wrong, you would get a very clear notion of what the blame game would look like.

So there are problems in terms of what we put in place. Security at Heathrow may be a harsh example, but harsh examples are important to get to the bottom of what the issue is. Hence, the important message is to look very long and hard at the evidence you have and how robust it is before formulating policy. And though transnational cases are sometimes very useful, transnational effectiveness varies tremendously. Ultimately you must learn your own lessons from your own disasters; but it can also be very useful to share information. It gives you an idea of what the prerequisites might be for future-proofing the state.

Effectiveness, too, varies. What we do learn from looking at global disasters, however, is that one prerequisite is a stable government and good governance systems. Enforcement, as I have already mentioned, is crucial. Corruption can be a major obstacle, as recent earthquakes in Turkey and China have demonstrated. In Sichuan in 2008 engineering and construction quality were major factors contributing to many thousands of deaths, especially of schoolchildren.

Central–local relations are also key to securing good governance. The central government of any state cannot achieve this on its own. It has to do it in partnership with local communities and local governments and business. Buy-in to the legitimacy of what is being done is crucial, as is the recognition of tacit knowledge, particularly tacit local knowledge.

Brian Wynn (1992), for example, has written a helpful academic paper showing that in the post-Chernobyl meltdown phase the UK authorities paid scant attention to the local tacit knowledge of sheep farmers in the Lake District who thought their sheep were not behaving normally, perhaps because of radiation fallout. The central authorities just didn't think this was possible; the farmers were in fact correct. As Wynn demonstrated, paying attention to local knowledge that may not be highly formal or scientific has actually been found to be rather important.

Increasingly, then, future-proofing the state is a multiparty activity. In the United Kingdom recent coastal and river defence schemes have involved the Department for Environment, Food and Rural Affairs (DEFRA), the relevant environment agency, the regulator, local authorities and the insurance industry. The insurance industry plays an increasingly important role of course, and there are a number of different schemes in which the insurance industry can partner with governments in terms of trying to deal with mitigation measures, incentivising people to invest in mitigation measures and helping facilitate post-disaster recovery. The way these scenarios pan out when the insurance sector is called upon to act may, however, be very different to those that were previously anticipated. Again, this highlights the need to learn from events that have already happened.

Not wishing to end on a gloomy note, I want to emphasise that there are important benefits to be gained from risk regulation, other measures and the mitigation of natural and other disasters. These benefits can be considerable, but they need to be used strategically. It's crucial in deciding policy options to look at the quality and the accuracy of the information you have about the levels and the location of risks. Where levels of certainty are high then more detailed risk-regulation measures and planning are possible and can be put in place. But where they are not, you may simply be wasting resources and giving false assurance. At a macro level, it is important to understand that we can place far too much faith in our ability to govern the future. We need to keep an eye on our limitations and expectations.

And although the state is an important player in future-proofing, we need a mix. We need to empower different participants in the regulatory process, including national and local governments, and businesses and local communities. If this is achieved, future-proofing of the state will be a cooperative endeavour with an emphasis on governance rather than on government.

Note

This chapter is based on a transcript of the author's presentation to the 2012 ANZSOG Conference.

References

Beck, U. 1992. *Risk Society: Towards a New Modernity* (London: Sage).

Douglas, M. and Wildavsky, A. 1982. *Risk and Culture: An Essay on the Selection of Technological and Environmental Dangers* (Berkeley: University of California Press).

Giddens, A. 1999. *Runaway World: How Globalization is Reshaping Our Lives* (London: Profile).

Hutter, B. M. 2009. 'The role of regulation in mitigating the risks of natural disasters', in H. Kunreuther and M. Useem (eds), *Learning from Catastrophes: Strategies for reaction and response* (Philadelphia: Wharton School Publishing).

Hutter, B. M. 2010. *Anticipating Risks and Organising Risk Regulation* (Cambridge: Cambridge University Press).

National Commission on Terrorist Attacks Upon the United States. 2004. *The 9/11 Commission Report*, 22 July. Available from: <http://govinfo.library.unt.edu/911/report/911Report.pdf>.

Perrow, C. 1999. *Normal Accidents: Living with High Risk Technologies* (Princeton, NJ: Princeton University Press).

Perrow, C. 2007. *The New Catastrophe* (Princeton NJ: Princeton University Press)

Wildavsky, A. 1988. *Searching for Safety* (New Brunswick, NJ: Transaction Press).

Wynn, B. 1992. 'Misunderstood Misunderstanding: Social Identities and Public Uptake of Science', *Public Understanding of Science*, 1(3):281–304.

10. Risk Responses, Emergency Management and Community Resilience in the Aftermath of the Recent Victorian Natural Disasters

Neil Comrie

This contribution focuses on risk responses, emergency management and the development of community resilience in the context of two natural disasters in Australia: the 2009 Victorian bushfires and the 2010 Victorian floods. My contribution arises from experience as a police officer of 35 years' service, including eight years as chief commissioner of Victoria Police and on-the-ground practical experience; also relevant is my experience of reviewing the 67 recommendations arising out of the 2009 Victorian Bushfires Royal Commission, and with reviewing the 2010 Victorian floods. From my perspective, I would argue that in recent years our capacity to deal with natural disasters has been tested more than at any point in the history of the Australian nation; however, while natural disasters are damaging events, they also provide an opportunity to learn.

Following these two major natural disasters in Victoria—the bushfires and the floods—there has been some critical analysis of our preparation and planning before the disasters and our subsequent responses to them and recovery. Consequently, we now have a substantial body of recent evidence we can use to inform our decision-making for the future. And there are two broad conclusions we can draw from the many reviews that have been conducted: first and foremost, we cannot always prevent or avoid major emergencies; and second, we realise they will continue to occur in the future. We can, however, reduce the risk and mitigate the damage of these emergencies through improved planning, preparation and coordination of response. And an important lesson that comes out of the two major events in Victoria is that the State Government must overhaul the flawed approach to managing emergency resources that has prevailed across all relevant agencies.

My most significant argument here, however, is that our communities must be equipped to be better able to survive and recover from disasters. Changes in legislative policy processes are needed, but it is clear that the most important improvement we can make to existing emergency management is to ensure our communities are more capable of looking after themselves. I will try to explain the rationale for these comments below.

Many lessons are to be learnt from the 2009 Victorian Bushfires Royal Commission. The most important issue to arise from the royal commission is the need for everyone in the community, from the individual right through to government, to play a role and take a share of the responsibility for dealing with emergencies. We have known for some time that probably the best means of emergency prevention is the education of adults and children. In fact, it was suggested some decades ago that fire prevention be made a part of the curriculum in every school. This was the finding of the Stretton Royal Commission after the 1939 Black Friday bushfires, in which 71 Victorians lost their lives. Now 73 years after this recommendation was made, and after the tragedy of the 2009 fires has been digested, it appears that education about bushfire safety will finally be included in the national curriculum.

I undertook the Victorian Floods Review in 2011, which turned into a protracted investigation into the factors associated with the floods. A large body of evidence was gathered from extensive community consultations. We visited all of the flood-affected areas in Victoria, held public meetings, spoke to those people directly affected by the floods, met with the local governments in those areas, received 150 written submissions, and undertook operational debriefings with all of the agencies involved in responding to the floods and which had extensive consultation with stakeholder agencies. Out of all of these consultations, the major issue of concern that emerged was that our communities were largely unaware of the risks they faced; consequently, they were ill prepared and incapable of looking after themselves in the face of adversity.

Evidence of a lack of community resilience included a poor understanding of their risk environments, despite the fact that people were living on floodplains. In many cases, they had no idea they were at risk of flood. Hospitals and community centres were built on floodplains and, as with the hospital at Charlton, were basically destroyed by the flood. Moreover, flood-mitigation plans were inadequate: people living in those locations were given no prior warning by the authorities that they lived on floodplains. There was little local planning or preparation for a response to an event of that nature. The structures for local responses were poor: they were disorganised and therefore extremely ad hoc. Two findings from the consultations were particular to some smaller, often isolated towns. First, emergency services found it difficult to access these areas. Second, emergency services personnel who happened to reside in the towns were forced to divide their attention between looking after their own properties and families on the one hand and trying to do their job on the other. The reality was that because of this isolation most people had no real idea of what they should do to look after themselves.

People did not know where to go for advice and knowledge about what should happen, and in many instances they simply were unaware of who was in charge and who was able to give directions. There was also poor capacity for mitigating the flood once it struck. In some cases, elementary procedures were adequate, but many people did not know how to fill sandbags or how to stack them. Despite their best efforts, in a lot of instances when the sandbags were placed in rows, they were washed away because they were not placed properly. Simple processes such as sandbagging often go unnoticed by policymakers, but the Victorian floods demonstrate that we must consider the need to provide education in the basics of disaster mitigation.

There was also confusion resulting from inaccurate and untimely warnings. A new facility called Emergency Alert, a telephone-based warning system that sends SMS information messages to local residents, was not in place for the Black Saturday bushfires of February 2009, but it was for the 2010 floods. Yet, emergency managers still had a lot of work to do because in a number of instances the warnings sent out were unclear and confusing. In some instances people were not sure whether information was a warning or simply advice; they became confused about what it was they were being told. Perhaps the most concerning aspect, from my perspective, was that many people were completely reliant on the emergency service organisations to give them some support and direction when they found themselves in trouble; successful disaster management requires that people who are threatened by the disaster have some autonomous capacity to resist its effects.

So what do we make of that lack of resilience and why has it occurred? The evidence indicates that many people felt they had been completely disempowered from the process of looking after themselves in an emergency, that the Government had centralised all the resources and the authority to deal with those situations. This created an expectation that, in the face of adversity, the State authorities would save residents—even at the last moment. Many of the respondents we spoke to in the community said the State Government had dictated to communities on emergency management rather than working with communities on such management. There is absolutely no doubt that apathy and complacency had developed in the communities affected by the Black Saturday bushfires and the Victorian floods. One relevant example about community apathy was demonstrated 12 months after the Black Saturday bushfires in Victoria, when the Country Fire Authority of Victoria (CFA) conducted a survey of communities affected by bushfires. Even though 173 people had lost their lives in this disaster, 80 per cent of the respondents to the survey said they would still wait to see whether there was smoke and fire on the horizon before they left their homes—by which time it is too late to leave. We have a serious problem trying to deal with community apathy. And the real problem is that the more government does for people, the more they expect of it. Government has created and encouraged a relationship in which the community is dependent on it and is unable to fend for itself.

After the review of the Victorian floods, one of the recommendations I made in the report was that Victoria should establish a network of community resilience committees to develop and administer community resilience plans based on an 'all hazards' approach and tailored to the specific needs of each community.

The 'all hazards, all agencies' maxim is one of the core issues Victoria needs to address. The term means that a flexible integrated arrangement is in place between the relevant emergency agencies so that an integrated response is forthcoming— regardless of the agency emergency officers serve in or the particular hazard they are confronting. In Victoria we are going through a major reform program because some of the inherited shortcomings of the previous emergency response regime have been identified. The legislation in Victoria for the Metropolitan Fire Brigade and the CFA was created in 1958. Apart from a few adjustments, the legislation clearly reflects its age. It created a set of silo structures where the critical firefighting agencies each have separate boards; from a governance viewpoint they are required to make sure the organisations deliver against the legislation, but they can do so with little regard for agencies in neighbouring areas or other sectors. Ideally, when faced with major disaster events such as widespread bushfires or floods, all the emergency services agencies, irrespective of their primary role and responsibility, have to come together and work as a collective; however, with separate, disparate communication systems, different equipment that is not interchangeable and with cultures that are quite different, a range of barriers prevents the concept of cooperative response. I hope the ongoing review of the legislation, including a white paper consultation process, will provide some overarching policy and structure that will drive that sort of philosophy.

More importantly, one of the key things is to train our people in an environment in which they understand each others' roles and are trained to work together from the outset. Let me use the examples of the police and military services, although similar examples are found in most of the emergency professions. To become a police officer or a soldier, basic training equips the new trainees to do the basic functions in those services. Afterwards, as officers, they specialise in whatever it might be, perhaps detective work or the artillery or as engineers. All emergency management workers should go through the same fundamental training and emergency management and then specialise in a firefighting team or a State emergency service. That should do two things: it would ensure shared consistent training at the fundamental level; and it would act as a barrier to some of the distinctive cultural problems that exist and inevitably develop over time. So when people come together in a major event they already know each other because they have trained together, and the cultural barriers disappear quickly in that environment.

Shared basic training does not necessarily mean, however, identical arrangements across all towns and regions. One of the issues that became apparent when we inspected the sites of the floods and talked to communities was that a one-size-fits-all plan is not feasible. And so I recommended that the emergency service organisations should be *required* to consult and engage with local community resilience committees in the preparation, planning, response and recovery phases of emergency management.

It was interesting that while we were doing the flood review, the Council of Australian Governments (COAG) released the National Strategy for Disaster Resilience, which reiterated many recommendations about shared responsibility made by the bushfire royal commission.

In undertaking research and compiling our report on the flood disaster, it became evident that the idea of community resilience was not a new one—resilience models have been established around the world, including in New Zealand, Canada, the United Kingdom and the United States. These models inform the community that immediate assistance by emergency service responders *may not* be readily available and that they should be prepared and able to cope on their own for up to three days. All these models include information on understanding the risk that natural disasters pose to the community, on making an emergency plan and assembling an emergency supply kit. One example that prevails in New Zealand schools is that the threat of earthquakes is a dedicated topic addressed early in the curriculum. It is not clear why such models have not been replicated elsewhere.

Further, during the course of our investigative review, the Queensland Government, which had managed its own emergency response to Cyclone Yasi at the same time as the Victorian floods, launched a new website called 'Harden Up Queensland'. On the front page of that website is the following statement: 'Weather events are getting more severe and when a major weather event hits you cannot rely on government and volunteer organisations to help. You need to harden up by preparation, awareness and helping others.'

That was a courageous stance for the Government to adopt because, prior to that in Australia, a 'softly, softly' approach to informing people of their responsibilities and power to resist disasters had prevailed. The Bligh Queensland Government was really the first State government I had seen stating directly to people that they had to take some responsibility of their own during natural disasters.

Across Australasia we must now formulate a multi-pronged approach to achieving community resilience to natural disasters. The first step is for governments and emergency service organisations to realise that they cannot protect our communities in all circumstances. We have to disabuse people of the notion that emergency service organisations will save them at the last moment; to pretend otherwise is not only deceptive but also dangerous, because it will cause people to become complacent and stay in their homes until it is far too late to evacuate before the oncoming disaster. The royal commission into the Black Saturday bushfires found that in several cases people died because they stayed in their homes too long. We must also ensure that our communities are informed of the characteristics and capacity of their emergency services. For example, it would be worth publicising that in regional Victoria, more than 90 per cent of our emergency service organisations are staffed by volunteers who have other responsibilities.

Governments must also invest in good *forward planning*, which should include specific, practical, risk-related policies that can be implemented to reduce loss of life and community damage. We need realistic integrated flood plans that are based not on artificial municipal boundaries but on the footprint of the floodplain itself. Floods ignore artificial jurisdictional boundaries. Our State and municipal authorities need to revisit their flood-mitigation plans. We also need to plan infrastructure with the risk of flooding in mind. One of the problems here is that our forebears deliberately built along rivers so they could have access to water. Towns lie on floodplains; farmers farm on floodplains for the fertile soil. Hence, we cannot claim that all the consequent risks can be eliminated, but if the areas of highest risk are identified this can be built into future planning strategies to deal with them.

In relation to the risk of further fires, we need to better use our existing infrastructure. The Fire Services Commissioner in Victoria appointed after the bushfire royal commission is now looking at a strategy in which all public buildings in fire-prone areas such as schools and public halls in the future will be built to a specified standard, permitting them to be used as community fire refuges. Because of the high cost of retrofitting buildings or trying to adapt buildings in high-risk areas the Victorian Government decided to buy back some land where homes were burnt and other properties damaged; this is to prevent rebuilding in fire-prone areas. The central authorities are working through this process, but some councils have other pressing needs and agendas, including a rate base that they are trying to protect. In a couple of instances, new estates are being developed almost adjacent to those areas where the Government is buying back land—a truly bizarre phenomenon. Strong decision-making must come to the fore; retrospective correction is very difficult but taking a hard line and making decisions to ensure we do not repeat those mistakes again are necessary to reduce the chances of future disasters.

Another important element in community resilience will be to include private enterprises in planning. There is a real challenge here for communities to pick up where they have privately owned infrastructure that impacts on the wellbeing of the whole community. In Victoria the owner of an electricity substation located on a floodplain had no protective measures in place to keep electricity flowing to the community. That is why it is important for the community resilience strategy to identify such potential risks (even when it involves private installations) and to try to put some strategies in place to plan for them in ways that *involve* not exclude the private sector. My assessment is that if the private sector is engaged early enough and its members understand the community priorities they tend to become more involved more quickly than if they just see it as an inconvenient cost factor that will disappear in due course. It is just part of that process of involving every stakeholder in the planning process so that communities can have contingencies in place should an event arise.

We also have to make a long-term commitment to address the apathetic culture demonstrated by many in our communities and raise the level of awareness of their role in combating natural disasters. In other policy areas we have been able to do this. For instance, significant cultural change has taken place on Australian roads through things such as the Victorian Transport Accident Commission advertisements, which have been major contributors to the reduction in the road toll; and the QUIT campaign has seen a significant reduction in cigarette smoking throughout Australia. Long-term social education programs like these are critical to developing a strong sense of community resilience for natural disasters. We need similar campaigns to focus on community preparedness.

I have argued strongly that I do not think we need to create a whole new separate community structure to achieve this, because in every country town in Victoria there are pre-existing community service organisations looking for opportunities to serve their community. Lions clubs, Rotary clubs and Country Women's Association branches are among a wide range of organisations which, if appropriately engaged, would be a powerful force in building this community resilience.

We need to facilitate the education of communities so we can empower them. We need to work in conjunction with them, rather than directing them when disasters strike. We need to encourage communities to discover their own learning about resilience in preparation for natural disasters. Moreover, local governments must play a much more active role in emergency management than they have in the past—this is certainly the lesson from the Victorian natural disasters.

In conclusion, we still need to make a whole range of structural policy and legislative changes. In Victoria the Government has started to do this by commissioning various green and white policy papers on this issue. These will propose a range of options for the development of a new emergency management environment. In my view, the most effective and significant improvement in emergency management will flow from strong and resilient communities that are not absolutely dependent on emergency services at times of crisis.

Communities that have involvement in and ownership of plans for their own safety have a much greater capacity to look after themselves. Moreover, this actually presents governments with additional opportunities to use those arrangements for other community capacity building. In Australia over the past few decades, a lot of social and community structures that existed in small country towns have declined. This absence of social capital militates against governments effectively communicating with local communities. Reflecting on the aftermath of disasters, like the Victorian fires and floods, and thinking about future emergency management systems provide an opportunity to build those community social structures again.

The major challenge for government and its agencies, however, is to have the courage to relinquish the long-established practice of central control of emergency management and to devolve it to local communities. For some that will be a very difficult challenge, but from the Victorian perspective it is obvious that maintenance of the status quo is not a viable option, for as Margaret Mead once said: 'Never doubt that a small group of thoughtful concerned citizens can change the world. Indeed it's the only thing that ever has.'

11. Understanding Resilience and Reducing Future Vulnerabilities in Social-Ecological Systems

Brian Walker

I begin this contribution by examining what resilience means and then considering the implications for future vulnerabilities. The use of the term 'resilience' has risen markedly in recent years in response to growing awareness and uneasiness about looming shocks. They include global and regional financial crises, climate and weather shocks, pandemics, social unrest, regional wars and refugees, among others. These are rising in frequency. The frequency of such events worldwide is reminiscent of Winston Churchill's famous volume *The Gathering Storm*: we have that sense of the gathering storm and wonder what we can do. Will we be able to cope? That question is worrying many people, and that may suggest why we find the term resilience so much in use today. So, will we be able to cope?

Two recent surveys of the Australian media have checked thousands of sources for every occurrence of the word 'resilience' to look at what it meant, and they show how its use is rising and how very different are two common uses. The first one suggests the view that if authorities try to help people too much they do not bother to look after themselves, while the other is exactly opposite, expressing a hope that the concept of resilience does not erode into a justification for denying help to communities. So, there are two ends of a continuum about what to do and how much to help people. Nevertheless, this term has greatly different meanings in the minds of many people. In essence resilience is a framework for understanding how persistence and transformation coexist in living systems. In Chapter 5 of this volume, Peter Ho has talked about 'complex systems'; I call them 'living systems', but 'complex adaptive systems' is what they are.

Complicated systems and *complex* systems are different. Complicated systems are relatively simple in the sense that they have linear dynamics; they are entirely predictable. If you prod something and you know about it you can predict what will happen. Predictability is not possible in complex adaptive systems because they self-organise. Its parts themselves are capable of change. They can change their own behaviour and therefore they can adopt different things; their unpredictability has to be taken into account. I was told of a wonderful example of trying to enhance salmon fisheries in British Columbia where the industry thought: 'If we could just get more young salmon down to the sea then more salmon would come back to spawn and we would have more salmon.' So they enhanced production in the nurseries and put lots of young salmon in the rivers that went down to the sea; but on the way down to the sea these fingerlings went past another type of fish that had never eaten salmon because they ate other things. But when an enormous volume of little salmon fortuitously came by they switched their predation behaviour and ate the salmon, so fewer salmon actually made it to the sea. A complex system had become totally unpredictable. Complexity is a change in the behaviour of the system because the system self-organises in response to changing circumstances.

So the definition of resilience is the *capacity to absorb disturbance, to reorganise so as to retain essentially the same function, structure and feedbacks, to have the same identity*. 'Identity' is what brings the world of psychologists and the world of ecologists together. Psychologists talk about people losing their identity when they go into a catatonic state or shift mentally, while we talk about ecosystems having a different identity—they change from one kind of operational system to another, not just another phase of the same system.

In layperson's terms, resilience is the ability to cope with shocks and to keep functioning in a similar way. The addition of 'feedbacks' is a key idea because the feedbacks in a complex system determine its self-organising capacity. The Resilience Alliance[1] has compiled a database of what we call 'threshold shifts' or 'phase shifts' in systems. In each case where we have been able to gather enough data we have identified a threshold crossing that shows a change in a critical feedback; so understanding the feedbacks, especially across domains and scales, is an essential part of resilience thinking.

Resilience has three critical components. There is 'specified resilience': the resilience of one thing relative to another, which has to do with threshold effects. Then there is 'general resilience', where no particular part of the system or particular shock is identified because it has more to do with the total adaptive capacity of the system. And third, there is 'transformability', the capacity for transformational change to a different kind of system. I will now deal with each of those components to deepen our understanding of the way resilience can operate.

Specified Resilience

Specified resilience is about thresholds or tipping points or critical transitions—they are referred to in many different ways. The commonly assumed response of the equilibrium or stable state of a system to a change in its controlling variables suggests no threshold effect, as shown in Figure 11.1 (a). Its trajectory might be curvilinear or linear but the change is continuous. In fact, there are four kinds

---

1   The Resilience Alliance is a research organisation of scientists and practitioners from various academic disciplines exploring the dynamics of social-ecological systems. See <www.resalliance.org>.

of possible responses, as shown in Figure 11.1, including a step change in (b) and two nonlinear types of change in (c) and (d). These involve what are known as hysteretic effects. In these two cases, as you increase a controlling variable the stable state of this system moves gradually and then jumps up. If you then decrease the controlling variable it does not drop down at the same point as it jumped up. It needs to decrease a long way further down. The crucial point here is that this allows alternative stable states for the same amount of the controlling variable. So the state of the system can exist in either of two states for the same amount of the controls on the system.

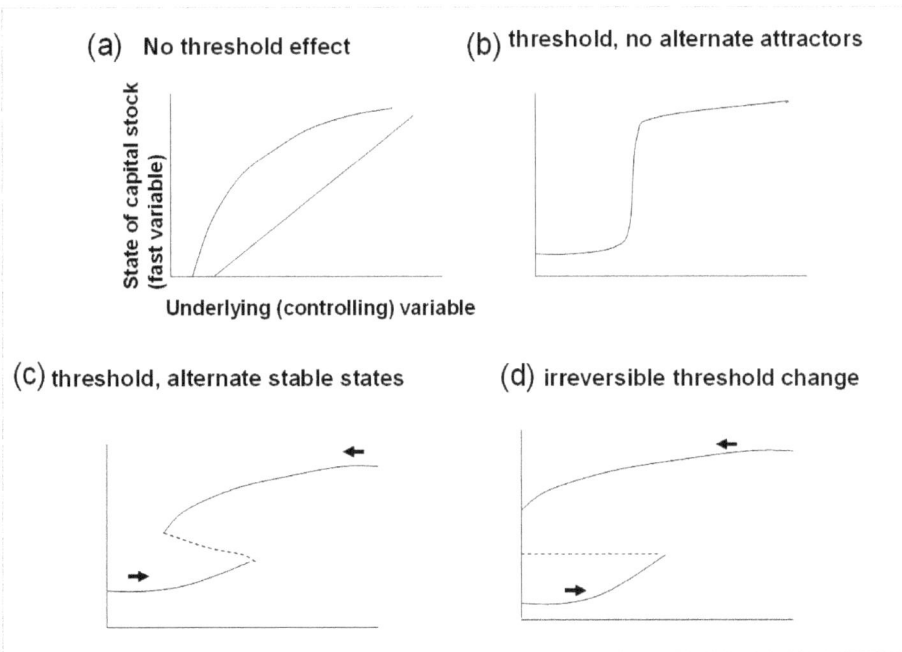

Figure 11.1 Kinds of Thresholds (Tipping Points)

Source: Author's summary.

An example of a step change is a landscape where the controlling variable is the percentage in its natural habitat, and the state of the system we are interested in is the number of fauna species that persist there. For instance, if one were to start clearing a landscape the fauna would gradually decline but then suffer a sudden drop. Many published papers from different parts of the world show that about 30 per cent landscape cover is a critical level (it varies depending on the pattern and the area, but there is a sudden, critical change at some level). There is another one at about 5 per cent so there are a number of step changes. It is not a smooth change.

An example of the kind of changes in Figure 11.1 (c) is algal blooms in lakes, where the lake suddenly becomes eutrophic (full of algae and foul smelling).

The controlling variable is phosphate in the sediment at the bottom of the lake. The state of the system is the amount of phosphorous in the water, which determines the amount of algae. The chemistry is quite complicated, but it has to do with the solubility of phosphate under different levels of oxygen. As the algae increase, they die and then sink to the bottom where oxygen is used up in decomposing them. When there is no oxygen in the water phosphorous becomes very soluble and is released from the sedimentary mud in large quantities and the algae numbers suddenly shoot up. The amounts of phosphorous in the water and sediment have to be brought way down before water phosphorous (and therefore algae) can return to the pre-jump level.

The fourth kind, in Figure 11.1 (d), is an irreversible threshold, where the system never comes back to the pre-jump level. An example of this is topsoil salinity. Catchment salinity is a big problem in Australia and the controlling variable is the depth of the water table below the surface; salt in the topsoil is the state of the system. As the water table rises, because of clearing the landscape, it brings salt with it. When the water table reaches a critical level— about 2 m below the surface for most soils—capillary action pulls the water up to the surface and brings the salt up with it. Salt disperses clay—making it soapy—and the water will not seep back down again. After the water table drops again, it takes a great deal of rainfall to eventually leach the salt down, so the topsoil stays salty. Effectively once the system passes that threshold it is in an irreversible salinised state.

All four of these kinds of thresholds or tipping points occur in all kinds of systems. Fortunately, many of them are smooth, as in Figure 11.1 (a). But if any of the other three occurs in a system it is important to know about them because they define the critical boundaries within which that system has to operate—or, if not, it will soon look very different and have a different identity.

The thresholds I have described exist in ecological systems but they also occur in social systems. In economic systems there is a debt-to-income ratio that everyone knows about; it has a very strong threshold effect and once you increase debt beyond a threshold level it is very difficult to get below that debt-to-income ratio again. There are many examples of research on threshold effects of behaviour in crowds, such as riots; also in fashions and fads where they suddenly take off. Some systems do not have a hysteretic effect in the return path but crowd behaviour does. For example, with a rioting crowd if the threshold level of rioters is below a certain number the riot dies away if the provocation ceases; however, once over the threshold (seemingly around 20 per cent), the riot takes off and continues even after the provocation is removed.

Social, ecological and biophysical systems exhibit nonlinear threshold behaviour, which results in alternating stable states of systems (or alternating stability domains). One could ask: what variables reached threshold levels or tipping points in the 'Arab Spring' political outbreaks in the Middle East recently? What was building up? One proposition may be that the threshold was brought much lower than before due to social media: mobile phones enabled it to take off at a much lower level of provocation than would have been required earlier. This is an interesting idea because it reinforces one of the next three points I want to stress.

First, a threshold occurs where there is a change in feedbacks, and feedback effects can be counterintuitive; they can be quite puzzling, as illustrated by the following example.

Salvinia molesta is a weed from South America that filled lakes in northern Queensland. After some tests, a little weevil (*Cyrtobagous salviniae*) was introduced from South America (where salvinia originates), which eats only salvinia, and it cleared the lake. Papua New Guinea also has lakes with the same salvinia problem and when the weevil was introduced there nothing happened. An Australian scientist studied this and discovered that the weeds actually needed to be fertilised to grow even more. What he found was that the protein level in the weeds was just below the critical amount needed for the weevil to breed; the protein level had to be raised. Nitrogen fertiliser was added; the protein level went up and the weevils took off and bred and controlled the weed. What was interesting is that once that had happened and the weevil numbers increased above a threshold number of their own, the effect of grazing on the weed was to increase its protein level, and so it never needed to be fertilised again as long as the weevil numbers remained high enough to control the salvinia.

The second point is that thresholds interact and can move—they are not necessarily constant. As an example, coral reefs can be healthy or stressed. They can exist in the normal coral state as well as a macro-algal state, and various others, the worst being slime. The two controlling variables determining these states are the amount of fishing, particularly of herbivorous fish, and extra nutrients flowing onto the reef. The nutrients promote algae, while grazing by herbivorous fish reduces algae, so if you go above a certain threshold of fishing and extra nutrients the reef goes from the coral state to the macro-algal state. Even if the fishing is reintroduced, it stays in the algal state unless something else intervenes that can get rid of the algae.

A point I underline in this example is that the threshold level is not fixed. Climate change has an effect on the threshold positions. The threshold is lowered by climate change, carbon dioxide and the acidification of the water. So the effect of climate change is to reduce the resilience of the reef to fishing and nutrient inflow. It will take less fishing pressure and fewer nutrients to flip a coral reef into the algal phase as climate change increases because that threshold, like most, is not fixed but can shift and change.

The third point about thresholds is that they occur across scales and domains that can have cascading effects; by domains I mean the ecological, the economic and the social subsystems. In the Goulburn–Broken catchment in south-eastern Australia 10 thresholds were identified by researchers, together with the local people, that occurred at three spatial scales—farm to landscape scale, landscape to catchment, state to nation—and in three domains: the social, the economic and the biophysical. These 10 thresholds have cascading effects. So once a threshold is crossed it can cause the crossing of another threshold or it can reduce the likelihood of crossing another threshold.

So from a resilience perspective, a linked social-ecological system is viewed as a set of interacting thresholds across domains and across scales, subjected to external shocks—price shocks, changes in markets, climate, diseases and so on—and, depending on the shock, one or more of these thresholds are likely to be crossed, which can set in chain a cascading effect. That represents a different way of thinking about systems other than trying to optimise some particular part of them.

General Resilience

General resilience, involving adaptability, is the capacity of all parts of the system to cope with many types of shocks. Many different studies show that having high diversity, and especially what we call response diversity, is important for conferring general resilience. It is often mistakenly called redundancy. In systems where economic efficiency is important redundancy means where there are two ways of doing something it is preferable to get rid of one and keep only the one that is doing the job best. Scientists do not see that as undesirable redundancy. Rather, they say if a system has several elements that do the same thing but in somewhat different ways, that confers response diversity. If one element is knocked out the other one can begin to do it. So if five species in a forest can fix nitrogen and something happens to one of them the other four can take up the slack. If there is only one legume species (nitrogen fixer) and a disease wipes it out the whole function of nitrogen fixation will be lost.

Being modular in structure and not overly connected is another contributor to general resilience. An overly connected system means problems and diseases can be transmitted rapidly through the system as a whole, while having no connections at all implies isolation. A modular system indicates enough connectedness to exclude isolation, but not so many connections that defences collapse.

General resilience is enhanced by the ability to adapt quickly and effectively to change. Having tight feedbacks is one aspect of this: when the length of contributing components in a feedback loop increases, it decreases the resilience. If it takes six steps instead of three to record and respond to something, resilience is lost. Also, being open, allowing immigration and emigration (ecologically or socially) enhances resilience. And having reserves is necessary, whether physical reserves like seed banks or social reserves like memory. Several years ago when the massive tsunamis hit South-East Asia, those communities which did best had old people nearby who remembered that when the water goes out people should run away from the water. Such social memories conferred resilience.

Other important qualities of general resilience applying particularly to human systems are fostering innovation and novelty/experimentation. Social systems are more resilient when we promote innovation and experimentation, but so much of the way our systems work reduces the potential of these attributes.

The final attribute I will mention is having overlapping institutions and polycentric governance. We are talking here of building social capital through leadership, trust and strong integrated networks. The work of Elinor Ostrom has shown how they enable long-term persistence, as opposed to having highly efficient, non-overlapping and single systems of governance. Ostrom, as a founding member of our Resilience Alliance, found some wonderful stories about small, long-term irrigation and forestry systems that have persisted for 500 years or more. What rules enabled that system to persist over time? These rules are incredibly interesting. Ostrom (1990) identified boundary conditions of the rules that have to be in place. What happened with many of them is that they evolved under a variable, uncertain environment and coped. Spanish agriculture (a persistent system) has now been opened up to the European Union. Spaniards now must allow cheaper oranges from elsewhere into their region and they can sell their water outside their region. This has entirely changed the rules that enabled that system to persist—globalisation has disrupted the rules. We still have to think of it as a complex adaptive system and also need now to think: 'How is the world changing?' Or, to put it differently: 'What are the rules for changing the rules?' Rules are going to change, so the issue is whether we can put in place rules to change our own rules so that we can transform through time instead of becoming an economic basket case.

I will now emphasise four additional points about general resilience. First, resilience is not about avoiding change. Trying to keep a system constant reduces resilience. If you never burn a forest it becomes increasingly prone to dying as a result of fire. The only way to make a forest resilient to fire is to burn it occasionally because otherwise the species capable of coping with fire will be outcompeted, will disappear and the forest will lose the ability to handle a fire.

Next, making a system very resilient in one way at one spatial scale can cause it to lose resilience in other ways or at other scales. There is a trade-off. A social-ecological system cannot be understood or managed at only one scale; there are trade-offs when resilience is applied in practice.

The third point is that general resilience is neither good nor bad. Often people talk about resilience as obviously good; however, undesirable states of systems can be very resilient, such as dictatorships and saline landscapes. Resilience is a *property* of a system. A very resilient 'bad' state is incredibly difficult to deal with and a system that was once considered desirable can become very undesirable through changes in external conditions to which it has adapted.

And finally, most losses in resilience are the unintended consequences of narrowly focused optimisation, mostly stemming from failure to recognise cross-scale and cross-domain feedbacks.

It comes down to the trade-off between specified and general resiliencies, which are both important. The 'rule of hand' states that at any one scale there are no more than three to five controlling variables that are really important at any time. If there were many variables the system would exhibit chaotic dynamics and wouldn't persist over time. It would eventually degrade until it became a simpler system. The handful of really important controlling variables defines the boundary conditions that limit the system so it keeps functioning as it is. It is necessary to understand what those variables are and that's where you should put your money. The way to get at those is to do a 'feedbacks' kind of analysis. You need to think that if you change this then what feedback loops follow? What controls the dynamics when you change any one part of it? This eventually simplifies down to a handful of controlling variables that define the axes of the system in which its behaviour remains. If, however, you put all your money on one variable, saying 'water depth is really an important controlling thing so we should put all of our money into controlling that, keeping it below that threshold', and if in doing that something else that is important is changed and you haven't really thought about it, you could come unstuck. You might end up with a massive disease outbreak because of a consequence of that action that had nothing to do with water depth. So you must constantly bear in mind general resilience. How do you remain generally resilient when you cannot predict what shock might occur and what the uncertainties are, and where the possibility of transformation is?

So although there is some trade-off between general and specified resiliencies you can prioritise because in each case you can identify where the weaknesses are. I run resilience assessment workshops with catchment management authorities and I find the easiest issue to come to grips with when they start working on specified resilience is to identify where the thresholds are. We use a process called state and transition models, which ask: 'What states can the system be in?' It can be in one of several states. This requires another question: 'How does it get from one to the other?' When you ask those questions people bring their knowledge and indicate what needs to happen for it to go from one state to another. So you can start by looking for a threshold level to get to grips with a particular part of the system. For general resilience, however, it is much fuzzier.

Transformability

Being able to adapt and being generally resilient will undoubtedly be very important in what we do in the future for our society, for ecosystems and for social-ecological systems. But when does further adaptation simply amount to digging the hole deeper? The first rule about holes is that when you are in one, stop digging. Getting past the state of denial is not easy. I have heard irrigation farmers in areas of the country that are drying out say: 'No, we just need to get a bit more efficient.' Their adaptation is to dig the hole deeper, making it much harder to shift to something else, as they probably will have to do.

So, if a shift into a bad state has occurred or if one clearly is going to happen then the only option is transformation, which is the third big property or concept of resilience: the capacity to become a different kind of system, a new way of living or making a living. This is not just another phase of the same system but a system that is defined differently.

In most of the world today the rates of change (social, ecological and climatic) demand a process of continuous transformation, not adaptation; that is a deeply uncomfortable idea because most people hate fundamental change. Adaptation people can do, though it is hard, but they hate fundamental change. So if communities are told they can no longer be irrigation farming producers, but must do something else, they will fight tooth and nail. Yet fundamental change is being demanded of us because the rates of change occurring in the world today require it.

Transformability has three determinants. The first is preparedness to change—getting beyond the state of denial is the most difficult stage. The second determinant is options for change. What new trajectories are possible? This emerges from support for experiments, for novelty, for continual learning to identify the options. The third is the capacity to change; even if a good option can be identified can it be adopted? The capacity to change is largely about the levels of capital: human, financial, knowledge and natural capital and higher-scale support, such as appropriate institutions. Higher-scale support includes governance, but governance, which is so important, is often lacking or disappointing.

So if we look at the options for change it is especially important to support creativity and identify new options. An idea that comes out of transition theory in The Netherlands is about 'safe arenas'. A group of social scientists is trying to transform five stressed policy areas in The Netherlands. They say The Netherlands cannot keep doing what it is doing in terms of energy, transport, old age, agriculture and water. The country has to change fundamentally. To change energy in The Netherlands requires getting all the stakeholders together, including the major energy company, which is likely to prevent anything it dislikes because it is the big, powerful player. So this group of social scientists proposes creating safe arenas for experimentation that are protected from the dominant regime, allowing people to do unusual things. Many of those will fail, but those that succeed will start to become mainstream and then you will get a trajectory shift.

It is also important to encourage change rather than help prevent change. All too often help from government seems to be help to keep doing the same thing. When people want to do something different they are told: 'Oh no, you can't use money for that. The money's dedicated to do this and you can't use it to do that.' So government effectively prevents communities from doing anything novel.

Resilience and transformability are not opposites. In Australia's Murray–Darling Basin it is now clear there is not enough water in the system to meet the water allocations communities were originally given (even in a wet period), so in order for the whole basin to support viable, sustainable, long-term farming communities with high wellbeing, parts of the system have to transform. Not all of the existing communities can keep doing what they are doing—and of course the tough question is: 'Who has to change?'

The questions that apply to these communities, spatial areas and even nations are: 'Where is there a need to build the resilience, and where is there a need for transformational change?' If as a society we can distinguish between adaptation and transformation, and try not to build resilience everywhere, we will make considerable progress forward.

Almost every time we have done the exercise the weakest part is in the governance. Achieving transformational change depends on the kind and strength of governance that is in place. I keep coming back to that. Often, those responsible for it are the root of the problem. I met one very perceptive person working in one of the catchment management authorities who was complaining about the intransigence of the levels above her—and many of them were intransigent. She then said perceptively: 'But hang on: you know, when we get the power to do something we don't want to distribute it down either, we want to keep control.' There is a kind of urge at every level to keep control and power, to consolidate power and not to distribute it. A distributive governance system allows a decision to be made at the level at which it is most appropriate. That level may change over time and depending on context. Under certain circumstances you should make it at a higher level, at other circumstances at a lower level; but keeping it always fixed is not going to work and will be particularly consolidating because then there is the natural tendency for control to creep upwards.

Current global governance efforts are largely failing because national self-interest and the silo structure of international agencies suppress and mask the secondary feedback effects of sub-global activities. This issue is of great concern to people in the Beijer Institute in Sweden and the Stockholm Resilience Centre, where we have been trying to look at how the planet is functioning at the moment. We see as a major problem the inability of international institutions and agencies to connect in a collaborative, self-organising way. Changing the planet's current unsustainable trajectory will require a process of continuous transformational change, not adaptation, and a new social contract; and that needs to be informed by a resilience perspective of what is happening.

So, to conclude: how do we operationalise a resilience perspective? Well, there is no single recipe. Applying resilience amounts to putting a resilience lens over what is already being done and whatever planning or management frameworks are being used. This is the challenge ahead.

Reference

Ostrom, E. 1990. *Governing the Commons: The Evolution of Institutions for Collective Action* (Cambridge: Cambridge University Press).

12. Improving Resilience through Environmental Scanning in Western Australia

Nicole Eastough

The public sector's resilience to change is dependent at least in part on its capacity to anticipate change and its preparedness to respond. This is the case whether change occurs gradually and progressively or as major shocks. In the public sector, environmental scanning is a technique for identifying prospective policy challenges—and opportunities—that might arise from current and emerging issues and trends. It attempts to answer questions such as: how do we identify relevant issues and trends? How do we present these as snapshots? How can we translate that information into flexible strategies and priorities *and* prepare decision-makers for change?

The WA Department of Treasury introduced an environmental scanning process in the aftermath of the Global Financial Crisis that hit Australia in late 2008. A new strategic policy unit was created to 'make space' to provide advice on longer-term and crosscutting policy issues. Part of its remit was to start producing regular environmental scans. The unit developed its first environmental scan in 2009 on a fairly small scale. The approach was refined with two subsequent environmental scans conducted in 2010 and 2011, with a broadened consultation base within Treasury and across State public sector agencies.

This case study describes how environmental scanning has been realised in the WA Department of Treasury, and is designed to encourage public sector officials to consider current and emerging trends and how they might impact on their agency, or the public sector more broadly. Specifically, this case examines

- the definition of environmental scanning used by the WA Department of Treasury
- the approach to environmental scanning and the methodological considerations adopted by the Department of Treasury
- the scanning mechanisms to identify relevant issues and trends
- approaches to undertaking strategic analysis of those issues and trends
- how the results of environmental scans can be used to inform public policy.

Defining Environmental Scanning

The WA Department of Treasury's approach to environmental scans was initially informed by reviews of definitions, approaches and formats for environmental scans undertaken in other Australian jurisdictions and internationally. This informal desktop study suggested that the key features of environmental scans were that they were outward looking, focused on change or possible change, considered the policy implications, explored the opportunities and challenges, and emphasised the issues that were most relevant to the organisation.

Over the past four years the WA Department of Treasury has developed its own, more prescriptive definition of environmental scanning that encompasses both the process and the use of such scans. First, environmental scanning is a formal and systematic exploration of the external environment to identify potential opportunities, challenges and likely relevant future developments that could or should inform government policy deliberations. Second, as a discipline, environmental scanning guides the development of flexible strategies and priorities that prepare the government and its decision-makers to respond quickly to change. This is an assertion of how the products of environmental scans might be used.

Environmental scans encompass both the potential for crises, which may include large-scale disasters, and softer, progressive processes of change. In this context, the essential nature of environmental scans is that they are

- formal and systematic investigations
- have an external focus
- investigate likely relevant future developments
- inform government policy deliberations
- provide for flexible responses to change.

The department's intentions in producing environmental scans were to use them to

- raise awareness of key strategic issues, particularly crosscutting issues that might impact on Western Australia's public sector, either in the short term or over the longer term
- inform the development of strategic plans and operational work plans, and policy development within Treasury
- prepare the Government to respond quickly to change.

Scans have also proved a useful means of introducing new staff to a 'big picture' view on key issues and trends that affect the public sector and more specifically

Treasury business. A further benefit is that they can pinpoint areas of risk, and at the same time develop scenarios to test the impacts of change in external parameters or policy conditions.

Conducting an Environmental Scan

Comprehensive Project Planning

An environmental scanning process can be as large or as small a task as the agency's resourcing will allow. Ideally, it is a task for a team of investigators, not for an individual in an ivory tower. Comprehensive scans need input from people with a broad range of views and experience. It is vital to draw on the diversity of talent, knowledge and experience within both the agency and the public sector more broadly to identify relevant issues and trends.

Given the potential breadth of scope, environmental scans need tight project management, covering their scope, approaches, time frames, consultation mechanisms, format, team resourcing and the communication strategy. In the WA Department of Treasury, initial planning and brainstorming began in April–May 2011 with dedicated staff taken offline while the State budget was being finalised. In-depth research and analysis were undertaken in the aftermath of the budget. Dedicated resources for the project consisted of three staff, with additional input and advice from other areas within the department and from other agencies.

Several internal and external workshops were held to invite internal senior officers to share their views, and for key government agencies to present and discuss their agencies' strategic issues. Approximately 25 to 30 State Government agencies participated in the 2011 process. The process was initially expected to take about four to six months, but the time frames were extended to monitor the immense volatility and uncertainty in global economic conditions at the time of drafting. When taking into account the time involved to communicate the environmental scan, the entire process took close to a year.

Identifying Issues and Trends

Environmental scanners typically employ diagnostic techniques of the external environment. The WA Treasury chose to adopt 'STEEP' as an instrument to identify issues and trends. STEEP seeks to identify changes in *society*, changes in *technology*, changes in the *economy* (perhaps better phrased as the economic outlook), *environmental* change and *political* change—hence 'STEEP'. From our perspective, the particular choice of technique (for example, whether STEEP is chosen over other techniques such as 'PEST', 'PESTLIED', 'PESTEL', 'STEEPLE' or 'SLEPT') is largely arbitrary, as the success of the technique in identifying relevant issues and trends is contingent on access to and engagement with a diverse pool of people who are willing to share relevant ideas and expertise.

The key difference between these environmental scanning techniques and a 'SWOT' (strengths, weaknesses, opportunities and threats) analysis is that the environmental scan is focused on the external environment, including issues that can be largely outside the control of the public sector, and does not specifically examine the agency's capacity to respond to change. Examples of the types of public sector issues and trends that may be drawn out of facilitated group discussions using STEEP or a related technique are provided below.

Societal Change

In public policy there are no hard and fast rules about what should be provided by government, to what standard or at what price. Expectations change over time, differ between generations and are influenced by the availability of services and awareness of new or alternative services that may not be available locally. Expectations can be highly political and emotive, and are difficult to manage.

For individuals, preferences to use public or private services can be influenced by the capacity to pay, the ease with which they can access services and differences between the two sectors in the range of services provided and their respective service delivery models.

Societal change is largely due to demographic developments, through population growth, population ageing, immigration and regional residential variability across the State or country. Other changes in society can occur through the comparative living standards and evolving relations between the indigenous populations and the broader community.

These demographic changes can result in changes in community expectations about the quality of services provided or receiving access to them, security of the services and rates of utilisation. It can also raise operational delivery issues, workforce issues and equity of services between metropolitan and regional and remote communities.

Changes in lifestyle trends and behaviours can have a significant influence on demand for and utilisation of services. Such trends may include prevalence of chronic health conditions, prevalence of smoking and alcohol use, health behaviours or the risks of outbreaks of disease.

Technological Change

New technologies can decrease our reliance on labour to perform specific tasks, to address imbalances between the supply of and demand for limited natural resources, and to satisfy society's expectations of communication, entertainment and service delivery. Advances in technology can change the way people work by automating processes or reducing processing time (such as through using wireless devices), and the use of robotics in some services and industries. The adoption of new technology can also reduce labour and other costs through more effective service delivery. Other technological advances can offer the potential to respond to societal values (for example, renewable energy sources) or to challenge existing values (for example, attitudes to genetically modified crops).

Rapid growth in the use of social media and the availability of the web 2.0 technologies are challenging the traditional ways governments communicate with the public, opening up new possibilities of providing access to data and information, and mediums or platforms to consult over policy areas or legislation.

Economic Outlook

Considerations of the economic outlook over the short to medium term may take account of common economic indicators such as inflation, interest rates, employment growth, unemployment rates, household debt and forecasts for economic growth. More strategic economic concerns may include considerations of which sectors of the economy are performing more strongly than others, levels of sovereign (government) debt, indications of structural change in the economy, trends in the terms of trade, and economic trends occurring in major trading partners.

Longer-term considerations may be challenges to managing government debt, increasing productivity and developing a more competitive economy. This may also include consideration of supply constraints such as levels of investment in research, science and innovation, regulation and support for business and agriculture, infrastructure adequacy, housing availability and affordability, and skills and employment.

Fiscal issues at present tend to focus on the provision of fiscal stimulus measures announced by various governments in response to the 2008 Global Financial Crisis, and fiscal consolidation measures to either wind back fiscal stimulus or manage sovereign debt.

Environmental Change

Consideration of environmental issues and trends requires a balance between observed and projected changes to the environment (for instance, rainfall patterns, salinity measures, sea levels, drought) and the relative risks of major environmental events, including major weather events (such as cyclones or floods), seismic events or bushfires.

Strategic considerations include the risk of conflict between heritage and conservation interests, resource development interests and urban land-use interests. These issues may arise from population growth and housing demand, proposals or trends to develop resources in prime agricultural land, and trends in foreign ownership of or investment in domestic assets and land. In turn, these factors will have implications for planning in terms of transport networks, the rate of urban infill, water allocation and management, and economic infrastructure.

Political Dynamics

The public sector has a close relationship with politics and government, and it can be difficult to isolate the political dynamics from the ordinary machinery of public administration. The challenge is to step back from the day-to-day issues and relationships between the public sector and government and to observe broader trends. Political factors that may be relevant include: government stability, which parties are in power across the country, government relationships with the media, opportunities and interests in government to introduce and progress reforms, the relative balance of independence versus the responsiveness of the public sector to government priorities, and broader geopolitical trends elsewhere.

In a federation such as Australia the stability and effectiveness of relationships between different levels of government, including the equity of distribution of financial resources between and across levels of government, can be significant influences on the effectiveness of service delivery. It may also be important to consider recent trends in reforms to accountability frameworks, the extent to which they centralise or decentralise decision-making, their influence on fiscal flexibility and financial accountability, and the longer-term implications for State sovereignty.

Strategic Analysis

At the simplest level, an environmental scan can be limited to identifying a list of issues and trends of relevance to the agency. Some environmental scanners may also undertake a simple risk-assessment exercise to indicate the relative risk of each issue. From a policy perspective, scans are of increased value when some additional form of strategic analysis is undertaken on the issues and trends, in terms of categorising information, gathering supporting evidence, identifying and considering the potential policy implications, and constructing a narrative of change.

Strategic analysis is the meaty part of the environmental scanning process. It is an iterative process that does not require a big team but does need people who are strategic thinkers, who can take responsibility for a cluster of issues, and who can sift them for relevance. It demands experience in isolating the intangibles from group discussions, transforming them into tangible facts, figures, charts and observations, and drawing out the policy implications.

Categorising Information

Categorising information is a matter of reviewing and clustering issues and trends identified through workshops and consultation. Mind mapping can be a useful tool to help organise information and identify related themes. This might need to be done in several stages at different levels of complexity. It is the process of categorisation that contributes to the development of the structure and underlying messages of the environmental scan; however, attempts to mind map every issue raised through extensive consultation can be counterproductive. There will be many interdependencies and interrelationships between issues and trends, and it is likely that a complete mind map will resemble an inky blob of spaghetti. It is therefore often better to prepare very simple, high-level mind maps, or to produce detailed mind maps for narrowly focused selected issues and trends.

Categorising information is more a process of achieving consensus than of finding the 'perfect' themes, and should be undertaken with a view to identifying about five to nine themes that are clearly relevant to the agency. In the case of the WA Department of Treasury, there was a heavy bias towards economic and financial themes. The 2011 environmental scan consolidated the identified issues and trends to eight key drivers of change, which were the State's economic outlook, global economic uncertainty, fiscal consolidation trends, urban and environmental change, technological change, health and wellbeing, societal expectations, and demographic change.

Gathering Evidence

Environmental scans are typically reliant on secondary quantitative and qualitative data sources. The scope of potential sources is necessarily broad, with a first priority to access professional expertise from within the agency, including people, corporate records and data sources. Other potentially relevant sources of data include

- published and unpublished data from line public sector agencies (reports, reviews, budget statements, annual reports, online statistics and unpublished data collections)
- government statistics and reviews from sources such as the Australian Bureau of Statistics, the Australian Institute of Health and Welfare, the Productivity Commission, the Reserve Bank of Australia and the Australian Bureau of Agriculture, Resource Economics and Sciences
- other sources of government information (media statements, Hansard debates, reports from inquiries and audits)
- testing local trends against other jurisdictions, using sources such as the OECD, IMF, World Bank and the Productivity Commission.

These sources need to be tested for relevance and credibility in terms of their authority, accuracy, reliability, validity, bias and timeliness. The Productivity Commission's suggested methodological considerations and principles for evidence-based policy should not be overlooked in determining whether isolated data and information constitute sufficiently robust evidence to be included in the environmental scan (see Banks 2009).

It can be useful to test 'public sector thinking' against the views of others, including industry bodies and/or community stakeholders and representative bodies, academia, employee representative groups and think tanks. The choice of consultation will vary with the scope of the environmental scanning exercise and the agency's relationship with potential stakeholders. Media coverage of issues, including press releases from other agencies or jurisdictions, can alert scanners to new developments, different perspectives and recently published new data.

Drawing out the Implications, Opportunities and Challenges

The third stage of strategic analysis is to review the accumulated evidence and identify the key policy implications. Where and why might the public sector need to respond to the issues and trends? What are the risks and uncertainties? What are the potential positive impacts (opportunities) of the observed and predicted trends? What are the potential negative impacts (challenges)? Does the government have a role to intervene, or is the rationale for current interventions still valid? This review forms the basis of a discussion of the implications, opportunities and challenges presented by the issues and trends that are included in the environmental scan.

Constructing a Narrative

The final task is to construct a narrative. The environmental scan should tell a story of change, using a mix of quantitative data and qualitative information. The role of the scan's narrative is to provide depth, focus and context, and a platform for policy debate. It needs to set out the opportunities, the downsides and the risks. It should use an accumulation of evidence to lead the audience to the policy implications, opportunities and challenges and directions for further policy development.

If an environmental scan is to be used to inform policy development, it needs to present issues, supporting evidence and the implications in the form of a narrative that persuades the audience that policy change may be needed. Its arguments must be supported with judiciously selected evidence. It must synthesise what might otherwise appear to be randomly selected data to give it meaning and coherence.

Appealing to the Audience

Environmental scans can be lengthy documents intended to communicate vast quantities of information. The layout thus needs to be designed both to attract the reader's attention and to communicate information succinctly. In presenting information on issues and trends, it may be useful to focus first on presenting and explaining data and research findings. Discuss the policy implications separately. Stand-alone pages, with a message on each page, can be very effective. Message-based taglines are more effective as headings than single words, and can be threaded to integrate isolated data and observations into a broader narrative from page to page.

There needs to be a strong focus on making very complex issues relatively easy to digest. The text should be condensed to the key points, and visual impacts are important. At least one image, graph or chart on every page (provided they are clearly related to the text) helps to both engage the reader and communicate key points. Infographics are resource intensive to develop but effective to present information. A defined colour scheme can be an effective aid.

As environmental scans may be informed by a vast range of information, particularly secondary sources, which may be subject to change, it is essential to reference sources. It is useful to both hyperlink the text and include academic referencing to encourage readers to refer to the original source information to pursue more extensive policy research.

It is advisable to incorporate a disclaimer. Environmental scans are not predictive documents, use material from an extensive range of secondary sources, don't necessarily cover a particular period or horizon, and the data cited may be current only for a (sometimes brief) window of time.

Using Environmental Scans

Environmental scans, as high-level, broad documents, are not an ideal vehicle for delivering formal conclusions and policy recommendations. They cannot provide government with immediate solutions to the complex, interdependent policy problems they describe. Rather, environmental scans should encourage thinking, discussion and further policy work. They should allow frank and balanced sharing of a broad range of issues within the public sector.

In view of this, and depending on the format and scope of the environmental scan, it is important to consider whether scans should be classed as confidential documents. Public debate is an important feature of policy development, but environmental scans may be too broad in scope, and the future too unclear, to engage the public and the media effectively. A more appropriate opportunity for public engagement may arise from tightly scoped green and white papers that focus on selected issues identified in environmental scans. If a scan is to remain confidential, the communication strategy for an environmental scan still needs to encompass the key audiences of agency staff, stakeholder agencies and government.

Copies of environmental scans should be circulated to agencies which participated in the consultation process. Stakeholder agencies may also be invited to receive briefings or presentations, with opportunities to present highlights and key issues to small groups of agency chief executives. This assists in providing agencies with the 'bigger picture' view and developing relationships for input into future scanning work and policy reform.

Ministers or cabinets may wish to be briefed on key messages in the environmental scan. For instance, some of the key findings from Treasury's 2011 environmental scan that had the potential to impact on the State's financial position over the budget and forward estimates period were brought to the attention of the Economic and Expenditure Review Committee as part of the broader scene setting for the development of the 2012–13 budget. At the agency level, environmental scans can be integrated with strategic and operational planning to help define the agency's forward work program and resource allocation. For individuals, they are also an opportunity to develop insight into the 'bigger' picture of the complexity of policy.

Environmental scans can, and should, be used

- to raise awareness of issues and trends, especially longer-term trends
- to identify crosscutting policy issues that impact on multiple portfolios and require a coordinated policy response
- as a mechanism to engage with stakeholders and other agencies

- to pinpoint and highlight areas of risk and opportunity for the sustainability of public sector finances
- to identify opportunities for scenario analysis with high-risk issues
- to inform policy development.

Informing Policy Development and Reform

Environmental scanning is a part of the complex pathway of policy development and reform. As indicated above, while they are very useful to identify issues, and involve some limited policy analysis, they are too broad and high level in scope to present informed recommendations for change.

Based on the experience of the WA Department of Treasury, in terms of further work it is important to dig beneath some of the higher-risk issues and to monitor them closely. It is not realistic to expect an agency to have the capacity to conduct in-depth policy analysis on every issue raised in an environmental scan. Rather, the scan should be used to help pinpoint significant areas of risk that demand attention, to allow just a couple of key issues to be focused on at any point in time.

In taking these priority issues forward, it is worth giving consideration to some of the drivers of good policy reform processes, such as

- establishing a sound case
- bringing intellectually sound design to the policy reform
- being ready for and using windows of opportunity for reform as they are presented
- securing strong political commitment to reform
- building a broad base of support and consensus for reform.

It should be remembered that an environmental scan may raise many issues and trends that are relevant to the agency but are not the agency's primary policy responsibility. The forward view is to engage other agencies to isolate the issues and trends that are important to them, and within their remit (which could include crosscutting policy issues common to multiple agencies), and to work collaboratively in the next stage of the policy process.

Conclusion

The WA Department of Treasury's approach to environmental scanning is formal and systematic, outwardly focused and examines change that is relevant to the WA public sector. Some of the lessons to be learned from this experience are that environmental scanners should be encouraged to gather information from a wide range of sources, and to incorporate consultation and awareness raising as vital components of the process. They should think strategically. They should construct a narrative that leads their audience to see opportunities for further policy development, and that has the potential to manage policy challenges before they become crises. Their product—the environmental scan—should be used as a platform for debate rather than to communicate predetermined policy positions.

Environmental scans explore the potential to improve public sector resilience in a softer setting of change, and should give the audience an appreciation of the connections between public policy issues. Understanding these connections, and how change in these connections influences government policy, is integral to the public sector becoming more resilient to change.

References

Banks, G. 2009. Evidence-based policy-making: what is it? How do we get it?, Speech presented at the Australia and New Zealand School of Government/ The Australian National University Lecture Series, 4 February 2009. Available from: <http://www.pc.gov.au/speeches/cs20090204>.

Henry, K. 2007. 'Challenges Confronting Economic Policy Advisors', *Views from the Inside No. 3* (Canberra: Australia and New Zealand School of Government). Available from: <http://www.anzsog.edu.au/media/upload/publication/11_anzsog_inside_view_03.pdf>.

Lindquist, A., Vincent, S. and Wanna, J. (eds) 2011. *Delivering Policy Reform: Anchoring Significant Reforms in Turbulent Times* (Canberra: ANU E Press).

Ministry of Finance. 2009. *Guidelines for Environmental Scans* (Regina: Government of Saskatchewan). Available from: <http://www.finance.gov.sk.ca/performance-planning/201011EnvironmentalScanGuidelines.pdf>.

Productivity Commission. 2009. *Strengthening Evidence Based Policy in the Australian Federation: Roundtable Proceedings* (Canberra: Government of Australia). Available from: <http://www.pc.gov.au/research/conference-proceedings/strengthening-evidence>.

United Kingdom Strategy Unit. 2008. *Realising Britain's Potential: Future Strategic Challenges for Britain* (London: Government of the United Kingdom). Available from: <http://webarchive.nationalarchives.gov.uk/20100125070726/http://cabinetoffice.gov.uk/strategy/work_areas/strategic_challenges0208.aspx>.

13. Environmental Scanning Processes in Queensland's Department of Transport and Main Roads

Adam Rogers

I write this chapter not as an expert in environmental scanning, but in my role as a user of the outputs of an environmental scanning approach implemented in the Department of Transport and Main Roads in Queensland.[1] This chapter will investigate the kinds of future influences that might shape the direction taken in delivering a transport system. It focuses on three key areas of environmental scanning and its relationship to transport strategy: how we use environmental scanning to inform policy development; how we build capability; and how we use it to build capability for scanning and future thinking.

The department's environmental scanning function focuses on the sigmoid curves of ideas and strategies as applied to transport. Sigmoid curves represent the natural growth and death of an idea, product, concept or system. So, for instance, think of the horse and cart, the most common form of transport in the 1800s. We started domesticating horses, we took them as far as we could go, got the most out of them and then something else came along: the automobile. The use of horses began to decline as the use of automobiles increased. We look at this phenomenon in terms of: 'Well, where are the things we do poised on the curve?' We ask: 'Are they part of the old way of things or are they a new idea that has come along?' We use a scanning process to help us fill the gap in the middle, first to examine where we are on the curve, and second to try to identify what has not yet gained our attention that we might need to respond to.

The environmental scanning processes were adapted to the structure of the department and our business model. Essentially, there are three main areas of our business: planning, programming and delivery. The department uses several key questions to guide its projects: what does the Government want to achieve from transport? What systems do we need? How do we manage the systems we already have? What planning do we need to do for future avenues? How do we choose the areas in which to invest? Program development is really about: 'OK, we made a choice. Now, when are we going to do it? How are we

---

1   The process described is the one that was in place within the Queensland Department of Transport and Main Roads leading up to the July 2012 ANZSOG annual conference. As such, this chapter reflects that point in time and may not reflect current practice or direction.

going to do it? How are we going to deliver and finalise it?' Ultimately, our business model centres on our scanning process, which occurs in the short term (a process covering one to four years) and in the long term (a 10-year process).

Transport is a huge issue in Queensland, particularly in the south-east, but also in regional and rural areas. The State has a vast network of roads, many of which are remote, but they carry the heavy burden of handling the movement of produce, resources and tourism.

The journey of the Department of Transport and Main Roads towards environmental scanning began in 1999 when it was two separate departments: Queensland Transport and the Main Roads Department. The two directors-general agreed that the departments needed to look at the future of transport for Queensland and to envision the State's changing transport needs between 2000 and 2025. The two departments coordinated a project called '4-seeable Futures', released in 2000, which planned for the eventuality of four hypothetical scenarios.

The first scenario was that of the 'Super City': the transformation of the Gold Coast, Sunshine Coast and Brisbane into one conjoined mega-city. The second scenario was that of 'Coastal Bloom': the establishment of a series of medium-density urban centres up the State's east coast. The third scenario was that of the 'Carbon Crunch', and the fourth, 'Global Bust'. Since 1999 all four of these scenarios have transpired to some degree. They were literally foreseeable futures that were foreseen.

In the initial phases of environmental scanning we also examined unconventional approaches to transport. For example, the department examined research into flying cars. There was some incredibly good analysis done; however, the only attention this research received was a banner headline on the front page of *The Courier-Mail*: 'The Transport Department Predicts Flying Cars in Brisbane.' Of course, this resulted in some sensitivity about doing these sorts of exercises and caused a bit of pain for the senior management of that time.

The big question with this sort of analytical process is how to implement it and how to use it within the agency. Arguably this research did not end up being used that effectively in the agency because there was no real plan to do something meaningful with it.

Ten years later the Departments of Transport and Main Roads joined into one agency in recognition of overlapping roles and responsibilities, especially in relation to road building and transport network planning. The new, larger department adopted a wider lens in its approach; it no longer considered roads to be the only solution to a transport problem, and it had a more long-term strategic vision. As a result, the agency decided to have another look at the forecasting environmental scanning process; rather than doing it in a stand-alone report, the agency built in some capacity to keep it on the agenda all the time in order to refresh thinking about it.

The first steps of the department's environmental scanning model focused on the influences on transport as a way of understanding the needs of the transport system. From there, the department formulated a transport system vision that implemented its strategies, specific plans, investment process, program, activities and evaluation. Environmental scanning was embedded in that process. It also incorporated the shorter-term, one to four-year corporate cycle. In effect, the agency said: 'We need to do environmental scanning. It needs to be embedded in the way the department works and thinks about its place in the world.'

In 2009, when the new department completed its environmental scan, it analysed the greater environmental trends that had arisen over the past decade, such as world energy use. We also looked at various future time scales. We formulated objectives for the near term (up to 2020), the medium term and the long term (up to 2070). This initial scanning process was not about answering the questions or deciding what to look at. It was merely to highlight the issues. Some of the questions we looked at were quite useful: what are the most important infrastructure platforms of the twenty-first century? What does sustainable transport look like? What are the policies and strategies that support it? If our transport system is a product of the way we live how will we need to change to reflect the way we will live? How might our concepts and language change? For example, what does it mean when organisations like IBM talk about enterprise ecosystems? We considered the sorts of language and systems currently used, and which ideas, concepts and principles are at their use-by date. These were the kinds of questions that were in people's minds.

There are a few other tools we use: the environmental scan and the annual opportunities and challenges scan or 'scanning radar'. We do 'one-pagers', each of which is a very simple analysis. A small team in one of our branches finds interesting media snippets and does a 'one-pager'. This addresses questions such as: what's the issue? What's the time frame involved? What are the opportunities and impacts on the agency? Where do we think it might affect our various business groups? What are we doing? This is circulated to an email group within the agency. The 'one-pagers' are for departmental use only but we do have something called an 'eCompass' with a broader distribution. This is how we have embedded the process into our planning cycles. This also relates to the three areas I referred to at the beginning: how do we use environmental scanning to impact strategic planning? How do we impact policy development? How do we impact capability building?

When we undertake a 'scanning radar' exercise, we use a diagnostic methodology. It's a simplistic representation of the key impacts in a particular area that we are interested in and lists the key issues according to seven scanned categories. We look for changes such as economic shifts and changes in technology and infrastructure. We then attribute them with a level of impact—high, medium or low. It's a simple way of showing where things are going. They are then summarised onto a radar diagram, which lists the seven categories.

We did this scanning exercise recently with our senior leadership team: the director-general, the deputies and all the general managers of the different divisions. We highlighted what things are changing, where the shifts were and the opportunities and challenges the researchers saw as coming out of their analysis. We then asked the senior leadership team: 'Where do you think these opportunities and challenges fit on the sigmoid curves? Are they a part of the old way of doing things? When do you think they will impact us? How well prepared do you think we are for responding to the challenges that might come?' Similarly, we asked of the other changes that emerged: 'If we haven't started thinking about them, when are we going to and are we ready to respond? Are they a part of the new way of doing things?' Using the old 'post-it' note process, the senior leadership team plotted the most important challenges and opportunities they saw. The direct output of this scanning process went into our corporate plan. Each of the business divisions is required to respond in their business planning process to the strategic challenges and opportunities.

Informing policy development is the next thing. The scanning radar identified some issues in terms of what is happening in the freight space. Online shopping and intelligent transport systems are really driving changes to the way logistics firms use their trucks, move their freight around, how they load and unload and what sort of freight there is. The scanning team went to the Queensland Transport Logistics Council, a private sector body, to work through some of the issues that have been identified in the scanning and to get some industry input into our Queensland Freight Strategy. This was based on the changes that were likely to occur in the future. This is just an example of how environmental scanning is informing a Statewide strategy and helping us to engage with our constituencies a little more closely. This was quite useful.

The main question the department faces with scanning is: how do we translate it into direct action? It can seem too blue-sky, too airy-fairy. How do we actually make it work for people? Part of the process of educating our own people is to work with industry to see the practicality, connections and implications for them.

The third aspect is about capability building. We have a voluntary scanning reference group across the agency so people from every division who are interested in future thinking can be kept up-to-date with all the developments.

We use them to shape the scanning process each year. We run staff workshops. When we have done the radar we present it to the staff workshops, saying: 'Here is the radar; this is what it's telling us; these are the things we need to look out for as they might impact on us over time.' We also present it to senior management workshops. We have also done presentations to different divisional teams as they go through their business planning process. We have run various master classes where we get the foresight consultant in to workshop ideas and findings from the environmental scanning with various groups in the organisation. We are really trying to build that constant level of interaction and interest within the agency.

Outside the agency we play a part in various external networks around scanning. There is the Queensland future scanning network and the national one. We are working with agencies like CSIRO and the National Transport Commission. CSIRO in particular was interested in what we thought about some of the transport implications of mega trends. We produce the eCompass, which is the public version of all the latest trends and tips. This is distributed across the public sector and to various private sector individuals who have expressed an interest.

14. Resilience in its Historical and Contemporary Contexts

David Kirk

This contribution focuses on the concept of resilience as it is understood and used in a wide range of contexts. As a trained medical doctor, I graduated from the Otago Medical School in 1985. I therefore have some understanding of the resilience of the human body and mind. I also have experience as a professional rugby union player. My sporting experiences have given me insight into the resilience of sports teams.

I have a reasonable understanding of economics from later study in Oxford and am therefore able to say something about resilient economic systems. Some of you may also know I worked in Wellington in the office of the prime minister Jim Bolger for more than three years. In its second term, his government had a one-seat majority but survived the term, so I have some insight into the resilience of governments.

Most of my working life, however, has been in business management. I have worked in the oil and gas industry, in the pulp and paper business, in printing and media services, in newspaper and magazine publishing and in a wide range of Internet-related businesses. I am currently involved in the film entertainment business, the e-commerce business, the funds management and broking business, and I am the co-founder and managing partner of a technology investment firm. I therefore am able to say something about the resilience of firms and industries from firsthand experience.

I will begin by discussing the resilience of political institutions and processes. It is important, however, to understand that my belief about resilience is that it is, in all contexts, a function of redundancy and optionality.

Political Philosophy and the Configuration of Political Institutions

There are two long periods and one short period in the evolution of the political institutions and processes of which we are the inheritors (this is, of course, a simplification, but a necessary one given the limited scope of this chapter). The documented development of Western liberal political tradition began in Greece about 500 or 600 years before the birth of Christ and continues today.

This first period is what we call Antiquity. There is no defined end to this period but it is not uncommon to consider the emperor Justinian's closure of the Neoplatonic Academy in Athens in 529 AD—because he considered its teachings to be inconsistent with Christianity—as the date marking the end of Antiquity.

The political institutions of the Greek city-states, of Alexander's empire and of the Roman Republic and later the Roman Empire operated effectively, and proved themselves resilient, for a little more than a millennium. There was, of course, a great deal of disorder and change in the detail of the governance arrangements during this period, but it was a period in which art, philosophy, commerce, science and culture generally developed consistently and spread widely. It was therefore a long period in which political and administrative processes broadly worked to the benefit of the peoples of Europe.

The second long period in the development of Western political institutions and processes also lasted about 1000 years. This was the period we call the Middle Ages. The Middle Ages was a period in which Christianity was the dominant impulse in art, science, military matters and politics in all of Europe, from the cold north to the Mediterranean and extending east to Constantinople and the reaches of the Byzantine Empire.

During the Middle Ages, God's will determined all. Only God was not around to interpret His own will, so that difficult task fell to the Pope and his armies and to the kings and their armies. Life for everyone else was short, unpleasant and subject to sudden disaster. A noble family's squabble might result in the razing of your house and confiscation of your fields, or if you were at court quickly shifting alliances could result in your head appearing on a spike one fine morning. But no-one was allowed to consider the ghastly unpredictability of life in the Middle Ages as in any way arbitrary. It was, after all, God's will.

The sole source of goodness and authority was infallible and He had a plan and the Pope and the kings knew what that plan was: it was for them to rule. The doctrine of the divine right of kings and the ceding of temporal power to popes and other high ecclesiasticals, whose playbook was Scripture and personal revelation, worked to provide stable and reasonably resilient governance so long as the people were not completely starving and the authority's armies were strong. Religious faith was a source of personal and institutional resilience through the Middle Ages but it was also the source of much instability. Political instability in the Middle Ages was chronic because no-one really knew whose side God was on. Anyone who made a claim of divine inspiration and could raise an army devoted resources to war. Agreeing to differ was not an option. There could only be one divine truth and only war would determine who had it.

The poor serf or impoverished city-dweller at least had the hope of salvation in the next life. And Scripture made it fairly plain that the winners on Earth were likely to get their comeuppance in the next world. *Schadenfreude*, even if it was postponed, worked wonders as a spiritual salve in the Middle Ages. Dante Alighieri gave the best literary expression to the sentiment that must have fuelled the resilience of all of downtrodden Europe throughout the Middle Ages. This is from *The Inferno*:

> And so we passed along from bridge to bridge,
>
> With other talk, whereof my Comedy
>
> Cares not to tell, until we topped the ridge …
>
> So not by fire, but by the art divine,
>
> A thick pitch boiled down there, spattering the brink
>
> With viscous glue; I saw this, but therein
>
> Nothing; only great bubbles black as ink
>
> Would rise and burst there; or the seething tide
>
> Heave up all over, and settle again, and sink.
>
> And while I stood intent to gaze, my guide,
>
> Suddenly crying to me, 'Look out! Look Out!'
>
> Caught me where I stood and pulled me to his side …
>
> And then behind us I beheld a grim
>
> Black fiend come over the rock-ridge at a run …
>
> On high-hunched shoulders he was carrying
>
> A wretched sinner, hoist by haunch and hip.
>
> Clutching each ankle by the sinew-string.
>
> 'Bridge-ho!' he bawled, 'Our own Hellrakership!
>
> Here's an alderman of St Zita's coming down;
>
> Go souse him, while I make another trip …'
>
> He tossed him in, and over the flinty cliff
>
> Wheeled off …
>
> Down bobbed the sinner, then up in writhing knot.
>
> (*The Divine Comedy: Inferno*, Canto XXI)

The third period of political organisation and philosophy is relatively short. Observations of the natural world from which could be discerned cause and effect led to explanations of natural phenomena according to the laws of nature.

Predictions from these natural laws proved to be accurate and the authority of the Scriptures and God began to unravel. It did not matter that the Inquisition extracted a recantation from Galileo; it was a demonstrable fact that the Earth revolved around the Sun and so it would ever be.

It took nearly another century to conclude the process, but man-discovered laws governing the physical world were the natural precursor to man-created laws governing the constitutional and political worlds.

The 'Glorious Revolution' of 1688, the American Declaration of Independence, the proclamation of the rights of man, the doctrine of the separation of powers and all the institutional forms established as a result of these constitute our modern Western political systems.

All of the understandings of modern democratic government were in place by the end of the eighteenth century but that does not mean it was straightforward to give these understandings stable institutional form. Take France for instance. France is often considered the source of modern democratic ideas and impulses; however, the implementation of these impulses has proved to be problematic in France. In a nation in which rhetoric is sometimes inclined to exceed rigour, we should perhaps not be surprised that after the revolution came Napoleon and then an alternating stream of republic, empire, restoration, empire and then two more republics before the fifth and current republic emerged in 1958.

Germany declared itself a republic only in 1918 and in the east of the continent it was not until 1992 that the Russian Federation came into being and democratic processes and institutions were established.

It is only now, at the end of the twentieth century and the beginning of the twenty-first century, that we have, in most of Europe and in a variety of the colonies and other countries that the European powers occupied in the nineteenth century, the 'best' form of government. I put 'best' in inverted commas because we ought to ask why it is we consider the political institutions we currently have to be the best.

First, I think it is because we gradually invented them and everyone always likes best those institutions of which they feel they have some ownership. Second, it is because they are extant and have survived and no-one likes to think they live in a second-best world or under second-best conditions.

Third, and this is a better reason, it is because others are actively choosing them. Eastern Europe has recently chosen, in a variety of forms, representative democracy. Even Russia has chosen representative democracy. Unfortunately, the leaders of Russia and the very rich have chosen not to implement the system, but they have it nominally. Closer to home Timor-Leste and Burma are choosing Western-style political institutions and processes.

The fundamental reason why, finally, after 2500 years, we think we have arrived at the right combination of political processes and political institutions is, however, because these processes and institutions are consistent with our idea of the best political philosophy, which is a messy and shifting trade-off between individual freedom and a belief in human equality.

But if we look back to earlier times we can see that this consistency was always a feature of political regimes. Political processes and political institutions are always consistent with the prevailing ideal political philosophy. I would go so far as to say that, if they are not, they have no resilience at all.

Ancient Sparta had a different political philosophy to Athens. Athens had a different philosophy in the time of Pericles than in the time of Alexander. The philosophy of the Roman Republic differed from the philosophy of the Roman Empire. But while there were stable governance arrangements there was always an alignment between the political, and we could say just as easily ethical, philosophy of the people and those arrangements.

In the time of Marcus Aurelius (who died in 180 AD), the dominant personal and therefore political ethic in the rulers of the Empire was Stoicism. Courage, wisdom, temperance and justice were the chief Stoic virtues and lawmaking processes and their application were supposed to be consistent with these virtues.

In his *Meditations*, Marcus Aurelius summed up the Stoic's approach to the new day thus:

> Begin each day by telling yourself: Today I shall be meeting with interference, ingratitude, insolence, disloyalty, ill-will, and selfishness— all of them are due to the offender's ignorance of what is good and evil. But for my part I have long perceived the nature of good and its nobility, and the nature of evil and its meanness … therefore none of these things can injure me, for nobody can implicate me in what is degrading.

Well, that at least proves that not as much has changed in 2000 years as we would like to think!

The same consistency is true of the Middle Ages. Political institutions and processes were consistent with the ethical, and in this case religious, beliefs of the people. Middle Agers, if we can apply that term to a millennium as well as populations, believed God was the source of all authority and therefore His representatives should have authority on Earth.

A more modern example is communism, which lasted in Eastern Europe for about 70 years. It was another attempt to build political (and economic) institutions and processes consistent with a political philosophy. In essence communism is a throwback to a medieval religion-based system, only the God of the Middle Ages is replaced in theory with the dictatorship of the proletariat and in practice by a common-or-garden dictator and a sophisticated police state. I have often wondered if the mistake they made was to leave out some promise of life after death. I think it was the atheism that got them in the end. After all, if the economic system does not work to make life comfortable for the people and there is no hope of a better life after this, there is not a lot to lose by rejecting what you have.

The Characteristics of Resilience

The aforementioned historical overview is relevant to the modern governance problem of resilience. An important question to ask ourselves is what reasons do we have to believe that our current system of governance is resilient? After all, the ancient systems lasted 1000 years and those of the Middle Ages about the same time, whereas we moderns have been struggling along for only a few hundred years.

The first point I will make is that no system is resilient when people are starving. This is the extreme case, but more generally the point is that no system is resilient when the economy is failing to improve the livelihoods of the majority of the people.

I chose the phrase 'failing to improve' because an important part of the personal philosophy of the modern age is the notion of progress. This is partly a Christian concept—we are all progressing towards salvation or damnation—and partly an Enlightenment concept. Science in particular has given us the capacity to understand and modify our world. This has not always been for the better, but much technological advancement has made life more interesting and more comfortable for us. And successive generations being better entertained and better fed and living longer have ingrained in us the belief that progress is good.

At its most basic, and therefore at its most politically powerful, progress is about getting richer. There are two ways in which people in a certain country can get richer. One is that the whole country can get richer and they, like the proverbial boat on the rising tide, can rise with the general wealth accumulation, and the second is even if the whole country is not getting richer, so long as you can get a greater share of what is available you can be richer, albeit not now in concert with others but at the expense of others.

I have already answered the question regarding what produces resilience in a person, a business, an economy or a political system. If an economy is growing strongly it is increasing its redundancy (its spare capacities). Redundancy might be captured by the private sector as more plant and equipment, or higher retained earnings and less debt, or it might be captured by the public sector in the form of improvements in the quality of services or an improved fiscal position. In any event, the point is there is a greater capacity for the system to either invest in further growth creation (and so continue to get richer) or distribute the available wealth to people who are not 'progressing'—that is, those who are not getting richer.

This capacity either to invest or to distribute, of course, relates to optionality (the creation of further choices). Redundancy almost always contributes to the creation of optionality. In this way you can see that redundancy and optionality are not separate but are related elements in understanding resilience.

Resilient political systems must improve the livelihoods of the majority of the people if they are to survive. This is true in the medium term, but I accept that in the short term people will put up with a great deal of hardship and not throw out the political system. This is true largely because the collective prevailing political philosophy, which in our modern case is a belief in freedom and a form of equality, continues to be consistent with the political institutions and processes of the country. It is just that the politicians are useless. And there is a mechanism for dealing with that.

The heart of the resilience of representative democracy are periodic elections, and periodic elections are of course an optionality. This optionality only has value, however, if it results in some change for the better. We can chop and change our governments as much as we like but, if the next lot is as bad as the last lot and the one after that is no better, sooner or later something has to give. These are the circumstances in which democracy has been shown to fail in the past and a new form of government has been tried.

I am not saying that any of the major Western democracies is in danger of being overthrown any time soon but I do say that the United States and Europe in particular have precious little redundancy and that the value of the option of periodic elections is far lower today than it has been in the past. I am saying that representative democracy in the United States and Europe is far less resilient today than it has been at any time since the 1930s.

It is often not easy to recognise the signs of a lack of resilience. Consider, for example, the question of whether Germany today is more resilient that Greece. The popular response would be that Germany is obviously more resilient than

Greece. Greece, after all, is nearly bankrupt. It is a country burdened with huge public sector debt, dependent on Europe and particularly the powerful and resilient German economy for loans to prevent economic and social collapse.

Germany, on the other hand, appears to be the strongest state in Europe. The Germans pay their taxes on time, work hard, save their money and have a secure and resilient political system. German governments function effectively. German leaders are tough and resilient.

But we make a mistake if we conclude from the current situation in Europe that Germany is more resilient than Greece. I do not believe we have the evidence to draw any conclusions on this. This is because we cannot judge resilience until we apply the same stress to the two systems and the two peoples.

What if German banks had borrowed heavily in short-term loans from overseas banks and were subject to demands for repayment within 90 days? What if German banks were, as a consequence, failing? What if the unemployment rate in Germany was 33 per cent and what if the tax take was to fall so precipitously that German States did not have the money to pay unemployment benefits? And what if industrial production in Germany was to be just 40 per cent of what it had been three years previously? What then? Well then perhaps we could judge relative resilience.

But, in fact, we don't have to ask 'what if?' at all. The conditions I have described were exactly the conditions that prevailed in Weimar Germany in 1932. Thirteen years later, five million Germans were dead or missing and the country was a divided, occupied, smouldering wreck.

Of course I am not saying the same outcome would occur if the same stresses were placed on the German institutions and people today. There is no evidence for or against that proposition. But perhaps we need to give the Greeks more credit for their resilience and forbearance than we do. It is correct to conclude that public protest, even smashing things and lighting fires, is better construed as a contributor to Greek resilience than to Greek fragility.

Why? Because rioting to the Greeks is an option available to them by which they can express their frustration at the ineffectiveness of the political system and the governments it has produced.

The political system in Greece failed because governments were elected to do stupid things. They spent too much; they created an unsustainable pension system; they created an ineffective tax system. You might reasonably say it was not the Greek Government but the Greek people who were to blame. They elected these stupid governments.

But all electorates are uninformed. All electorates are gullible. All electorates will vote for what they believe is in their short-term interests. It is human nature. It is the responsibility of those who seek election to put in front of the electorate sustainable policies. Any fool can dupe someone into electing him to office. Only a wise and courageous politician can hold his course when things go badly.

The Greeks themselves can reach back thousands of years to their own proud heritage to understand what it takes to be a real leader in difficult times. Thucydides quotes Pericles, explaining his policies at a time when the war with Sparta is going badly:

> It is a policy which entails suffering, and each of you already knows what this suffering is; but its ultimate benefits are still far away and not yet clear for all to see. So, now that a great and sudden disaster has fallen on you, you have weakened in carrying out to the end the resolves which you made.

> When things happen suddenly, unexpectedly, and against all calculation, it takes the heart out of a man; and this certainly has happened to you, with the plague coming on top of everything else. You must remember that you are citizens of a great city and that you were brought up in a way of life suited to her greatness; you must therefore be willing to face the greatest disasters and be determined never to sacrifice the glory that is yours. We all look with distaste on people who arrogantly pretend to a reputation to which they are not entitled; but equally to be condemned are those who, through lack of moral fibre, fail to live up to the reputation which is theirs already. Each of you, therefore, must try to stifle his own particular sorrow as he joins with the rest in working for the safety of us all.

Resilience and the Political Ethic of the Populace

So I make the point that the resilience of political systems rests finally on the political ethic of the people. Political stability rests on the redundancy a nation has in the belief and commitment of its people to the political ideals the system is designed to embody.

The redundancy in belief and commitment to the political ethic upon which Western political institutions were founded is now low in many Western nations. This sinking store of ethical legitimacy of Western governments is the result of profound changes in the economic and social conditions in these countries.

In the United States, for instance, it seems that every week there is some commentary on the death of the American dream. The United States is a more unequal society than Australia or New Zealand, but the majority of Americans have accepted this inequality as the price of liberty. They have been told inequality is the Siamese twin of the opportunity to improve their own situation and they have believed this because, at least anecdotally, it has been true. Many people are now beginning to believe that the dream of owning a home and sending their kids to college is beyond them. And yet they see income inequality growing. The same is true in a less virulent form in Australia and New Zealand.

In Europe the resilience of individual states has been severely undermined by their lack of financial redundancy. They have simply run out of money. This has been compounded by the lack of optionality these states face as a result of their membership of the euro monetary zone. They cannot devalue their currency; they cannot manage their own monetary policy. Without redundancy and optionality, there can be no resilience.

Let me conclude this section with an analysis of the resilience of the political institutions in the three periods: Antiquity, the Middle Ages and the modern period.

The prevailing ethic in antiquity amongst the ruling classes was one form or another of personal virtue. In the Middle Ages the ethic was Christian virtue and in the modern period the ethic is, as I said earlier, a transient trade-off between freedom and equality, the result of which at any one time is a collective conception of a just society.

The political institutions of antiquity and the Middle Ages adapted and adjusted themselves to remain consistent with the political expectations of the people for more than 1000 years. It is important to clarify here that I refer to 'people' as the group who had the capacity to influence the political process.

This excludes, for instance, women, slaves, the faraway peoples in Antiquity, the disenfranchised and very poor of the Middle Ages. But the Ancients and the Middle Agers were undone in the end because their systems lacked optionality. The ethic of personal virtue, however much redundancy was built into it by the acceptance of all sorts of religious affiliation and personal philosophy, could not compete with the appeal of Christianity—the promise of life after death. Christianity outsourced virtue. God sent His son to die so that mankind could be saved and that trumped anything the ancient world could come up with.

A thousand years later, political institutions based on divinity collapsed because their system could not adapt to the newer, manmade laws and institutions.

Representative democracy seems to have a good deal of built-in optionality. Like the ancients' systems, it is based not on one core idea. It is, instead, founded on the flexible interplay of two ideas, liberty and equality, which are themselves flexible notions. But unlike the ancients, whose ideas of virtue were founded in superstition, ancestor worship and pure thought, the modern ethic is a derivative of empiricism and, at least in part, of the scientific method. Our modern systems are pragmatic and, if we can muster the numbers, always open to change within the limits of the majority's conception of a just society. This endows much resilience.

Conclusion

Finally, then, I will furnish a few brief examples of resilience as a product of redundancy and optionality from my other areas of experience. I work from the equation that resilience equals redundancy multiplied by optionality.

The human body has a great deal of redundancy. We have two lungs, two kidneys, two eyes, two legs, two arms, 10 fingers. And we have much, much more tissue in each of our major organs than we require for simple life support. The brain is the most significant option-generating device in the human. We can think our way around all sorts of problems. We can learn new things and endlessly adapt. The human is the most wildly successful creature ever and the most resilient creature the world has ever seen, largely because it has massive redundancy and option-generating capability.

The best sports teams are the teams that can do two things: they can play a given style of game better than their opponents and they have 'something in reserve' when it is needed to get them over the line. And two, they have the capacity to play multiple styles of game depending on the prevailing weather, the strength of the opposition and the attitude of the referee, among other things.

Resilient business organisations require plenty of redundancy. There are no new ways to go broke: running out of cash remains the only one. Low debt, high margins and diversified sources of revenue are hedges against inevitable market downturns, new competition and regulatory change. But these redundancies merely delay the inevitable. If companies are not able to adapt to the new conditions, using up their redundancy to create new options for growth then they will not survive. New geographies, new products, new customers and whole new businesses are all important optionalities that firms must have or develop quickly when they are needed.

Take one example: I joined the newspaper publishing business as the CEO of Fairfax Media in late 2005. I was late. The online classified advertising businesses that are thriving today in Australia at the expense of the big metropolitan newspapers were already established. I invested heavily in diversifying Fairfax's revenue, most notably by buying *Trade Me*, New Zealand's biggest online auction and classifieds website, for what was thought at the time to be a wildly expensive price of NZ$750 million; however, after Fairfax purchased *Trade Me* in 2010, the business had by then doubled in value.

The optionality I contributed to building into Fairfax has made the company more resilient, but it came at the expense of redundancy as I used up the balance sheet headroom. Ultimately, though, I had little choice. What I did has helped the company, but there remains no guarantee the business will survive in its current form. It is a competitive world in which we seek to survive and prosper, and we need to build resilience to do that.

Part 3: Managing Crises

15. Managing Crises Long Term: The challenges of preparedness and response

Paul 't Hart

The Heat of Crisis

The summer of 2011–12 was dry and hot in much of Australia. Coming on the back of the continuing drought of the previous five years, it left large parts of Victoria desperate for water. The long-term outlook of the Bureau of Meteorology was that the warm weather in most of Australia would continue in future Australian summers. In the summer of 2011–12, extreme fire risks existed in most of the south and south-east of the continent. The recorded temperatures between Monday, 25 January and Tuesday, 2 February 2012 were extreme, rising to 42°C or above in and around Sydney, Canberra, Melbourne and Adelaide on most if not all days of the week.

Summer is always a busy period in Melbourne, with a number of high-level events in progress or soon to begin. Various Australia Day festivities and small events throughout the city are held, culminating in a fireworks show in the centre of the city. The Australian Open tennis championships at the Rod Laver Arena take place between 18 and 31 January and attract more than 700 000 fans overall—up to 70 000 on a popular day. The 'Big Day Out' music festival was scheduled for 26 January 2012 at Flemington Racecourse, with an expected turnout of 50 000. Most importantly, Melbourne was about to host the meeting of the G20 leaders at the end of the month, to be held at the Grand Hyatt Hotel in the central business district. Various national and international activist bodies intended to stage protests. Intelligence briefings suggested a small but hardcore group of activists planned to penetrate security perimeters and/or otherwise disrupt the summit.

On 25 January, various fires broke out in the Dandenong Ranges just east of Melbourne after a major thunderstorm that inflicted heavy lightning, but virtually no rain, passed through southern Victoria. The combination of extremely dry conditions, high temperatures and strong winds fuelled these fires. The smoke blew towards inner-city Melbourne, covering it in a thick haze. At 1 pm it appeared that various fires around the community of Healesville joined and threatened to jump containment lines on the eastern side of the town. Community concern and media attention were intense, partly in light of the still fresh memories of the tragic events of 2009 and the harsh judgments about the State's disaster preparedness and firefighting performance delivered by the bushfire inquiry.

During the night, new fires emerged on the north-eastern outskirts of Greater Melbourne, a densely forested area. Some fires blazed out of control and moved westwards. Hundreds of people were evacuated and two dozen homes were lost. The Chief Health Officer advised the Victorian Government that the combination of extreme temperatures and the blanket of smoke covering large segments of the city constituted a major hazard to public health, particularly among the elderly and the very young. Public announcements to this effect were made. He later advised the Government to consider imposing school closures if the hot weather persisted and also mentioned the risks these conditions posed to participants in large outdoor Australia Day and other events.

During the late afternoon of 26 January reports came in from the Big Day Out about an alcohol-fuelled altercation that escalated after security personnel attempted to break up a large group of young men moving around the grounds harassing festival-goers. When a uniformed police officer became involved, he was beaten unconscious by a group, which brought in other uniformed and undercover police on duty, who allegedly responded in a heavy-handed manner as paramedics attempted to extract the injured (including the police officer, who was hospitalised). News of the incident spread fast through the plethora of graphic footage from the camera phones of festival-goers caught up in the violence, along with accusations of police brutality and rumours that the brawl was fuelled by ethnic tensions.

There was intense media coverage of the fires, which had wrecked 45 homes so far, and possibly killed a group of missing hikers. The fires were still burning in force on Melbourne's north-eastern fringe—triggering public debate about the risks associated with holding the G20 summit in Melbourne under these conditions. Furthermore, the incidents during the Big Day Out led some media outlets to question whether the police were capable of dealing with G20 protesters. On activist websites, calls for retaliation against 'police pigs' gained a lot of support. Behind the scenes, some of the advance parties of the G20 delegations sought assurances that the situation could be controlled. The head of the US Secret Service contingent was particularly adamant, and the US Ambassador conveyed his concerns discreetly to the foreign minister.

Later in the day, the first international leaders arrived in Melbourne ahead of the weekend's summit. A joint press conference involving the British, Canadian and Australian prime ministers was scheduled for 5 pm at the Grand Hyatt Hotel. In the early afternoon, the temperature had reached 44°C, stretching the power system beyond capacity because of heat-related increased demand. Prior calls to the public to moderate consumption did not have the desired effect. At 4.31 pm the system suffered a major malfunction when a fire broke out in a substation, cutting off supply to most of the CBD and other inner-city areas. Almost immediately, hundreds of calls for emergency assistance from people trapped in elevators in extremely high temperatures clogged the switchboards of security firms and emergency services.

The blackout affected the Grand Hyatt just prior to the press conference. Backup generators did not function properly and the UK Prime Minister was trapped in a lift for 20 minutes before security could safely access the elevator shaft. Exploiting the initial confusion caused by the blackout, a small number of protesters managed to enter the security zone around the building, just as press conference attendees were ushered out of the building. The press conference was cancelled as power remained off and the temperature inside the hotel quickly rose. The media nevertheless managed to file their reports, featuring the blackout, trapped leaders, the failure of the backup generator and questions of security ahead of the major summit on the weekend at the same venue.

Traffic chaos ensued as the late-afternoon rush hour began with traffic lights not working. Emergency services reported great difficulties reaching urgent cases as a result. The power company said that given the extensive damage to the substation and the high demand for power throughout the city and the State, it did not expect to be able to fully restore power within the next 24 hours. Some limited capacity could be available by nightfall, but might cover only 25 per cent of the affected area. The Victorian Employers' Chamber of Commerce and Industry estimated the costs to businesses of the CBD blackout would run into more than A$200 million per day. It approached the Government asking to ensure that top priority be given to restoring power in that area. Likewise, the Australian Open organisers demanded power for the event to be guaranteed.

Ambulance services and hospitals reported they were in danger of being overstretched. Moreover, ambulance workers as well as police reported an increasing number of cases of heat victims in their own ranks. In parallel, medical authorities in the States of Victoria, New South Wales and South Australia affected by the heatwave reported steep increases in the number of deaths in the previous 36 hours. There were conflicting reports about the numbers involved, because it was not immediately clear how many people died on account of the heat. The reports ranged from 10 to 30 per cent increases in fatalities. The most common demographic of people who died in this period was old people—usually those living alone in residences without airconditioning.

In an impromptu statement, the Prime Minister said he had been fully briefed on the seriousness of the situation, but he nevertheless had full confidence in the emergency services' capacity to handle the fires and the heat-related problems, as well as guarantee security for the G20. He mentioned that as a precaution, additional personnel and equipment might be flown in from interstate. He also called on citizens to look after their neighbours, to make sure vulnerable groups (the old, the very young and the infirm) were sheltered from the heat and had plenty to drink. He offered 'any and all' Commonwealth assistance to State authorities.

The next morning, news bulletins and front pages moved on from the incidents at the Grand Hyatt. They instead were full of graphic pictures of the dead being removed from derelict apartments and old people's homes in the three capital cities most affected. Talkback radio was awash with callers desperately seeking help, claiming they could not get through to the emergency services. They were mostly elderly citizens living alone or their relatives fearing the worst after not being able to reach them. Other news outlets reported 'extraordinary scenes' of panic purchasing of bottled water and soft drinks by nervous crowds at supermarkets around the capital cities. Local breakfast TV ran an interview with a disaster expert asserting that Melbourne in particular might be heading for a 'catastrophe' of historic proportions. Comparisons were drawn with Chicago's 1995 heatwave, when the city became 'an urban heat island', killing more than 750 people, and with the French and Italian heatwaves of 2003 and 2006, which were estimated to have caused more than 15 000 and 3000 deaths respectively. In each of these instances, severe criticism was directed at alleged government negligence in emergency preparedness and response.

Clearly, the signs of 'collective stress' were becoming stronger, and not just in Melbourne. There were increasingly vehement allegations on websites and local radio that critical electricity supply as well as police and emergency services resources were 'diverted away from ordinary citizens in need' to protect 'a talkfest for politicians'.

The G20 summit nevertheless unfolded without major incident, and the level of protest against it came out well below expectations. The reasons for this were grim: the heat and the fires created bigger, more acute problems to worry about. Early public estimates were that more than 1900 people across the three States died prematurely on account of the heat. Relentless live coverage of bodies being carried out of homes and offices produced a sense of shock and subsequently anger in the community. The occurrence of multiple power outages in three jurisdictions as well as the long duration of the power outage in Melbourne raised questions about the resilience of the power grid, and State and Federal governments' roles as regulators.

Thinking about Crisis Management

This scenario—a fictionalised but all too plausible combination of several real events—shows how even in otherwise prosperous, peaceful and stable communities 'business as usual' can give way to critical conditions of disaster, conflict and breakdown. When this happens, something akin to 'un-ness' reigns supreme: citizens and policymakers alike face *un*planned, *un*wanted, *un*certain and *un*pleasant prospects and choices. Crises act as pressure cookers: they arouse interests and emotions to higher levels of intensity. The more threatening, surprising and acute they appear, the stronger is the collective stress they elicit. They defy normal structures and routines of collective problem solving. They test the resilience of communities and their governments. They raise intense and awkward questions for policymakers. How could this happen? Why didn't we see this coming? Who is to blame? How do we move on from here?

We should therefore ask how governments, organisations and leaders prepare for and perform under the intense pressures generated by crises; however, we should not assume that crises are simply bad news for leaders, whose crisis management is focused purely on damage limitation, both operationally and politically. Crises may also provide leaders with unique opportunities to discard old policies and commitments, kickstart new ones, reform public organisations and reshape the political landscape by forging new coalitions. To understand the complex challenges of crisis management, we should also look very strongly at the social-psychological dimension of crises in a society. We should approach crisis management not just as an elevated form of practical problem solving, but also as a profoundly political activity with intense strategic implications for the positions of elites and institutions.

Moreover, we often think of a crisis as a sudden event, an approach that might inadvertently lead us to take a rather myopic view of just how long and dynamic a crisis might turn out to be. This is because the shocks and effects of the initial crisis will accumulate, not just in 72 hours or a week, but across a month, or two or three months. That's how crises escalate. And then the long shadow they create can last for years.

Consequently, the people who study crisis response ask, 'Although much initial focus has always been on this first stage, what happens when the proverbial shit hits the fan?' The study of this subsequent stage—how crises actually impact on institutions over a much longer period—has been relatively neglected, in planning effort and preparedness effort, and in research. I will try to cover this topic in my chapter.

What really sets a crisis apart from business as usual? There is significant consensus in the literature that from the perspective of government or the management of organisations which must respond to these events, it is the combination of three situational characteristics that makes crises particularly tricky. First, the idea that something really bad is going on, or might happen, generates a significant level of collective stress and requires a large-scale, multidisciplinary, unconventional and possibly interjurisdictional and intersectoral response. Second, there's a sense of time pressure: policymakers feel (rightly or wrongly) that something must be done about the threat or damage right now or very soon. So this leaves them no time for conventional processes of public problem solving such as research, broad consultations, lawmaking or incremental reform paths. The third crucial component is that many aspects of the crisis are deeply uncertain, as are the possible consequences and ramifications of one's own past and present actions in relation to the events. In other words, the unknown unknowns can be a large part of the picture in a crisis.

So from a policy or managerial perspective, leaders need to take highly consequential decisions in a context in which they do not have all the numbers, they can't delegate the issue to a commission, and can't get the experts to study it for a few months. They have to act much faster than governments normally act. And often that acting involves doing quite unpleasant things, or disappointing a lot of people, or making tough decisions about the allocation of scarce resources. That's what makes crisis management tough from an operational and tactical point of view.

If, however, we also look at crises from a more strategic point of view, the picture shifts somewhat. Crises generate a form of hyper-transparency: everybody, including the entire media, is focused on the issue. There is an explosion of tension and scrutiny of what the relevant policymakers and organisations are doing during the crisis and what they have done or failed to do in the lead-up to it. The idea, then, that some things are natural disasters and the evaluation of our response to them is going to be determined by the response alone is becoming increasingly remiss. Natural disasters are almost immediately being reframed as regulatory failures one way or the other—for example, questioning why inundated houses had been built on a floodplain, or why earthquake-ravaged buildings had not been better equipped to deal with such a natural disaster. So there is an immense concentration of scrutiny of behaviour during and before the crisis; momentum builds for a move away from this discredited state of affairs to something new and better. And quite bluntly, there's a lot of pressure on people in high positions to fall on their swords one way or another. So from a more strategic political point of view, this is also a reality that people will factor into their actions.

A crucial point to remember here is that it is the *strategic* crisis after the operational and tactical one—the crisis after the crisis—that will go far to determining the long-term consequences of the disturbance, and the subsequent long-term policy and institutional implications. It means that a trade-off is created during what is essentially the post-acute stage of a crisis: a trade-off between the need to learn (everybody pays lip-service to this idea of learning) and the strategic reality of managing the blame that is going around.

If we juxtapose operational-tactical and strategic thinking about how to respond to a crisis two logics of action emerge. The first is the logic familiar to most readers, and which is written in all official planning documents, however aspirational or fictitious they might be. Citizens are cast as victims in this kind of perspective. The media is considered part of the communication picture. They report what's going on, they can be your ally in getting messages across, and so on. Crisis management then happens on site—it happens in line agencies, in coordination centres and so on, and the key stakes are to control the physical damage and to have community resilience and rebuilding kick in as smoothly and energetically as possible.

But there is also the other logic of action in which a crisis unleashes powerful emotions—blame games, if you like—in which citizens have a voice, become advocates for positions and will form interest groups which can be vocal, well connected and influential. Such a situation can arise when the media has axes to grind, and when stories about the crises are fitted into ongoing political narratives about good guys and bad guys. Take UK prime minister Gordon Brown's handling of the Global Financial Crisis as an example. For a short while in late 2008 the British media typecast Brown, who had just taken over from Tony Blair as Labour prime minister, as the wise and heroic international statesman crafting a global solution to an unprecedented financial catastrophe. But when solutions proved elusive and painful, the media reverted back to the story frame they had already imposed on him, which was that of a no-hope prime minister, one who even had been asleep at the wheel in his long years as chancellor when the risks of bad debt were building up throughout the British financial sector.

Key crisis-management arenas are also somewhat different in this strategic perspective: they are partly the media, including the social media; they involve parliament and inquiries—in other words, the more political arenas where the action is. And obviously the key stakes are political and institutional: elite careers, programs and organisations are at a critical juncture. A crisis can be enormously consequential politically, both in terms of threats and in terms of opportunities. Think of the famous photo of Margaret Thatcher riding a tank at the time of the Falklands War, which transformed a weak prime minister into an unassailable prime minister for many years after the conflict ended. Conversely, think of Thatcher's later successor Tony Blair, whose decision to commit British armed forces to the Iraq War proved to be a significant factor in his political undoing.

Perhaps even more poignant was former US president Jimmy Carter's response to the Iran Hostage Crisis (1979–81), when 52 staff members were held hostage at the US Embassy in Tehran for 444 days. Carter met with his advisors every day for those 14 months at 7 in the morning to discuss what could be done, before any other business of government was conducted. The hostages were released the day Carter's term in office ended, and the experience was widely considered to have broken the man. If you compare photos of Jimmy Carter taken the day he took office with those taken on the day of Ronald Reagan's inauguration you see a stark contrast. There were many reasons for this, but a significant one was the emotional toll of Carter's involvement in the hostage crisis, and particularly his micromanagement of it.

All these cases demonstrate that the stakes are high. A leader can be the hero, the villain or the victim of a crisis, politically speaking. The same goes for public institutions. For example, the Roman Catholic Church has taken a big hit over recent years on account of the widespread incidence of long-term, covered-up child molestation in Catholic institutions such as foster homes. It was damning evidence of an institutional lapse of morals too big to ignore, forcing a 2000-year-old institution into public contrition, damaging compensation battles and—hopefully—critical self-examination.

Key Leadership Challenges

Up to this point I have principally been providing context. For the remainder of this chapter I will focus on what I consider to be the five key recurring challenges of responding to crises once they have emerged. My colleagues and I have identified these challenges from comparative analysis of a couple of decades of crisis responses—whether it be to disasters, terrorist events, riots or some other crisis. In so doing, we have tried to ignore the specifics of those various types of crisis scenarios and instead tried to look at the commonalities from the perspective of strategic and tactical management of these events (Boin et al. 2005, 2008).

The first challenge is *making sense of the crisis*. If uncertainty is a big part of the picture, making sense of what is actually going on—and updating that diagnosis in the face of dynamic developments—becomes a key challenge.

The second challenge is that those in management positions must *make decisions*—particularly strategic decisions—about the overall direction, nature and limits of the response.

The third one is the need to *marshal organisational capacity* both within the public sector and beyond it to address the crisis. And it is critical that this is done more quickly, and at a much larger scale, than that at which these organisations had previously operated.

The fourth challenge is what we call *meaning making*: persuading the public, other actors and the media of one's own interpretation of what is going on, what can be done, how people can increase their own safety, how we should deal with questions of accountability, and how we should deal with questions about the future.

And finally there is adaptation. This refers to the idea that we need to *move on from the crisis and look beyond it to reflect and draw lessons*. And here 'renewal' is a more appropriate term than 'rebuilding', because the term rebuilding (or even 'recovery') suggests a return to the status quo that existed before the crisis, which is a fanciful and unrealistic proposition in the face of consistent evidence that crises always act as catalysts for change at one or more levels. I will now elaborate on each of these five challenges in turn.

Sense-Making

This first challenge refers to the initial comprehension of a crisis—the moment encapsulated in the photo of George W. Bush learning of the 11 September attacks, sitting in a school with his chief of staff whispering in his ear. Of that moment Bush has said he was calculating not just what to do about 9/11, but also what kind of impression it would make on the public if the American President left a class full of schoolchildren. It was a controversial decision, but it illustrates the kind of dilemma that crisis managers face: in real time, starting to think about what is going on, what it means and what can be done about it.

In fact there are several 'sense-making' dilemmas that arise during a crisis—for example, the dilemma of speed versus accuracy. If there is a seeming imperative to act very quickly, how long are you going to wait until you get a richer picture of the situation? Are you going to take immediate action and run the risk that it is ill directed or suboptimal? But if you wait too long to respond, there is the risk the action may not be meaningful. This is a recurrent dilemma. An example of this was Jimmy Carter during the Iran Hostage Crisis. By constantly meeting with the families of the hostages, Carter lost the ability to maintain a cold, analytical picture of the situation. Though such an approach may have been a very noble thing to do, you're not the US President to be noble; you're there to be clear-headed. And if you place yourself so deeply into the emotion of a crisis it becomes very difficult to engage in that kind of dispassionate analysis.

Where do you get the expertise you need? There is a tendency for people to draw on the old hands, the experienced people, those who have been there before. This can be a very good thing; we have to respect experience and the professionalism it brings. Quite often, however, it is also beneficial to call upon people who have not traditionally been part of the crisis-management picture, or who are not known specialists in the area or part of the same old network. How do you create space in your organisational setup for bringing in and amplifying these so-called 'soft voices'? How does this tacit knowledge (which is often local knowledge) find its way to the centre of the decision-making process during a crisis?

What do we know goes wrong in sense-making? I will mention two things. One is myopia—that if the present becomes so all-consuming because buildings are collapsing and people are dying, etcetera, it is extremely hard for decision-makers to not just address pressing concerns, but also keep perspective on what's going to happen in one week, two weeks, three months, or a year. If you don't organise this long-term plan it won't happen. And even prime ministers and other senior crisis managers lapse into an operational or, at best, tactical stance and ignore the strategic stance.

I have observed this myself in various cases where I was in the command centre during a crisis. One example was on 4 October 1992 when El Al flight 1862 crashed into the Groeneveen and Klein-Kruitberg flats in the Bijlmermeer neighbourhood of Amsterdam. All the local politicians and local administrators who meant anything were put into a crisis centre where they could govern without a counsel looking over their shoulders. In these situations all the bureaucratic politics disappear because everybody is motivated to 'do the right thing'. And these people grow comfortable in this space where they are all of a sudden at the top of a pyramid. In normal life they are at best a node in a network and they have to bargain to have an impact on governance. But in a crisis you can suddenly be government, and you know best, and you're surrounded by basically your trusted and liked sources. It can be very difficult for information from outside that bunker to penetrate the reality that these people are forming with one another.

How do we improve sense-making in a crisis? There are many recommendations I could cite from the literature but I will highlight one here: the power of harnessing the wisdom of the crowd. As I previously mentioned, there is a danger of governments listening only to themselves in the context of a crisis, whereas now with social media and other forms of new technology we have a unique opportunity to gather rich pictures straight from the community level, filter it and use it.

For example, in a bushfire situation the firefighters and the people directing the firefighters usually have no idea how bad things are in affected locations. With this kind of logic transformed into a communications design, it would be possible to know a lot more in real time about what is going on if you can somehow get the individual citizen to become a co-producer of information that the crisis responders can act upon.

Sense-making should not be limited to the crisis itself, either, but should extend to institutions or aspects of your society that are brought under the microscope as a result of a crisis. Often we allow the strategic aspects of crisis management to be taken over by small politics, so it becomes more about the politics of managing tough accountability questions, saving skins, protecting paradigms and so on. But what you are then missing is the opportunity a crisis presents to learn something about your own society and about your own institutions that you didn't already know. This might cause you to rethink the design of that society and the design of that institution. It may sound lofty, but every major crisis reveals something you didn't already know. In this way, crises are potential teachers.

Take the El Al flight 1862 incident as an example. It took an airplane coming down in Amsterdam for city authorities to realise they had no idea who was actually living where in their city. Surely it would have been easy to answer some simple questions: who had died when the plane crashed? Who was living in the Groeneveen and Klein-Kruitberg flats at the time? But not in a multicultural neighbourhood like Bijlmermeer, with its high concentration of refugees, asylum-seekers and illegal aliens.

Consequently, the authorities had to go to the public and say, 'Look, we've been digging in the rubble for three days, we've found 10 bodies, there are about 100 apartments obliterated by this airplane, we don't know where you are, if you've survived this. If you happen to be illegal in this country and you are somehow victimised, please come forward.' And in doing this, they used very careful language, hinting that those victims without official papers would be allowed to stay in the country.

The next day, 1500 people showed up at City Hall. This case illustrates how a crisis can teach you about the adequacy of your registers, and about public communication; the challenge is to draw out those lessons and be open to them. Such an approach is taken by so-called high-reliability organisations (HROs). They study operators of power grids, nuclear facilities, airlines and so on, because they approach every incident as a possible teacher, and they don't rest until they find out what those lessons are. But you can only do that if you make the learning process safe from the politics of blame. And so a strategic approach to crisis is on the one hand to deal with those accountability issues while not allowing it to be the only game in town.

Decision-Making

Consider now the challenge of decision-making. Once it has been established that there is a crisis, what next? There are some tough choices that can be made during this stage, and some potential dilemmas. Are we going to play this down, are we going to play it up? In a major case of child sex abuse in Amsterdam in 2011, the authorities had to decide whether they would limit their information to the parents of those 67 children affected, or whether they would also inform the rest of the world. They had to make a calculated guess. Obviously if you inform the rest of the world, particularly the rest of Amsterdam, you're going to create collective behaviour and collective emotions that will be very difficult to control. If you're not informing them, but you are informing 67 parents who are then going to talk to their families and friends, word is going to come out in an uncontrolled fashion and you may look like you've been trying to suppress information. The authorities in Amsterdam quickly realised they could not contain information regarding this case, so they acted on the presumption it would be a big deal, and prepared a large response accordingly.

The role of insurance companies can also present a dilemma for decision-makers. What, for example, if the insurance industry doesn't do its bit—or what government and citizens consider to be its bit—in assisting victims of crisis? Is government going to step in? This would be costly, and would set a precedent for the next crisis. So how do public policymakers decide whether or not to act? And how do professional public servants make sure that during the initial shock following the outbreak of crisis, their political executives don't go running around making heartfelt promises that the experts know cannot be kept later?

Such a situation arose on 28 September 1994 when the ferry *MS Estonia* sank in the Baltic Sea, with the loss of 852 lives. Most of the dead were Swedish nationals, and immediately following the tragedy the acting prime minister of Sweden, Carl Bildt, promised the next of kin they would get their relatives' bodies back. A few hours after Bildt made this commitment, however, his navy told him this would be extremely difficult to do. It is this kind of impulse generosity that crisis managers might have to think twice about, even at the risk of seeming callous and indifferent.

What can go wrong in terms of making those decisions? I have already covered quite a few, but I haven't mentioned lack of disagreement. Group-think can be a real issue, especially in a bunker situation where policymakers and their advisers face something very unpleasant and the world out there has no idea what pressures are on them. Outside advice does not necessarily come through to the 'inner circle' handling the crisis. It's a physical and an emotional setting that is conducive to tunnel vision and group solidarity. And it shows: we know from comparative research that more crises are mismanaged because of excessive consensus at the top than because of a lack of consensus there (Janis 1989; Schafer and Crichlow 2010).

A lot of the lack of consensus occurs below the top; agencies fighting each other can be a problem all on their own—something I will discuss later. But at the top it is more often this consensus, or assumed consensus, that isn't questioned under the pressure of the circumstances and the stress of the situation that leads to mismanagement.

What, then, are sensible things to do to improve crisis decision-making capacity? Those in crisis-management positions must think hard about the balance between their ambition and their generosity: the positioning of the government as the purveyor of solutions and the purveyor of around-the-clock care for everybody versus a restrained policy posture that emphasises self-reliance and that limits the government's liability and involvement in the crisis. Clear limits of involvement must be set because it is better to do that quickly, clearly and consistently rather than at a later stage when expectations may have already been raised.

Another way to improve decision-making is the realisation—and there is consensus about this among researchers—that you cannot aspire to control tactics and operations from the centre, whatever that centre might be. You need to have a far-reaching form of delegation and mandate to empower localised units to respond as they believe is best. Moreover, you have to rely on their professionalism, which is easy to do if you have invested in pre-crisis training and communication. But whenever we see a large and dynamic crisis being micromanaged by the centre of the centre, paralysis, misjudgments and a lack of tailor-made solutions ensue.

Organising Response

Consider the US response to Hurricane Katrina in 2005 as an example of how not to organise a response. It is a story of complete breakdown of intergovernmental relations, from the local to the State to the federal level. It's the classic case of how not to coordinate a major disaster response.

What, then, is the right way to organise a response? Is it best to coordinate by writing plans and, when the disaster strikes, applying the plan and seeing if it works? Or is it better to rely on improvisation because the situation calls for a move beyond the plans? This second option is facilitated by having relationships cemented by pre-crisis planning and processes of exercise and joint operations. How much centralisation is necessary? What should be centralised and what done locally? Is coordination about coordinating the machinery of government or about coordinating the collective effort of the affected society? Of course it should be the latter.

Why, then, is it that most of the coordination processes that my colleagues and I study tend to be of a myopic, government-centric nature, which fail to harness the resources of NGOs or the private sector? One only need consider Hurricane Katrina, where some of the major corporations, particularly supermarkets, had an impeccable logistical operation and were able to provide more direct care to the community than were the entire government operations. And yet they were never part of the official crisis response. This was a great shame and it shouldn't happen, but it happens all the time.

And finally, how much of our organising energy do we concentrate on that immediate acute response phase and how much on planning ahead to the recovery phase? My rule of thumb is that 80 per cent of the time the energy is focused on the response phase. Recovery is always the stepchild of a lot of the pre-crisis planning and coordination efforts. And yet, the recovery phase is the one that will ultimately stick in people's minds. After all, any heroism of the response phase will be quickly forgotten if you're still waiting for shelter five months after the crisis occurred.

What traps should be avoided? One is that if people involved in the crisis management meet only in a crisis setting trust doesn't immediately build up among strangers. Trust builds on familiarity with who the person is, what their organisation represents, what they can do, what their operational logic is, and so forth. I cannot emphasise enough the importance of bringing about that familiarity by organising preliminary crisis-response exercises. This needs to an ongoing, very broadly organised process so that the people who will be thrown together to manage a crisis are on familiar terms long before the crisis. And it needs to be done every one or two years.

Finally, if you tolerate turf wars the way they were tolerated in the aftermath of Hurricane Katrina, you are setting yourself up for nastiness. And so, despite everything I have argued in favour of a decentralised response, somewhere in the centre of the centre managers should still be observing the quality of interaction that's going on. And if they see infighting taking over, there needs to be a short, sharp and unmistakable intervention to stop it.

Meaning-Making

The fourth key challenge to crisis management I will highlight is meaning-making. How do you regulate public distress? The 2011 Fukushima nuclear disaster was an interesting case from a meaning-making perspective. The world did not get to see the Japanese Prime Minister for the first eight days of the crisis. The public face of the Government's meaning-making effort was a cabinet secretary. The man was competent, but the public nevertheless began to wonder why their leader was so eerily absent from the story (though he was frantically active behind the scenes to the point of attempting to micromanage not just the governmental response but also that of the private energy provider Tepco which operated the Fukushima plant).

The example raises interesting questions about the choices governments make about who will be the public face of the crisis. Usually the head of the government is assigned this role—which may or may not be a good idea. In Queensland, Premier Anna Bligh's political capital was very low at the time of the 2011 floods; but she managed to do the meaning-making so well that suddenly she experienced a political comeback, if only briefly. I suspect there were some personality and stylistic issues involved in the decision to keep the Japanese Prime Minister in the background immediately following Fukushima. But there may also have been a strategic calculus at play. Prime Minister Kan's political stock was low at the time and plenty of bad news had to be delivered; perhaps the Government thought it should hold the prime minister in reserve for when there was some good news to tell. The problem with Fukushima was there was never any good news. And after a few days people started to wonder who was actually leading the country.

The Japanese Prime Minister was not the first national leader not to communicate publicly to citizens that something bad had occurred. It took Mikhail Gorbachev seven days to acknowledge the Chernobyl nuclear meltdown incident; Vladimir Putin arrived at the site of the *Kursk* submarine disaster nearly a week after it had occurred. Even in the limited democracy setting of Putin's Russia, not showing up—he had to be dragged to the *Kursk* scene—was a public relations fiasco. It's not just about what you say; it's also about where you say it, when you say it and with whom you engage. They are all part of the meaning-making process.

One must also be wary of letting the experts do all the talking. At the time of the Chernobyl incident, we had a radiation expert on Dutch television reassuring the public that radiation levels were only 10 000 times higher than normal. This may have been reassuring in his mind, but not necessarily in the mind of the public. But he couldn't conceive of that because he's not a member of the public—he's an expert.

Another difficult issue surrounding meaning-making is what we in the industry call the 'creeping crisis'—whether it be some form of slow environmental degradation, a possible pandemic about to emerge or another slowly unfolding crisis. I occasionally attend the lectures of Dutch epidemiologist Hans Lusthaus, who never fails to scare me by pointing out that at any one time five or six potentially lethal pandemics are bubbling away under the surface. How can meaning-making be done in such scenarios? You don't want to run the risk of succumbing to 'cry wolf syndrome': going out with all guns blazing, alerting people to the enormous danger they're in, only to have the supposed danger not materialise quickly, which destroys your credibility.

Consequently, building up a solid evidence base is a critical part of the sense-making process. This enables you to convince the public that although they may not be able to see buildings burning or people dying right now, there is a high probability that they will be able to in a certain amount of time. If you don't have that evidence base, shut up.

If you do have that evidence base, what is the strategy to persuade governments, corporations or whoever is in charge that something is 'rotten in Denmark'? Is it best to use really powerful hyperbole and perhaps even go public so as to surround those potentially affected by the crisis with information? Or is it better to inch them slowly towards awareness that there's a big problem going on?

I will always remember Peter Shergold, then the secretary of the Department of Prime Minister and Cabinet and head of the Australian Public Service, describing to one of my student audiences the way in which he incrementally persuaded John Howard that he should do something about climate change in the latter years of his prime ministership—a challenge, given that the former prime minister was at best not interested in climate change, at worst a climate change denier. The approach Shergold took was to casually slip little bits of information that pertained to climate change into his daily meetings with Howard. 'Oh, Prime Minister, have you noticed that the CEO of this mining corporation is now saying we should do something about climate change?' Slowly Howard got annoyed, but he could also not deny what was going on; he eventually agreed to create a taskforce to look into the issue, with Shergold as its chair. This was a sensible strategy, and perhaps in retrospect a more sensible strategy than Al Gore going to Hollywood and scaring us in 2007 with *An Inconvenient Truth*.

Meaning-making presents some dilemmas. Do you project certainties or do you also project your uncertainty? If you have unknown unknowns, do you tell the public you have them? And again, a lot of the research suggests that governments err on the side of not informing the public about things they don't know to prevent the public from panicking. The problem with this argument is that there is no academic evidence to suggest the public panics. In fact, the evidence suggests the contrary: the public does not panic. It's a form of governmental, paternalistic bias that the public can't handle bad news. It's a real source of concern.

How, then, do we improve our meaning-making capacity? These days it's crucial that you have not just the resources but also the skills to sustain real-time multimedia communication for a very long time. Many governments are making good progress in this area because in a way it isn't difficult to acquire the relevant hardware, media people and so on. Yet I don't want to play this down: it's a necessary but not sufficient component of a resilient meaning-making capacity.

It is also important to have people involved in the meaning-making effort who have an understanding of human behaviour in extreme situations—people who understand the social-psychological perspective and not just the economic or physical infrastructure perspectives. Quite often people with this experience are not harnessed to the task, with politicians instead devising their public communications strategy on the basis of the advice of either politically focused media advisors or economists—both groups liable to making stupid and crude assumptions about human behaviour. I could cite many examples of ill-conceived public communication because the socio-psychological expertise is not around the table.

A final point to make about meaning-making is that it is not a one-sided show that the government can run. Other actors in the political context of crisis management are engaging in their own meaning-making. My colleagues and I use the term 'framing contest' as a way of describing what happens as we move from the acute stage towards investigations. It becomes a contest between different frames of interpreting what went on, why it went on, who is to blame and what we can learn from it. So as part of that contest, you have to really work on your credibility; you have to be careful not to say or do anything that undermines your credibility even further than it will have been undermined by the sheer fact that the crisis has happened on your watch.

Adaptation

Only weeks after Hurricane Katrina had destroyed coastal areas of Louisiana and Mississippi, Hurricane Rita entered the Gulf of Mexico. When the projected trajectory of Rita included Houston (the fourth-largest city in the United States), the Texas authorities quickly ordered an evacuation. The lessons of Katrina had been learned! In the chaotic evacuation, more than 100 people died. Hurricane Rita changed course and never reached Houston.

The extent to which lessons are learned after a crisis (if they are learned at all) is one of the most under-researched aspects of crisis management (Birkland 2006). A crisis or disaster holds huge potential for lessons to be learned about reforming contingency planning and training to enhance resilience in the event of similar episodes in the future. In an ideal world, we might expect all relevant players to study these lessons carefully and apply them in order to reform organisational practices, policies and laws. In reality, there are many barriers to lesson drawing.

Organisations tend not to be good learners, certainly not in the aftermath of crises and disasters. One crucial barrier is the lack of authoritative and widely accepted explanations of the causes of the crisis or disaster. Potential factors encompass individual, organisational, technological and societal shortcomings, all of which can be subject to many different interpretations and assumptions about their significance. Yet even if explanations could attract common agreement, many organisational factors such as an excessive focus on core goals at the expense of 'looking for trouble' can act as barriers to preventing future crises and improving coping capacities in the event that they do occur. Most public service organisations are focused strongly on delivering front-line public services, rather than on scenario planning and crisis training. Worst-case thinking is rarely high on agendas.

In addition to cognitive and institutional influences on learning lessons after a crisis, the political and social aspects can also be crucial. A dominant political depiction of a crisis as the product of failures of prevention or lack of foresight in contingency planning can set the agenda for rethinking policies, processes and organisational rules. Other players in the lesson-drawing game, however, might attempt to use the political reform rhetoric to advocate very different types of reforms from those put forward by leaders. Therefore, the stakes are high for leaders in their capacities to steer lesson-drawing processes. The key challenge is to ensure that in the wake of a crisis, they have a dominant influence on the feedback stream and that existing policy networks and public organisations follow the leader's desired pathway.

Despite complex barriers to post-crisis learning, crises also present opportunities. They can create windows of opportunity for policy reform, institutional overhaul and even leadership revival (Boin et al. 2008, 2009). The 2001 foot-and-mouth disease crisis in the United Kingdom led to the abolition of an insular and backward-looking agricultural department. Barack Obama's victory in the 2008 US presidential elections was helped by a perception that he was better placed than his rival John McCain to lead the country's economic revival. A word of caution is necessary here. Leaders need to be careful of 'knee-jerk' reactions that are high on symbolic value because they create the impression of swift and decisive reform action, but are not based on considered deliberation or sound rationale. Sweeping reforms and the rapid replacement of key officials in response to a crisis or a critical inquiry report may help create the impression that a leader is 'in charge'; however, such action may severely limit the capacity for genuine lesson drawing, and may create new vulnerabilities or reinforce old ones.

Table 15.1 Components of Crisis-Response Capacity

A. Sense-making capacity
1. Absorbing surprise, shock and uncertainty
2. Exploiting experience without being captured by it
3. Mobilising and utilising comprehensive expertise
4. High-velocity and continuous monitoring and updating
5. Safeguarding the long-term view
B. Steering and synthesising capacity
1. Delivering strategic direction
2. Empowering operational agility
3. Forging concerted action across jurisdictions and professions
4. Safeguarding consideration of values and ethics
C. Meaning-making capacity
1. High-speed, all-channel public communication
2. Acknowledging and channelling public emotions
3. Mobilising pro-social community behaviour
4. Maintaining authority in the face of criticism
D. Consolidation capacity
1. Proactive recovery planning
2. Balancing solidarity and restraint in service provision
3. Resilient response–recovery transitions
E. Adaptive capacity
1. Proactive management of external accountability demands
2. Safeguarding institutional self-reflection
3. Exploring and exploiting learning opportunities
4. Fostering collective memory and a culture of awareness

Source: Author's summary.

Three Paths to Improving Crisis Management

In this chapter I have listed a broad catalogue of factors that together constitute what one might call the strategic capacity of a crisis-response system (see Table 15.1). Trying to put this into practice involves a broad and long-term capacity-building agenda, but let me highlight the three most important factors. First, it is important *to open up crisis-management planning*. By this I mean taking it away from the monopoly of experts, operational agencies and specialists. Obviously they are pivotal in a crisis situation, but if we are to take community resilience seriously, surely the community—in whatever form—should be part of the planning process rather than being relied on only when government meets its own limitations.

Second, it is imperative to *focus on the crisis after the crisis*—the so-called recovery phase. This requires focusing on the adaptation process of learning the right lessons rather than becoming obsessed with fighting the last war— something the average inquiry report is often overly concerned with. Because while it is important to be prepared for the last war, it is even more important to be prepared for a whole range of possible wars you have to fight in the future.

My final recommendation is to *upgrade the capacity to learn from a crisis* rather than simply engage in the blame game. This requires embracing the best practices available (which are extremely well documented) from so-called high-reliability organisations (Weick and Sutcliffe 2007). Doing these things will go a long way towards creating a culture of learning in an organisation that routinely has to make extremely dangerous decisions in the context of a crisis.

There is evidence to suggest that crisis-response capacity will become even more important in the future as the nature of crises changes. Two rather sweeping developments demand our attention. First, crises are becoming increasingly interconnected and trans-boundary in nature (Boin and Rhinard 2008; Helsloot et al. 2012). Contemporary crises such as pandemics and mega computer viruses transgress functional, geographical and time boundaries that used to keep crises and disasters more or less contained. We are facing crises that escalate across policy domains and countries, combining long incubation times with long-term effects. Such crises are harder to manage through conventional means and strategies.

Second, the political-administrative capacity to deal with such crises has been gradually eroding. The current downsizing of the state, the inheritance of two or more decades of New Public Management insistence on leanness and efficiency, and the fragmentation of the political consensus about 'bottom-line' issues of safety and security—are all phenomena that can be easily exaggerated, but it is hard to see how they contribute to the type of political-administrative capacity required for dealing prudently with the crises of the era.

Many things may change, but one thing that will remain the same is the call for leadership that follows the onset of a crisis. It is time that crisis management is viewed as an integral and crucial dimension of leadership, in both the public and the private sectors.

References

Birkland, T. A. 2006. *Lessons of Disaster* (Washington, DC: Georgetown University Press).

Boin, A. and Rhinard, M. 2008. 'Managing Trans-Boundary Crises: What Role for the European Union?', *International Studies Review*, 10(1):1–2.

Boin, A., McConnell, A. and 't Hart, P. (eds) 2008. *Governing after Crisis: The Politics of Investigation, Accountability and Learning* (Cambridge: Cambridge University Press).

Boin, A., 't Hart, P. and McConnell, A. 2009. 'Towards a Theory of Crisis Exploitation: Political and Policy Impacts of Framing Contests and Blame Games', *Journal of European Public Policy*, 16(1):81–106.

Boin, A., 't Hart, P., Stern, E. and Sundelius, B. 2005. *The Politics of Crisis Management: Public Leadership under Pressure* (Cambridge: Cambridge University Press).

Helsloot, I., Boin, A., Jabobs, B. and Comfort, L. K. (eds) 2012. *Mega Crises* (Springfield, Ill.: Charles C. Thomas).

Janis, I. L. 1989. *Crucial Decisions: Leadership in Policymaking and Crisis Management* (New York: Free Press).

Schafer, M. and Crichlow, S. 2010. *Groupthink versus High-Quality Decision-Making in International Relations* (New York: Columbia University Press).

Weick, K. and Sutcliffe, K. M. 2007. *Managing the Unexpected: Resilient Performance in an Age of Uncertainty* (New York: Wiley).

16. The Public Service in the Aftermath of the Global Financial Crisis: Future-proof or future shock?

The Honourable Bill English

I wish to give a reasonably broad, high-level view of the way the New Zealand Government is currently thinking about public service, as well as to offer some of my own thoughts that are going to continue to influence us. The first point is that all organisations, public or otherwise, are dealing with a number of what are increasingly appearing to be permanent changes. I will highlight three here. The first is debt reduction in the developed world, which is a generation-long project. We really have no idea of what the ongoing dynamics of this are, because we have never done it before, and no-one else has done it under the circumstances the developed world currently faces. This makes constraint permanent.

Ubiquitous data and free information form a second, greater force. Traditionally, the power of government was as a holder and controller of information. That has gone. Not only can anyone (including nine-year-olds) now access information for free, they can do it immediately. Moreover, citizens no longer think governments should hold information as power over people in the way they used to accept.

A third feature I see as a permanent change is the ongoing shift of wealth, power and therefore influence from our traditional markets and allies to the Asia-Pacific region and other emerging economies.

In this context, the New Zealand and Australian public services are in a unique position to harvest ideas for change—a change that is inevitable. On the one side we have the developed world, which has begun and will continue to undergo for a couple of decades radical experimentation and crunching the costs of its public services. This process has only just begun; those who think the current debate is only about austerity are wrong, as debt levels are still rising across the developed world. All they are really doing in these countries (particularly the Eurozone) is shuffling around their balance sheets. The image I have in my mind is of staff in an emergency department standing around a bed discussing how much adrenalin to pump into an ailing patient. The approach they are taking is far from a cure.

And while on the one hand much of the developed world is going through radical experimentation, on the other hand the developing Asia-Pacific economies and other emerging economies want more consumption-led growth, and are therefore developing an appetite and a need for public services which they don't have. This makes us ideally positioned both to harvest the ideas from the more radical experiments from economies that are under more pressure than Australia and New Zealand and to on-sell our expertise on public service to emerging economies, who will want them. In such emerging economies there is scope for massive and rapid growth in the provision of effective public services.

We are entering an age of experimentation on a scale we haven't seen since World War II and its aftermath. What does the government of little old New Zealand think about this? Our approach is to try to create sufficient stability so as to get even more change. By this I mean that it is hard to make change in large, sophisticated organisations with customers who are sensitive to service levels when you are working from a short-term budget process. In such systems there is often confusion surrounding the divisions of responsibility, and a lack of focus on what you are trying to achieve.

Consequently, we have taken the opportunity over the past few years to make a number of changes that are part of what I call the 'responsibility model'. Under the responsibility model, organisations themselves—not treasury, not the minister of finance, not central agencies—are responsible for making change and delivering services within fiscal constraints. They are in the best position to do this, because they know best what they are doing. Politicians and central agencies often don't know, and their culture tends to be one of watching what's happening, compared with the people who actually have to do it. In other words, according to the responsibility model, your destiny is in your own hands and how you handle pressures is up to you—although of course we have a whole public service and it can provide support.

There are a number of features we put in place to try to create the sense of stability and responsibility that we believe leads to better long-term decision-making. The first is to avoid the temptation of rushing in and grabbing savings in an irrational and random manner, which is actually the long-term habit of treasuries. This is because treasuries have to meet a target, so they simply go and get the money—something that preoccupies everybody about their short-term survival and decision-making, and prevents them thinking about the longer term and the real fiscal drivers.

That, then, is my first point: focusing on the longer-term fiscal costs, accepting deficits in the shorter term with the view that if we think very hard about what we're doing, two, three or five years down the track we can actually be spinning out hundreds of millions of dollars of spare cash, not just the NZ$20 million that is preoccupying us now. After all, the long-term focus works best when we know what we're trying to achieve.

There are a couple of critical aspects to this approach. One is that we are trying to get the strength of having targets without the weaknesses. The second is that our results are focused on communities and populations, not government departments. This is because people don't live in government departments. They don't measure the success of public services by the success of a government department; they measure it by looking around in their street and their suburb and the particular public service they happened to use yesterday. This point—relating to where people are rather than where we are—is critical. For while the parliamentary accountability system is about tracking a dollar, not whether something works, we have to also keep track of the real world.

To focus on results, another thing we have done is break the annual budget cycle and move consciously to four-year budget plans. A recent survey of chief executives suggests that this is now leading to the right kind of conversations about the longer-term effects they are trying to achieve, and about the sectoral relationships they need across government to achieve those results.

Another factor we have been looking at is what I would call judgment not process. By this I mean that leadership in the public service should ultimately be about judgment, not about going through all the right processes. After all, as we move into a more adaptive environment, we don't have time for all the processes; we need people who are willing and able to quickly take a position and make a judgment in tough situations, rather than waiting around for the next budget cycle or whatever.

The changes we have put in place are starting to have some effect, and we have unashamedly taken a long-term view—longer than an electoral cycle and the life of one government. Ideally, government departments would not take part in our budget cycle, because they would have their own four-year revenue track and their own plan, allowing them to just go off and do it. We would simply keep an eye on them—something that would probably free up half of senior management's time, from what I can see.

That, then, is what we are trying to do to create stability. But what are the implications for the kind of change that is going to actually happen, not just at the macro level but also within public services? There are four I would like to propose.

The first is that the usual political boundaries don't apply anymore—not in New Zealand anyway, and not, I suspect, across the world. What do I mean by that? The other day I read one official's report, which kept referring to the political risks of a particular proposition. But it was wrong because it was based on what everyone used to talk about five years ago, but not today. I would argue the public today is much less susceptible to lobby groups and self-interest; the public today is much more interested in politicians and public servants just getting on with their jobs. They are much less worried about whether they were consulted, and they are not nearly as concerned about sacred cows.

That doesn't mean that everything is up for grabs, but the sense of caution and risk management built into public servants from the time of plenty is now quite outdated. In fact, we are finding, as politicians, the only constraints on getting things done concern our own internal processes, not the public's attitudes or aversion to risk. The public is not marching in the streets against change, because they know change is necessary. They've been doing it in their homes, they've been doing it in their businesses. They think central government is just catching up with it, and they know local governments are about another two years behind, but that eventually they will get there.

In that context, the public is very focused on the economy. They want their public service to work well—they actually expect that—but they also want their public service to focus on growth. And I know this is a radical idea for some, but as we write our regulations and our policies we need to know that the people to whom we are applying them—who actually pay for us—have as their top priorities: one, job security; two, a job for their teenager; and three, a bit more income, so they can increase their savings and pay off their debt. Everything else comes after that. We have quite some way to go for that strong focus on economic opportunity to filter right into every corner of the New Zealand Public Service.

The whole world is headed in this direction. I have been in discussions in the past year where countries like Canada and Japan, whose governments of all political persuasions have been for generations opposed to free trade, are starting to advocate free trade. Why? Because they need a growth story for the middle class, and there's nothing much else around that is working. Our public in Australia and New Zealand is where the public of most of the developed world is right now—that is, they know the world has changed, they expect us to behave in different ways that reflect their much deeper sense of economic insecurity in doing what we can to reinforce a sense of security.

The second implication of the changes that are occurring is that policy is now a commodity. My twelve-year-old son can print off world 'best practice' policy from the OECD website in 10 minutes flat if you asked him to. He doesn't need a degree, he doesn't need highly trained policy thinking; he can get this kind of information now from anywhere for free. What matters now is not the ability to sit around and think about high-level policy; what matters now is a detailed understanding of how policy applies to a particular setting and how to make it work. Our public services in Australia and New Zealand have some way to go to realise this. They need to ask themselves the question: why would someone pick the best thing to do? This process is often largely accidental in the public service at the moment.

Why would public servants get out of bed in the morning and try really hard to make something work? How do they tell whether it's working, and if we found out it wasn't working, would we do anything about it? The answer to that last question has traditionally been no. Instead, we go and find another good idea and put it on top of the one that's not working, and if that doesn't work, we go and find another one. The result is that over 30 years we accumulate a very expensive failure. After all, if we're going to fail, let's do it at low cost. Policy, then, is a commodity, and the critical knowledge that has to be built in our public services should be centred on the institutional arrangements that are going to make policy work. The public is not going to tolerate us spending money on stuff that doesn't work; five years ago they would have, now they don't, and what's more our lenders are not going to lend us money for stuff that doesn't work.

So if we want to maintain service levels for the public, we must flush out what doesn't work, and often that requires a change in our institutional incentives, and some basic institutional economics. To do this we need to determine what incentives people face and what signals are out in our public service market to tell people how to behave. We need to better understand the institutional arrangements that are about success, and this has become a current focus of the New Zealand Government.

A third implication of this world we are going to change is that other people can help us. In New Zealand and to some extent in Australia, we have had a period where the political climate discouraged any further privatisation. Until 2008 we had a Labour government in New Zealand which put a huge premium on who did the job. Their view was that the public service had to do it, because they are apparently the only ones who care, and those other nasty people who are not in the public service are going to rip you off, make excessive profits and not care about anything. By taking this approach, the Government cut itself off from a vast pool of knowledge, particularly knowledge about something that everyone is coming to understand now: how to manage risk.

In the public service over the past 20 years, risk has effectively meant avoiding embarrassing media stories. In the next 20 years, by contrast, it will mean whether you can manage the operational and financial risks of the vast expenditure and the vast capital expenditure that we control. But we don't have those skills: governments are terrible at managing assets. Given that there are people out there who have spent billions of dollars building up investment and the intellectual property of managing assets, why don't we use some of their knowledge?

Similarly, we don't know much about how social programs impact on communities, or whether much of what we do undermines the natural collectivism of the non-governmental community. Consequently, we better work with those people who do understand it. After all, while they don't have public policy degrees and are not paid a lot, they do know a lot about the places in which they live and how the dynamics of those places work, and we need to see them as equal partners.

In New Zealand, we have had a fantastic little experiment in this recently with something called the 'Social Sector Trials'. The idea is simple: we go to six small towns with problems with youth and find someone—essentially anyone who will turn up—and tell them that they control the government spending related to the services supporting youth; they make the decisions. In mid 2012, after just 12 months of this experiment, we had a presentation to cabinet of these young people from small provincial towns—none with a population of more than 10 000—telling us what they had achieved with about NZ$100 000 and some control over other government spending. It was fantastic.

The presenters had a fully blended grip of all the public policy issues associated with the financing, delivery and effectiveness of services for quite a difficult part of the community. They gave exemplary presentations and descriptions of what they were doing. This kind of capacity is everywhere, and public services have to learn how to use it, because most of our approaches don't work when we ignore that capacity in communities and in families. Outsiders can help us, and in fact unless you are working with other people, you probably have it wrong.

If, as a public servant, you are still living in a bubble where you believe 'the public service cares and they are the only ones who know what they are doing', you are wrong, because I haven't come across a single example in the past three and a half years where that's the correct diagnosis of the situation. I have come across many examples where by reaching out, viewing society as a network not a hierarchy and acknowledging that other people know stuff we don't know, we have been able to make fantastic advances in the quality and the economy of our services.

And this of course leads to a different kind of leadership. We are in the same situation as much of the private sector, although we can't move as quickly to change it, where a lot of our skill sets come from the time of plenty. How to get in the minister's office door, how to crank out more cash, how to manoeuvre the strategy out there—all these skills are now redundant. Such approaches may have been applicable at the time, but that is no longer the case. Instead, the kind of leadership we particularly need is the kind of leadership that allows disruptive talent to emerge, and by this I don't mean chaos.

I mean, instead, that we are after leaders who, in spite of pressures associated with the financial squeeze, can have fresh analyses, think laterally and have a different set of relationships than were previously needed to succeed in an organisation.

If we rely only on incremental adaptation then changing technology and increasing public demand are going to squeeze our capacity, push the anxiety levels through the roof and the morale through the floor so that in the end someone else will have to come in and do the job. There are a lot of other aspects of leadership that are very important in the public sector; it involves quite specialised skills, but is easily disparaged by those outside the public sector. The people who come in, however, find it's a good deal more complex. The public service is not a business, but we must have room for disruptive talent.

In New Zealand across the board, we are implementing a range of significant changes: our defence forces are going through probably the biggest reorganisation of any defence force in the developed world; we're making significant changes to our law and order system, which means we're closing prisons for the first time in a generation; we're looking at welfare reform, which has aspects that are quite unique, and are already changing our thinking about our welfare population. In addition to these changes we have another massive challenge that we haven't made much progress on yet: the affordability of social housing—the Government's single biggest asset. We are also attempting to change the way we deal with information and privacy, and we expect to make some real progress in these fields over the next three or four years.

The reason we have been able to get as far as we have without significant disruption, and the reason we have confidence we can get quite a long way further, is that we think most of the talent we need in our public service is already there—it just needs to be given a clearer sense of direction. To do this we need to nurture a culture that allows different talent to come to the fore.

A good illustration of this was demonstrated following the 2011 Christchurch earthquake. In the first week after the disaster, I got to see New Zealand's public service adapt to a high-stress situation that demanded rapid action across a number of issues that were not simply complex, but also of a nature we had not dealt with before. A small group of people did a magnificent job of this in the early stages, and that level of excellence has been maintained.

We are fortunate in New Zealand to be able to undertake our own radical experiments; it is a place where you can break all the rules. And I hope that much of what I have covered in this chapter will serve as lessons for what you should do when you're allowed to break all the rules. We hope to harvest the product of that experiment and spread it across our public service, because we think that's the only way we are going to be able to achieve better public services when we have less resources to do it with.

Part 4: Disaster Recovery

17. Disaster Recovery: The particular governance challenges generated by large-scale natural disasters

Bruce Glavovic

I will share some of my reflections on disaster recovery by drawing on lessons learnt from recent international experience. I will focus attention on post-Hurricane Katrina recovery experiences. Since 2005, I have spent a lot of time in Louisiana, for periods of anywhere from two to six weeks at a time on an annual basis, in order to track the recovery process and learn from their experience. I have also conducted fieldwork in Indonesia and the Maldives after the 2004 Indian Ocean tsunami; and have been studying the recovery experience after the 2011 Tohoku earthquake and tsunami in Japan. My goal is to learn from these large-scale disasters to understand the nature of risk better, how to build more effective institutions for risk reduction and post-disaster recovery and, ultimately, how to build more resilient and sustainable communities.

I will introduce the notion of a political ecology of recovery and frame this concept in the context of the 'wicked problem' of post-disaster recovery that presents society with 'wicked choices'. Drawing on examples from disaster experiences around the world, and in particular the post-Katrina and Canterbury earthquake recovery experiences, I will argue that recovery presents a distinctive governance challenge that goes far beyond 'fixing levees' (in the context of the New Orleans levee failure) or bridging fault lines (in the Canterbury context).

The topics I will cover include reflections on disaster narratives and what they teach; the complex challenges of leadership and governance in the face of disaster risk; the political ecology of recovery; responding to and recovering from disasters in ways that build resilience to future shocks; and finally a word or two about future-proofing society.

Hurricane Katrina

You will have seen the graphic televised images of the impacts of Hurricane Katrina on the people of New Orleans and their plight in the face of the dismal response and protracted recovery process. I am sure you are all aware of the many challenges faced by people in this region. Hurricane Katrina was not a 'natural disaster'. It was a natural hazard event that became a human-induced catastrophe because of failings in the design and maintenance of the levee system that was compounded by the response failure in the aftermath of the flooding of New Orleans. This multifaceted failure continued into recovery.

The immediate drivers of the disaster have historical roots that go back more than 200 years of well-intentioned efforts to 'wrest the city from nature' (Colten 2006). The Mississippi River was channelled, levees were constructed, navigation channels cut through the wetlands and resources exploited as if they were infinite. The construction of the levee system opened up the possibility for suburban development in former swampland. The wetland ecosystems that sustain livelihoods in the region and act as a natural defence against coastal storms have been degraded and transformed over time. To compound matters, more and more people live in harm's way as people move into suburban developments that depend on the levees to keep out floodwaters. Over time, these choices have resulted in more and more people being exposed to natural hazard events like hurricanes. To make matters worse, New Orleans and the Mississippi Delta have a disproportionate share of people living in poverty. As a consequence, the region and New Orleans are fractured by layers of social vulnerability that were exposed by Hurricane Katrina.

Attention is usually focused on the story of the storm or the post-storm response narrative. Freudenberg et al. (2009) persuasively argue that a critical narrative predates the landing of Katrina: choices were made to locate people in places exposed to storms and flooding. They argue that a 'growth machine' of self-interested property developers, business tycoons and public officials secured public funding to undertake projects that profited a few in the short term but have caused extensive environmental degradation and spiralling disaster risk as people moved into low-lying suburbs on former swamplands.

Burby (2006) describes the paradoxical consequences of endeavours to reduce moderate risk—for example, through levees that safeguard people from low-level frequent events such as river flooding—but that generate a false sense of security, encourage intensified development behind the levees and result in catastrophic consequences if an event exceeds design standards. This is often referred to as the 'safe development paradox'.

Early settlers stayed on relatively high ground but with the expansion of suburbs into low-lying areas behind levees, the flood risk increased exponentially. New Orleans was flooded in the aftermath of Hurricane Betsy in 1965, and, despite improvements to the levee system, it failed again in 2005 when Katrina struck. Now repaired and improved, it provides category three protection; but this is insufficient to protect the city from a breach by a category four or five storm. Tragically, New Orleans will flood again when a category four or five storm strikes the area—we just do not know when it will happen. The people of New Orleans and the wider gulf region thus face waves of adversity from coastal storms and hurricanes.

There are other waves of adversity that face the people of this region. The 2010 BP oil-spill disaster devastated the wetland ecosystems of the Mississippi Delta and has had profound negative impacts on coastal livelihoods in the region. To exacerbate matters, the region is a global hotspot for climate change impacts, particularly sea-level rise, and consequently the waves of adversity will be magnified and intensified in years to come.

Choices made in recovery have profound implications for exposure to these coming waves of adversity. Future disasters are inevitable if pre-event exposure and vulnerabilities are entrenched in post-disaster recovery choices.

Mitch Landrieu, who was lieutenant-governor of Louisiana in 2005, made a statement in 2008 that captures the essence of the recovery challenge:

> The challenge is to keep and secure those things that are good: our food, our music, our architecture, our people, our faith and our families, our love of life and our love of country. And at the same time, [to] discard that part of our culture that strangles us: crime, bad schools and the inability to move beyond race.

In 2010, Landrieu became mayor of New Orleans, a place with an amazing array of 'good things': the birthplace of jazz, incredible cuisine, amazing architecture—a city that resonates with ritual and culture. It is, however, also a place that has a longstanding slew of social, economic and political challenges—including deep poverty, social inequity and racism. As Landrieu points out, the recovery challenge boils down to discarding that part of our culture that strangles us. Confronting the root causes and drivers of social vulnerability lies at the heart of reducing disaster risk and enabling recovery—a theme I will build upon. Hurricane Katrina and disasters in general expose the skeleton, the 'bones', of society: the good and the bad. Working out how to secure that which is good and discard that which strangles is a critical but complex undertaking.

Many lessons have been learnt from Katrina. You might remember the televised images of people looting, and the reports of rape, pillage, plunder and mayhem; but it has subsequently been shown that many of these media reports were based largely on rumour and unverified sources that resulted in misinformation.

Yet we do not hear enough about the stories of Katrina's heroes: the people who brought their boats into the city to rescue people, who broke cordons to get through to the needy, the incredible role played by the US Coastguard, and many more stories of heroism and altruism. It is the same in every disaster. The first responders are local people, and beyond that response there are those who dedicate themselves to the recovery process, working tirelessly through very, very difficult circumstances, often with their own homes and families disrupted. It is important not to lose sight of these stories of selfless commitment and dedication.

A series of studies and reviews reveals the systemic failure of the post-Katrina response, some of which persisted into recovery. There are many lessons that have been learnt. One review described the post-Katrina response as a systemic failure of initiative (US House of Representatives 2006). Another contribution in this book speaks of the need for imagination in disaster situations. You could say the same thing about post-Katrina New Orleans. Analysts and reviews describe a failure in leadership at every level of society—from the White House down to the lowest level of government, and in key domains of civil society and the private sector. Of course, it is not as simple as that because there are examples of success and effective leadership despite the fraught circumstances. So it is important to acknowledge that Katrina is not a simple, 'everyone did a bad job' story. It is a much more complex, nuanced narrative.

Particular attention needs to be focused on the pre-Katrina story to understand how to avoid recovery choices that put people back in harm's way and, fundamentally, how to confront the poverty and marginalisation that were endemic in New Orleans and the region; together these constructed the human catastrophe that was precipitated by Katrina.

Another recovery insight is the 'speed versus deliberation' dilemma: the conundrum of trying to progress a speedy recovery by making quick decisions so that a level of 'normalcy' can be restored and meeting the countervailing need to create opportunities for meaningful dialogue and deliberation to ensure that wise public choices are made that will be enduring and robust (Olshansky 2006). Resolving this dilemma has been very challenging in post-Katrina New Orleans. One of the tragic consequences of failing to resolve it has been the decision to allow rebuilding in places that are low-lying and exposed to future flooding. In short, the pre-event exposure and social vulnerabilities that characterised the pre-Katrina narrative have been entrenched by recovery choices so that a future disaster is a dismal inevitability. Post-Katrina demographics and socioeconomic conditions have changed. Many long-term New Orleans residents have left the city permanently. In some areas there is no tangible evidence of Katrina while nearly a decade later other areas are little changed from the immediate aftermath of the hurricane and flooding. Despite massive recovery efforts, social vulnerability in the city and wider region persists. Exposure is entrenched and disaster risk is escalating in the face of climate change. There are always winners and losers in disasters and in the recovery process. A key Katrina lesson is the imperative to address the needs of marginalised and socially vulnerable groups.

Another lesson is the need to anticipate and plan for waves of adversity that are likely to occur over time and subject the people of this region to multiple shocks. For those living in the bayous of Louisiana, there is no levee protection and they are dependent on the wetlands for their livelihood. But their way of life and, indeed, their lives are exposed to waves of adversity as they have had to weather a succession of events in recent years, including Hurricane Katrina, the

BP oil spill, the Global Financial Crisis, several other hurricanes and the prospect of flooding by the Mississippi River. To make matters worse, these waves of adversity will intensify in the future in this era of climate change. These waves of adversity are not unlike the series of earthquakes and aftershocks that have devastated the people of Greater Christchurch and the wider Canterbury region.

So, the challenge is: how do we fix the levees—not just the physical ones, but the levees of society—to build more resilient and sustainable communities? This is a 'wicked problem' that presents society with a set of 'wicked choices'.

The Canterbury Earthquake

I will now make some observations about Canterbury, based on a series of interviews I have conducted with key informants involved in the recovery process since late 2010. Here, like Katrina, you could argue that there are villains and there are heroes. There were people who stole, though I do not think we saw anything like the level of villainy in Canterbury as was seen in New Orleans. But we have seen many, many heroes in Canterbury, as we did in New Orleans and the wider gulf coast.

The story of leadership and initiative is quite different in Canterbury than the Katrina story. By all accounts the response worked very well in Canterbury and that is a real credit to those in positions of responsibility for the response. I understand from my key informant interviews that many dimensions of the recovery are going well. There is also room for improvement. So, does practice make perfect? I have heard some interesting commentaries. For example, a scholar from the University of Canterbury has argued that the university may not have responded as well in the major February event as it could have because it relied on practices learned in the September 2010 response that may not have been appropriate for the February 2011 circumstances. So that is ironic.

There are many stories emerging about our understanding of seismic risk and choices made to build on ground prone to liquefaction. We have learned about the notion of a 'class quake', as people describe how some lower socioeconomic neighbourhoods in Greater Christchurch were more exposed and vulnerable to seismic impacts and have borne the brunt of suburban damage. The dilemma of 'speed versus deliberation' in decision-making is an obvious reality in Canterbury.

A key challenge in the Canterbury recovery, as in major disasters elsewhere, is how to avoid entrenching pre-event exposure and vulnerabilities that inexorably lead to future disasters. The Government has made some bold decisions about not allowing rebuilding to take place in localities prone to a high risk of liquefaction. Not allowing rebuilding in 'red-zoned' areas is very different from the decision to allow people to rebuild anywhere—regardless of flood risk—in New Orleans. These 'red-zone' decisions were controversial and contentious. And there are winners and losers in Canterbury as a result of these decisions, but it took bold leadership and a focus on societal resilience, equity and sustainability to avoid putting people back in harm's way.

Inevitably, there are winners and losers in disasters and part of the recovery challenge is to support and enable those worst affected, and to avoid deepening the misery and hardship that many face. This has been especially challenging in Canterbury because the earthquake series has caused shock after shock after shock, quite literally. The people of the region have faced waves of adversity as they seek to recover and they need to build layers of resilience.

The recovery challenge in Canterbury thus boils down to bridging fault lines—not just geomorphological fault lines, but also societal fault lines. For example, bridges need to be built between civic, business and political leaderships. Bridging societal fault lines is, however, a wicked problem and presents wicked choices that must be made—and made well.

Lessons Learnt

So, what have we learnt from disaster narratives? Simply put, social vulnerability must be confronted—as was graphically exposed in Katrina. You cannot stop a hurricane or an earthquake, but we can do something about reducing social vulnerability—and this is pivotal for reducing disaster risk and enabling recovery.

Recovery is complex precisely because it involves much more than the physical dimension; it is overlaid with social, economic and political dimensions. There is no simple end point and it is certainly not a return to 'normal', or to what existed previously (International Conference on Urban Disaster Reduction 2005). Recovery begins when the community repairs or develops social, political and economic processes, institutions and relationships that enable it to function in the new post-disaster context (Alesch et al. 2009). That is the challenge. The hard part of recovery is rebuilding the human and societal architecture that underpins every community. The physical and economic infrastructure is important and is difficult to repair after a disaster; but it is much easier to repair physical and economic infrastructure than it is to repair the social and cultural infrastructure.

One way to frame the recovery challenge is to recognise that there are 'domains of uncertainty' that need to be 'shrunk' (see Figure 17.1). After a disaster uncertainty intensifies and expands. Reducing this proliferation of uncertainty is a key challenge for the recovery process. Domains of uncertainty include, first, uncertainty about seismic risk. The September 2010 earthquake took place on an unknown fault. The region has experienced a series of earthquakes and aftershocks since then, moving east towards the coast and offshore. A lot of work has been undertaken to better understand and reduce uncertainty about seismic risk in the region. It is not possible to finalise insurance decisions, for example, as long as there are aftershocks and uncertainty about when they will diminish. Consequently, as long as there is uncertainty about seismic risk it is very hard for people to make critical livelihood decisions—such as whether or not to repair their homes and businesses, or whether or not to relocate. Uncertainty about seismic risk thus compounds a second domain of uncertainty: livelihood uncertainty. A third domain of uncertainty is uncertainty about recovery governance. Shrinking this domain of uncertainty is critical for instilling confidence and building trust to progress recovery.

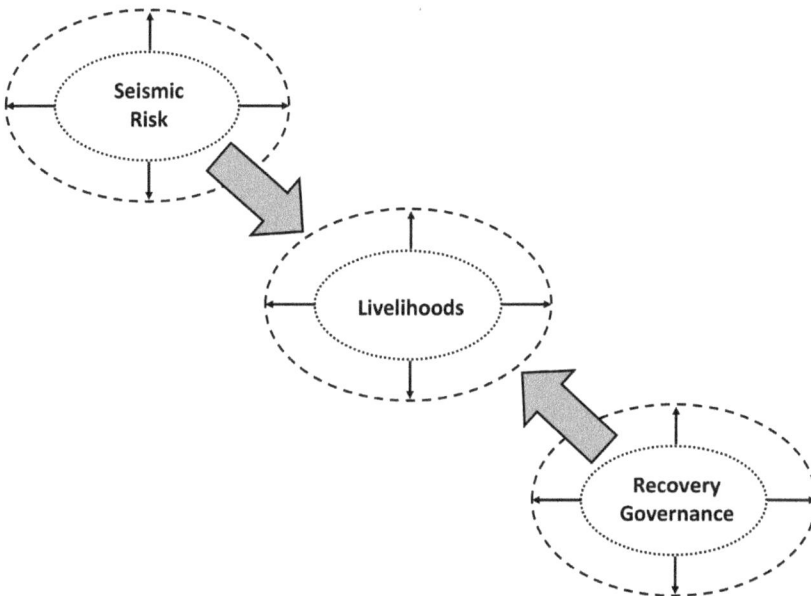

Figure 17.1 Domains of Recovery Uncertainty

Source: Author's summary.

The Government came in early to try to provide clarity about how to govern the recovery, enacting legislation to set up the Canterbury Earthquake Recovery Authority (CERA) to lead the recovery process in partnership with local government in the region. Despite these measures, however, and notwithstanding the good intentions and hard work of many politicians and government officials, there has been widespread and persistent uncertainty about the recovery governance process. Many of those I have interviewed lacked basic knowledge about the recovery governance process and expressed frustration about the perceived confusion and lack of clarity about who is responsible for different aspects of the recovery. A particular concern has been uncertainty about how citizens and business can contribute meaningfully to the recovery effort. Many have found it difficult to connect with CERA and local government recovery efforts. Many have felt excluded and marginalised from the process—notwithstanding the many efforts by CERA and local government to consult the public. Many would like to see more opportunities to contribute and collaborate in what they consider to be 'their recovery'. Any complex, large-scale disaster confronts this third domain of recovery governance uncertainty. The sooner recovery roles and responsibilities are clarified, and opportunities created for authentic public participation in the recovery process, the faster this domain can be 'shrunk', but as long as it persists it 'squeezes' the domain of livelihood uncertainty and people continue to feel they are in limbo. In sum, the recovery challenge is to reduce each domain of uncertainty.

We live in a time of escalating disaster risk, with an exponential increase in the number of people living in places prone to natural hazard events. Disaster is unavoidable in the context of exposure to natural hazards and historical patterns of vulnerability (Oliver-Smith and Hoffman 2002). Key international organisations are focusing increasing attention on reducing disaster risk: prevention is better than post-event cure and it pays dividends in the long term (UN-World Bank 2010). Disaster risk, resilience and sustainability are fundamentally interconnected and there is a compelling need to make sense of the relationship between these concepts. Among other things, there are complex interrelationships between sudden shock events, like a hurricane, and slow onset disasters, like climate change. Resilience and sustainability are about building the capacity of present and future generations to, among other things, cope with large-scale natural hazard events, and anticipate and adapt to a future characterised by change, uncertainty and surprise. Post-disaster recovery opens up opportunities to chart pathways to a more resilient and sustainable future.

I submit that recovery is community (re)development in a pressure-cooker situation. The stakes are higher and the circumstances are much more pressurised than in typical pre-event situations. Extremely important and complex social choices have to be made. Fundamentally, recovery is democracy in action under dire circumstances. It is about empowering local people—and some of the comments New Zealand Prime Minister, John Key, made are pertinent: how should central government engage and work with local government and local communities? An empowering recovery process is compelling but complex; it is a wicked problem that compels us to rethink how we make social choices in pressure-cooker situations.

I would like to provide a rudimentary contrast between 'simple', 'complicated' and 'complex' contexts or situations. One could argue that baking a cake is a simple undertaking. Sending a person to the Moon is more complicated. Raising a child is a complex task. So, what institutional arrangements and leadership qualities enable us to deal with these very different circumstances? In short, the implications for the kind of leadership and organisational characteristics required under these different circumstances are very, very different. That is not to say that disaster situations are always simple, complicated or complex. At different points in time circumstances vary from simple to complex.

In the response phase, there are probably half a dozen priorities: save lives, rescue people, secure buildings, and so forth. It is a relatively high-danger situation in which the response is made in a complicated set of circumstances that requires leaders to marshal resources, stabilise the situation and buy time. The archetypal 'alpha male' personality is the ideal leadership model. In fact, many females perform this role better than many men, so this is not a gendered comment. The traditional notion of an alpha male—a commander in control of his troops supported by a command-and-control organisational culture—works really well in these circumstances.

Transitioning into recovery is a very different reality. Recovery is a much more complex task; it involves building safe, resilient and sustainable communities. It is about empowerment. It is about making social choices in the face of deep uncertainty and ambiguity, so the appropriate leadership style is that of a nurturing female, where empowering, collaborative and adaptive ways of working are dominant.

The concept of risk lies at the heart of recovery choices and resilience and sustainability more generally. But prevailing risk discourse needs to be deepened and extended. Risk is typically defined as the probability and consequences of a hazard event (after Knight 1921)—or measurable uncertainty. But not all risk problems can be reduced to measurable uncertainty. There are situations that are dominated by ambiguity, which is when people disagree about how to frame options, context and so on, resulting in contending legitimate viewpoints about a particular social choice. Ambiguity cannot be resolved by a probability and consequence analysis. Some risk problems might be characterised as being dominated by unmeasurable uncertainty when the nature of the problem is effectively unknown and credible probabilities cannot be assigned. Other risk problems are best described in terms of 'ignorance'—where we lack knowledge, education or awareness of the problem. Andy Stirling (2010) from the United Kingdom distinguishes knowledge about possibilities from knowledge about probabilities, and categorises risk, uncertainty, ambiguity and ignorance into four domains (see Figure 17.2).

Uncertainty matrix

+ Knowledge about possibilities -

Risk	Ambiguity
- Risk assessment - Cost benefit analysis *Eg. Expert consensus*	- Interactive modelling - Multicriteria mapping *Eg. Participatory deliberation*
Uncertainty	Ignorance
- Interval analysis - Scenario methods *Eg. Evaluative judgment*	- Monitoring and surveillance *Eg. Flexibility, adaptability, resilience*

(left axis, bottom to top: - Knowledge about probabilities +)

(After Stirling 2010)

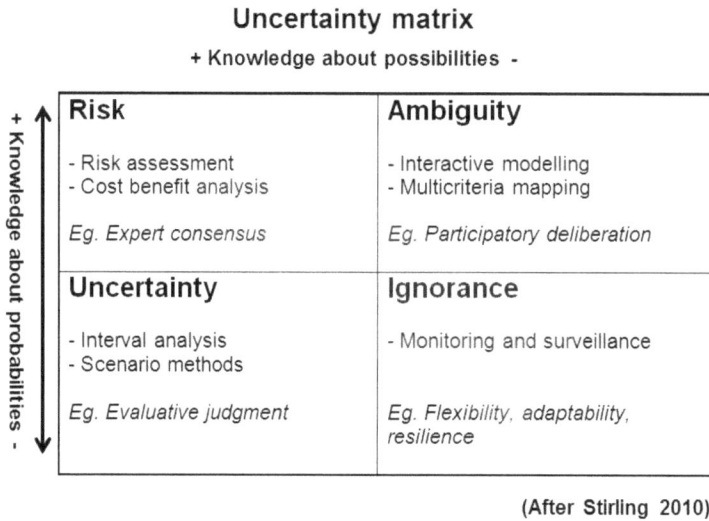

Figure 17.2 Risk, Uncertainty, Ambiguity and Ignorance

Source: Author's summary, after Stirling, 2010.

Importantly, different approaches and ways of working are needed to deal with each different risk problem. There is a tendency to try to reduce all risk problems to 'measurable uncertainty' and to rely on traditional assessment and treatment options for dealing with problems that cannot be resolved using these approaches. But ignorance, ambiguity and unmeasurable uncertainty cannot be resolved using probability–consequence calculations. Fortunately, there is an array of available approaches that can and should be used to deal with different classes of risk problem. It is imperative to match the assessment and treatment approaches to the particular risk problem under consideration.

Recovery is thus much more than rebuilding physical infrastructure and analysing all risks as if they can be reduced to measurable uncertainty. Yet such framing tends to dominate prevailing recovery governance thinking and practice.

Recovery governance needs to be reframed to suit the more demanding tasks of recovery. Governance is more than government. Governance is about making social choices and raises the question: how should key actors in government work together with key actors in the private sector and civil society to resolve societal problems? There is an important role for key actors in science and the media in recovery governance; and, together with other governance actors, they draw upon and develop vital institutions and relationships to navigate through the wicked problem of recovery. What constitutes appropriate modalities of recovery governance will vary from place to place. The challenge is to construct an architecture of recovery governance that engages and empowers those in recovery; this is a monumental but crucial challenge for all in pressure-cooker situations.

Figure 17.3 Actors and Institutions of Governance

Source: Author's summary.

Recovery governance needs to be an empowering and collaborative process that provides a solid foundation for addressing the pivotal questions of what kind of post-disaster community is desirable; how do we live with risk, uncertainty, ambiguity and ignorance; and who should make the critical recovery decisions? In short, I submit that there is a compelling need for deliberation, a non-coercive communicative process that encourages reflection, not only on the technical details, but also on the values, preferences and interests that underpin recovery. Recovery governance thus needs to be reframed as a deliberative process. This is not merely a philosophical reframing of recovery governance; it has important practical implications for how key actors and stakeholders in recovery negotiate their shared future.

My reflections on large-scale disasters and the recovery narratives of Katrina and Canterbury in particular have prompted me to explore political ecology as an arena of scholarship that is relevant to the challenge of recovery governance. For those who do not have a background in ecology, the term comes from the Greek '*oikos*' (house) and '*logos*' (study of), and means the study of the house or household ('household' being extended to include entire estates by medieval times). Ecology is the scientific study of the relationships between living organisms and their natural environment. Political ecology introduces the political dimension into the study of social-ecological systems, and it recognises that issues of global change, resilience and sustainability are essentially political issues. Political ecology is the study of the politics of environmental change that shape socioeconomic power relationships in society, which may be driven by natural and/or human-induced phenomena and development interventions. It is therefore constructive to think about a *political* ecology of recovery, which recognises the politics of recovery, the connection between people and places and the socioeconomic power relationships that are fundamental to understanding recovery as a process to empower local communities in the aftermath of disasters. A political ecology of recovery is the study of the politics of recovery that shape post-disaster socioeconomic power relationships impacted by natural hazard events and recovery interventions.

This framing of recovery governance has important implications for understanding the nature and role of science in post-disaster situations. The physical sciences have a vital role to play, and among other things to help reduce uncertainties such as the nature of seismic risk. The social sciences also have a tremendously important role to play, a role recognised by key players in the Canterbury recovery. The kind of science that is most relevant for answering urgent questions in a post-disaster situation is not, however, 'normal' or traditional science, which is appropriate when decision stakes are relatively low and a high degree of certainty prevails. In domains where there are high levels of system uncertainty and decision stakes are high, a different kind of science needs to be engaged. Funtowitz and Ravetz (1991) introduced the concept of 'post-normal science', which is an appropriate modality of science in circumstances in which facts are uncertain, values are in dispute, stakes are high and decisions are urgent. Post-normal science is especially relevant for a post-disaster situation (see Figure 17.4).

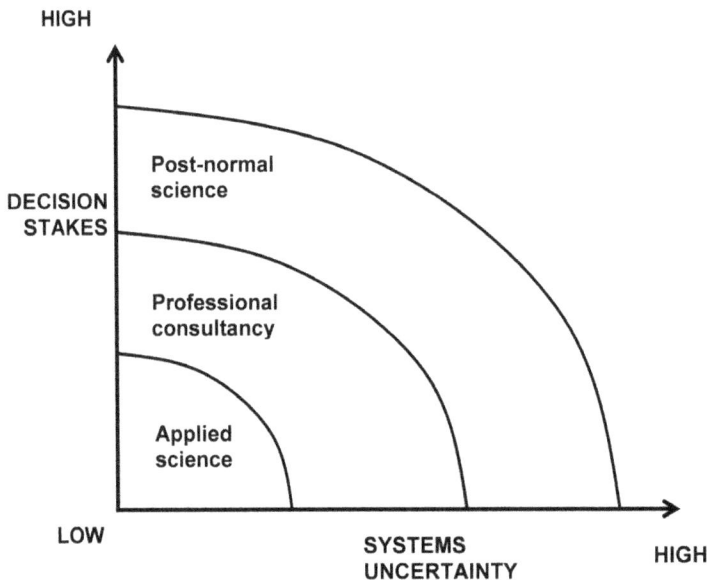

Figure 17.4 Post-Normal Science

Source: After Funtowicz, S. O. and Ravetz, J. R. 1991. 'A New Scientific Methodology for Global Environmental Issues', in R. Costanza (ed.) *Ecological Economics: The Science and Management of Sustainability* (New York: Columbia University Press).

In post-disaster circumstances—fraught with uncertainty and high decision stakes—an extended peer community needs to be engaged in post-normal science, including those affected by the disaster and willing to participate in a process of shared learning and understanding. Such participants can contribute to the process of scientific learning and also bring local, tacit knowledge to the table. An extended peer community is vital, not only for good process but also for good outcomes in a post-disaster situation.

One of the challenges of undertaking post-normal science in recovery is 'speaking truth to power'. Key informant interviews in post-Katrina New Orleans revealed that a number of scientists found themselves marginalised from key decision-makers and access to research grants ostensibly because they were critical of some of the recovery choices made. They were not necessarily critical of the individuals making those decisions but their research exposed flawed decisions. Many difficult choices have to be made in the course of the recovery and some of those choices stand up as being good decisions in the fullness of time; others, perhaps, will not stand up so well. So, in presenting their findings, some scientists and academics found themselves ostracised, and their ability to provide constructively critical input to the recovery process was marginalised—arguably to the detriment of recovery. This experience brings to the fore the need to develop a new social contract for science (Lubchenco 1998) in which the role of science is not simply to produce 'reliable knowledge' but for science and society to co-produce the knowledge required to navigate the uncertainty and the high decision stakes of the post-disaster setting.

So, to begin to bring this to a close, I want to highlight some of the conundrums and challenges revealed by the disaster narratives I have recounted and the spectrum of wicked choices that needs to be faced.

First, we tend to focus on the 'readiness' and 'response' phases of the hazard cycle, but we need to extend these efforts out into the 'reduction' and 'recovery' stages (to use the four rs of the New Zealand hazard cycle). Second, we need to go beyond the physical and economic dimensions of recovery to engage the social, cultural and political dimensions. Third, as important as the technical details are, attention needs to be focused on the ethical or moral dimensions of recovery. The last dimensions are fundamental for resolving the 'speed versus deliberation dilemma'—the fourth set of wicked choices. There are no simple or easy answers; post-disaster recovery poses a wicked problem and presents society with many wicked choices. Fifth, the question arises of whether recovery governance should be top-down or bottom-up. Should government establish a centralised agency to take charge of the recovery process? If so, how can those at the local level be empowered to recover? Invariably there are no easy answers and there is no panacea. Sixth, another conundrum is the issue of 'insiders' versus 'outsiders'; according to some there is antipathy to outsiders driving recovery in Canterbury. In post-Katrina New Orleans, there was strident objection to academics who came in from elsewhere to do research but were experienced by local people as syphoning off information from disaster victims, were never seen again and thus did not contribute to the recovery process. But outsiders can and do make invaluable contributions to recovery efforts. Seventh, another issue that arises in post-disaster situations has been described by some as the 'opening up' and 'closing down' of bureaucracies. The post-disaster pressure-cooker situation means that recovery agencies have to manage the tension between focusing all their energy on getting on with the manifold urgent tasks at hand versus setting aside time and effort to learn from past experience and reflect critically on what they are doing and how well it is working and, where appropriate, making adjustments to improve future practice. Eighth, the conundrum of rights versus responsibilities arises: whose recovery is it and can government 'do' recovery on behalf of disaster-struck communities? How does one reconcile local, regional and national interests in large-scale disasters? What are the responsibilities of current generations for the safety, resilience and sustainability of future generations? The conundrum of rights versus responsibilities thus has both geographical and temporal implications. Ninth, to what extent does the recovery entrench 'business as usual' practices or move towards transformative change? Should recovery efforts address the structural or embedded systemic problems that lead to marginalisation and social vulnerability? Can a post-disaster window of opportunity be opened to build back better, safer and more sustainably or will it stimulate exploitative practices that are ultimately antithetical to recovery? Will the choices made be ones that are expedient or will they leave a legacy that future generations will appreciate? Tenth, and finally, the imperative to expedite and operationalise an efficient and cost-effective recovery must be reconciled with the imperative to adopt reflexive practices that stimulate learning-by-doing and build resilience and sustainability.

In order to future-proof society, we need to recognise that society will continue to face waves of adversity, and the challenge is to build resilience in the face of the financial and social realities that Prime Minister Key describes in his contribution to this book. Risk, uncertainty, ambiguity and surprise are the 'new normal'. They will not go away, but will accelerate, intensify, deepen and proliferate in an era of global change. We live in a world that is complex and contested; and we face protracted, wicked problems that generate wicked choices. Deliberation is fundamental to understanding risk, resilience, sustainability and the political ecology of recovery. Recovery governance needs to be reframed as a deliberative governance process that is reflexive, collaborative and empowering. This is a challenging endeavour for individuals in the organisations that are charged with recovery because there is so much pressure on them to meet such compelling immediate needs. But the need to reframe and engage in new modalities of recovery is clear from post-disaster narratives around the world.

Finally, we face a series of complex, contested realities in post-disaster situations. Dealing with them requires deliberation and collaboration. Community wellbeing lies at the heart of recovery. We need a deeper understanding of what constitutes community and, recognising the heterogeneous and contested nature of community, we need courage to engage in new modalities of disaster risk reduction and recovery governance. We need political leaders, and leaders in business and civil society and science, to show courage by engaging in deliberative and reflexive practices in partnership with local communities to enable their recovery.

References

Alesch, D. J., Arendt, L. A. and Holly, J. N. 2009. *Managing for Long-Term Community Recovery in the Aftermath of Disaster* (Washington, DC: Public Entity Risk Institute).

Alpert, Bruce. 2008. 'Landrieu: National lessons are in La. – State is "where we can test what works"'. The Times-Picayune, 23 July.

Burby, R. J. 2006. 'Hurricane Katrina and the Paradoxes of Government Disaster Policy: Bringing about Wise Governmental Decisions for Hazardous Areas', *Annals of the American Academy of Political and Social Science*, 604:171–91.

Colten, C. E. 2006. An Unnatural Metropolis: Wresting New Orleans from Nature (Baton Rouge: Louisiana State University Press).

Freudenburg, W. R., Gramling, R., Laska, S. and Erikson, K. T. 2009. *Catastrophe in the Making: The Engineering of Katrina and the Disasters of Tomorrow* (Washington, DC: Island Press).

Funtowicz, S. O. and Ravetz, J. R. 1991. 'A New Scientific Methodology for Global Environmental Issues', in R. Costanza (ed.) *Ecological Economics: The Science and Management of Sustainability* (New York: Columbia University Press).

International Conference on Urban Disaster Reduction. 2005. *Report of the World Conference on Disaster Reduction*, UN World Conference on Disaster Reduction, 18–22 January, Kobe, Japan.

Knight, F. 1921. *Risk, Uncertainty and Profit* (New York: Houghton Mifflin).

Landrieu, M. 2008. Speech, 23 July 2008.

Lubchenco, J. 1998. 'Entering the Century of the Environment: A New Social Contract for Science', *Science*, 279:401–7.

Oliver-Smith, A. and Hoffman, S. M. (eds) 2002. *Catastrophe & Culture: The Anthropology of Disaster* (Santa Fe: School of American Research Press).

Olshansky, R. B. 2006. 'Planning after Hurricane Katrina', *Journal of the American Planning Association*, 72(2):147–53.

Stirling, A. 2010. 'Keep It Complex', *Nature*, 468:1029–31.

United Nations (UN)-World Bank. 2010. *Natural Hazards, UnNatural Disasters: The Economics of Effective Prevention* (New York: The World Bank).

US House of Representatives. 2006. *A Failure of Initiative: Final Report of the Select Bipartisan Committee to Investigate the Preparation for and Response to Hurricane Katrina* (Washington, DC: US Government Printing Office).

18. Missing the Opportunity to Promote Community Resilience? The Queensland Floods Commission of Inquiry

Jim McGowan

The Queensland Floods Commission of Inquiry (QFCOI), established in 2011, was given broad terms of reference for its investigation. It included: floodplain management, State and local government planning, mining industry issues, the performance of private insurers, the emergency response and dam management matters. In adopting a regulatory approach to disaster management, however, it regrettably ignored, or was unaware of, recent intergovernmental policy developments, particularly the strategic intent of the Council of Australian Governments (COAG) of building individual and community resilience. Moreover, it did not address the most significant and pressing policy issues for disaster management in Australia: the imbalance in the allocation of government resources to *response* and *recovery* through the Natural Disaster Relief and Recovery Arrangements (NDRRA), and a genuine commitment to increase investment in *prevention* and *mitigation* strategies. It might also be argued that the inquiry's dependence on greater and more prescriptive regulation in its recommendations potentially conflicts with the agreement to reduce 'red and green tape' made at the COAG meeting of 12 April 2012.

The Queensland Disaster in Context

The QFCOI's interim report of August 2011 argued that:

> The floods of December 2010 and January 2011 strained the resources of a state more used to coping with drought than floods. The consequences were shocking; no one believed that people could be swept by a torrent from their homes and killed … that nine motorists could be drowned in an attempt to negotiate floodwaters; that some towns could be completely isolated for weeks, or that every last citizen of others would have to be evacuated; that residents of cities like Ipswich and Brisbane could lose everything they owned in waters which wrecked thousands of homes. (QFCOI 2011:6)

Then, on 3 February 2011, north Queensland communities were subject to the fury of Tropical Cyclone Yasi, the largest and most intense cyclone to cross the Queensland coast in living memory.

The cumulative impact produced Queensland's most serious and geographically extensive series of natural disasters that occurred sequentially over four months. Together they impacted on more than 78 per cent of the State. Thirty-five people died and the cost to individuals, businesses and the State has been conservatively estimated at A$7.5 billion.

Reviewing Disaster Management Performance

In the aftermath of any natural disaster (or indeed any significant event), it is both good public policy and good practice to debrief and review the preparation for and response to that disaster. In particular, it is important to identify what worked, what did not work and what could have been improved in order to better prepare for the next event. In most cases, these reviews are relatively low-key internal processes gauging the response of agencies: police, fire, the State Emergency Services (SES) and other emergency services staff and volunteers. Other service agencies such as local governments and utilities companies (for example, electricity, telecommunications and water suppliers) whose services on the ground are critical during a natural disaster usually adopt a similar approach.

In Queensland, the disaster management framework has institutionalised this review practice with the local, district and State disaster management groups. After Cyclone Larry in March 2006, annual cyclone and storm season workshops were initiated along the Queensland coast as part of the preparation for each cyclone and storm season and involved the Bureau of Meteorology (BOM), State government agencies and local authorities.

Given the significance and tragic impact of the flooding events in Queensland in 2010–11, however, a major and external review was expected. There are commonly two options: 1) an external and public review panel led by an eminent person(s); or 2) a formal commission of inquiry utilising royal commission or judicial powers.

The eminent-person model was exemplified by Mick Keelty's review of the Perth Hills bushfires in 2011, by Neil Comrie's Review of the 2010–11 Flood Warnings and Response in Victoria and by the Brisbane City Council's panel headed by former Queensland governor Peter Arnison to investigate in the aftermath of the Brisbane floods in January 2011. Generally, the eminent-person model is focused on lessons learnt and the recommendation of improvement strategies.

The more formal commission of inquiry processes were adopted by the Victorian and Queensland State governments in the case of the 2009 Victorian bushfires and 2010–11 floods in Queensland. This is understandable given the significant loss of life and acute consequences of these events.

Queensland Floods Commission of Inquiry, 2011

On 17 January 2011, just four days after the floods swamped Brisbane and Ipswich, the Queensland premier Anna Bligh announced the establishment of the Queensland Floods Commission of Inquiry (QFCOI). The inquiry (QFCOI 2011:251–3), led by Supreme Court Justice Cate Holmes, was given broad terms of reference including

- the preparation and planning for the flooding by governments at all levels, emergency services and the community
- the supply of essential services during the floods
- the adequacy of forecasts and early warning systems, with particular reference to Toowoomba and the Lockyer Valley
- compliance with, and the suitability of, dam operational procedures for safety and flood mitigation
- land-use planning to minimise flood damage
- the performance of insurers in meeting their claims responsibilities.

The commission presented an interim report on 1 August 2011, which generally focused on the operational and planning requirements to better prepare for the 2011–12 storm and cyclone season. The final report, presented on 16 March 2012, made 177 recommendations, 119 of which centred on floodplain management, State and local government planning and building controls and related issues, and mining industry planning and environmental issues. Five recommendations related to the performance of private insurers, 12 to the emergency response and the balance of 41 to dam management matters (QFCOI 2012:12–29).

Intergovernmental Policy Developments: Resilience and shared responsibility

The focus of the commission's recommendations—emphasising greater local and State government responsibility and more prescriptive regulation—is at odds with the February 2011 COAG-approved plan, the National Strategy for Disaster Resilience (NSDR). The NSDR (COAG 2011:2) represents a whole-of-nation *resilience-based* approach to disaster management, which recognises that a national, coordinated and cooperative effort is needed to enhance Australia's capacity to withstand and recover from emergencies and disasters.

The emphasis on resilience is founded on a far broader policy approach to emergency disaster management. It relates to strategies to build community and personal resilience so that communities and individuals are better prepared to mitigate the impact of natural disasters, respond to them and recover more effectively from them. In simple terms, resilience to natural disasters can be compared with an infection or virus. The healthier, fitter and more prepared an individual is, the quicker and more complete their recovery is likely to be.

It is a major disappointment that the Queensland floods commission provided no policy support for the NSDR or engagement with its approach. In contrast, the Comrie Victorian Floods Review (VFR) into the 2010–11 Victorian floods formally acknowledged the importance of the national resilience strategy. It stated up-front in its executive summary:

> [T]he VFR is of the firm view that the most effective means of making our communities safer is to build their resilience to natural disasters … [The NSDR] is an important reference document in this regard and the VFR offers strong support for the objectives of the strategy. (Comrie 2011:5)

Shared Responsibility

In building community resilience to disasters, a strengthened regulatory and planning framework is an important element, but there is much more. 'Shared responsibility between governments, communities, businesses and individuals' (COAG 2011) is central to an effective resilience strategy. Resilience necessitates a focus on an 'all hazards, all agencies' approach in which risk information and responsibility are shared across the community.

In its final report, the Victorian Bushfires Royal Commission (2010:303) commented that 'shared responsibility' translated to 'increased responsibility for all', including State agencies and municipal councils, communities, individuals and households, and that they all need to 'take greater responsibility for their own safety'.

The Queensland floods commission has not recognised this nationally endorsed policy intent in its approach or its recommendations. As noted by the Monash Injury Research Institute in its *Review of Recent Australian Disaster Inquiries* (Goode et al. 2011:25): 'the concept does not come across explicitly throughout the [interim] report … The shouldering of responsibility by individuals and communities is ambiguous … When taken together … the recommendations advocate shared responsibility only in the sense that responsibilities of different agencies are clarified.'

Prevention as the Major Policy Gap

The serious gap in disaster management policy in Australia is the lack of integrated policy and funding frameworks focused on 'all hazards' and on building resilience. This involves developing effective, practical strategies to limit the impact of disasters with more effective integration of policy and programs across the *prevention*, *preparedness*, *response* and *recovery* phases of disaster management. Governments should perhaps approach disaster management as they do counterterrorism, where up-front resources are expended on preparation and prevention, and lessons learned in response and recovery are integrated back into both operational response planning and the prevention and preparedness phases. Each phase should provide feedback loops to improve performance, policy development and resourcing priorities. These feedback loops are currently weak in disaster management, as evidenced by the disproportionate allocations between the response and recovery phases and the prevention and preparation phases. In short, the latter are badly neglected.

A simple 'risk and impact' model comparing how we prepare against terrorism with how we prepare for natural disasters demonstrates significant differences in approach, creating a major policy gap and funding distortions. Table 18.1 captures three aspects of the different policy management approaches to such disasters: the calculated risks, the possible impact of a disaster and our relative investment priorities. In the case of counterterrorism policy, the investment priority is in the preparation and prevention phases, yet the risk is relatively low. In the case of natural disasters, which are arguably inevitable in Australia and far more common, the allocation of government resources devoted to disaster management is heavily weighted to response and recovery.

Table 18.1 A Risk and Impact Model of Disaster Management and Investment Priorities

Potential threat	Risk calculation	Most likely impact	Investment priority through policy
Terrorism threats (human-induced)	Low (perhaps medium on occasions)	Localised to widespread/ extensive	Investment mainly in preparation and prevention
		Minor to catastrophic	
Natural disasters (physical phenomena)	High (repeated events almost inevitable)	Localised to widespread/ extensive	Investment overwhelmingly in response and recovery
		Minor to catastrophic	

Source: Author's summary.

Ferris and Petz (2012:38) summarise the present policy imperative for disaster management thus:

> With a disaster landscape where the past might no longer be indicative of the future, policy makers and mitigation specialists will need both foresight and guidance from ever more sophisticated climate models to take the necessary decisions to prevent and prepare for future disasters. This might require major investments in disaster mitigation measures and upgrading infrastructure as part of a climate change adaptation agenda.

The QFCOI: A missed opportunity

The allocation of resources to response and recovery through the NDRRA has grown exponentially in response to disaster events, from about A$40 million in 2003–04 to A$600 million in 2009–10, and to about A$1.9 billion in 2010–11. The estimated costs of the 2010–11 flooding and cyclone events in Queensland are reported to be in excess of A$7.5 billion. As a consequence of the serious financial impact, the Federal Government resorted to a 1 per cent levy on taxable income in 2011–12 to assist funding the Queensland recovery.

The commitment to, and investment in, prevention and mitigation, however, has been miserly in comparison, despite evidence of the economic returns and resilience benefits that can be expected from such investments. Research in the Australian context by the Bureau of Transport Economics in 2002 showed that flood mitigation can provide a 3:1 return on investment through the avoidance of response and recovery costs (Bureau of Transport and Regional Economics 2002). In the United States there is further research that claims a 5:1 average return on flood-mitigation investment (Rose et al. 2007:103).

The Natural Disaster Resilience Program (NDRP) is the funding source for grants to councils and other bodies 'for emergency management activities intended to build resilience and to minimise the impact of natural disasters in Australia, including the priority areas [of] disaster mitigation, support for volunteers and consideration of the impact of climate change' (Attorney-General's Department 2011). It expresses a grand vision—but the funding is mere crumbs!

By way of stark comparison with the NDRRA's costs, the entire NDRP funding of A$145.9 million was allocated over the five-year period from 2009–10 to 2013–14. In Queensland this program translates to a total of A$44 million across five years, with equal contributions coming from the Queensland and Australian governments. The financial imbalance is staggering when one considers that in the same year, when the estimated cost of repairing the damage caused by flooding and cyclonic events was A$7.5 billion, Queensland's allocation of NDRP funds for disaster mitigation was just A$9 million.

Regrettably, too, there are examples where roads, bridges and other critical infrastructure have been repaired using NDRRA funds only to be swept away in the next flood. Previous policy was simply to restore these assets; this is short-sighted and ultimately more expensive. More recently, there has been some acknowledgment that this infrastructure needs to be rebuilt to mitigate future risks. This approach is referred to as 'betterment' or 'Building Back Better' (Queensland Reconstruction Authority 2011:7). Despite a policy change to accommodate 'betterment' projects under the NDRRA in 2007, practical examples are rare, perhaps non-existent, and a significant injection/redirection of funds is needed to give effect to this aspiration.

The former Commonwealth attorney-general and minister for emergency management Robert McClelland (2012:1) has gone on public record to question whether the allocation of some of the individual hardship grants of A$1000, which were made regardless of assessed impact, would not be better used for preventative measures:

> The trouble is that politicians at all levels tend to focus (and want to be seen) after a disaster occurs because that's when it has most media attention ... [and] there is a lot of money that goes into post-disaster compensation payments ... I have consistently said we need to evaluate how efficient these payments are, these $1000 compensation payments. Firstly to streamline them so that we target them to those who are most in need, but secondly to look at shifting a substantial amount of that money into preventative measures.

He pointed out that A$840 million was provided in A$1000 payments to people affected by the 2010–11 floods and Cyclone Yasi. Just 10 per cent of that A$840 million would have resulted in a tenfold increase in the funds for disaster-mitigation programs in Queensland!

The president of the Local Government Association of Queensland supported McClelland's stance and called for a review of the disaster funding priorities, indicating that government investment 'in infrastructure offered better protection from flood, fire and cyclones' (Bell 2012).

It may be that the State and federal budget processes are what actually frustrate other policy attempts to change the relative allocations. Robert McClelland (2012:1–2) speculated that:

> Part of the problem is your pre-disaster expenditure is a budget line item. In circumstances where spending that money upfront is going

to save money downstream but at a time when the Government is, understandably, trying to achieve a balanced budget, they don't want budget line items that involve … not insubstantial expense.

This policy impasse ought to be resolvable. The evidence in support of a change in government policy with significantly greater injection of funds into mitigation and adaptation initiatives is overwhelming. The QFCOI *could* have made a significant and influential contribution to the public policy debate, but it did not.

Stuck in the Regulatory Mode

The QFCOI's report identified that regulatory failures relating to local government land-use planning and dam management, for example, contributed to the scale of the disaster. That is not in question. What is open for debate, however, is the prescriptive nature of the proposed regulatory requirements.

It is hardly surprising that a royal commission/commission of inquiry would present a case for greater regulation. It is the 'nature of the beast'.[1] Such commissions are legal constructs in which the key players are highly experienced and well-credentialed lawyers. This was the case with the QFCOI as it was with the Victorian Bushfires Royal Commission. Legal training dictates such commissions will take a forensic, inquisitorial and sometimes adversarial approach to the examination of evidence, frequently in pursuit of guilt or a scapegoat. The end game seems to be to find those responsible, fully or partially, for the human tragedy and economic costs of events.

Moreover, governments which establish royal commissions/commissions of inquiry are largely obligated to accept the recommendations of the body they establish. The community would expect no less. Consequently, the State Government's commitment to implement whatever recommendations were made was widely expected.

The QFCOI opted for a very prescriptive set of regulatory recommendations with multiple subsets of formal requirements, rather than a risk-based approach based on principles of floodplain management and planning. Its recommendations relevant to planning, building controls and the mining industry will involve much greater regulation at the State and local government levels. Its recommendations relating to flood studies and land-use planning led the commission to suggest that the Queensland Government should be

1   See the *Australian Journal of Public Administration* (Vol. 69, No. 4, December 2010), especially contributions by Allan Holmes and Susan Pascoe.

responsible for these actions, but if it did not accept these responsibilities then local councils should. The rationale for this approach is unclear, but does seem inconsistent with the detailed and prescriptive nature of many of the other recommendations. This lack of clarity is likely to result in ongoing arguments over which level of government should bear the costs of the implementation of these recommendations. Many local councils are simply not in a financial position to meet these additional costs. Future blame shifting between tiers of government following incomplete implementation of these recommendations seems inevitable.

To give one example, one of the QFCOI recommendations proposed an extensive flood study of the Brisbane River catchment, with the commission describing in detail the required methodology and contents of such a study almost in a checklist fashion. In this and other recommendations, the report recommends the specific criteria for sophisticated flood modelling that are unlikely to be evident in any existing flood models or maps in Queensland or nationally. In passing, the QFCOI noted that a review of 'best practice principles' for flood modelling has been initiated by the National Emergency Management Committee through the National Flood Risk Advisory Group (NFRAG), a group of technical experts from Geoscience Australia, the Bureau of Meteorology and a range of relevant professional disciplines. Yet the QFCOI (2012:14) seemed to believe its expertise in the area outweighed that of these expert bodies. It argued that 'in the event the [NFRAG] review does not adequately account for Queensland conditions, the Queensland Government should produce a document that provides appropriate guidelines for floodplain management in the Queensland context'.

This presumably meant that the QFCOI wanted a document produced consistent with its recommended prescriptive methodology.

Better Governance and Accountability?

More legislation and additional regulation are not on their own synonymous with greater accountability. Governments already have strongly documented governance arrangements and large and complex accountability regimes. The potential consequence of the Queensland commission's approach is that by focusing on process accountability, documentation is measured as an outcome rather than the performance of local authorities and government agencies.

By definition, greater regulation will increase costs, which would need to be met by the local and State governments through higher taxes and rates or by increased costs to developers and the building and construction industries. Inevitably these higher charges will be passed on to households and businesses.

Further experience would indicate that greater regulation increases complexity and consequently impacts on the time frames for the completion of projects subject to those regulations.

In this context, the April 2012 COAG meeting committed to a process to streamline the regulatory burden:

> COAG agreed to consider concrete measures to lift regulatory performance, including reducing complexity and duplication and increasing transparency and accountability ... COAG agreed the new agenda ... [which] will be supported by a *National Productivity Compact: Regulatory and Competition Reform* for a more Competitive Australia. The Compact ... will set out a high-level statement on principles for effective regulation and reform. (COAG 2012)

If we are serious about better governance and accountability, Boin and 't Hart (2010:367) have already challenged the effectiveness of the regulatory approach that was the basis of the QFCOI report. They have argued that 'the oft-observed importance of "hardware" (formal structures; technical equipment; legal frameworks) is overrated. It distracts attention from the often more salient and cost-effective, yet symbolically powerful "software" factors (leadership, training, network building, organisational culture).'

Hence, they suggest that '[i]nstead of going down the structural reform path, it is more helpful to identify a select set of administrative principles that have served policy-makers well in organising and managing a crisis response network'.

An alternative approach consistent with 'building resilience' and with COAG's chosen direction would be higher-level principles to cover land-use planning, and floodplain modelling and mapping based on appropriate risk management to encourage confidence and a more mature relationship between industry and government. Governments need to reduce direct control and aim for increasing returns to the economy through lower implementation costs, increased industry productivity and direct measurable accountability. Our capacity and resource-constrained local councils need to focus on strategies to mitigate their future risks during natural disasters. Under this approach, some of the resources earmarked for a prescriptive regulatory framework could be redirected to prevention and preparedness initiatives.

The issue of concern, however, and a potential consequence of the QFCOI's approach is that this becomes process accountability where the measure of accountability is the documentation not the performance of relevant agencies against their land-use and disaster management plans. Performance accountability, in contrast, would shift the emphasis to an assessment of the outcomes and performance, rather than focusing on formal processes that are voluminous, resource intensive, not linked to performance objectives or measures and often separate from the business of the local authorities.

A further issue is the relatively narrow range of expertise in the areas of flood-risk modelling, mapping and associated floodplain management, particularly at the local government level where it will matter the most. Currently this expertise is largely confined to a small number of specialist engineering companies and individuals. We might wonder how much relevance the sophisticated and detailed flood modelling and mapping will have to the owners of land and businesses and smaller infrastructure providers who really only want to know what the risks are to their properties in a range of scenarios. In practical terms, this would be on the basis of previous reported events and possible peak flood levels.

Interestingly, a number of governments in the region (Victoria, New Zealand and Queensland) in the aftermath of major disasters have established statutory reconstruction authorities with very wide-ranging powers based upon the mantra of 'whatever it takes'. In practical terms these authorities have focused exclusively on recovery efforts. To enable more effective post-disaster coordination, these recovery authorities have been given powers to override existing State and local government planning instruments and regulations. It can be anticipated that this approach will be replicated after each major disaster.

Paradoxically, the capacity of these recovery authorities to override existing planning instruments and regulations stands in stark contrast with the philosophy embraced by the QFCOI, favouring stronger and more prescriptive regulation.

Other Missed Opportunities

Notwithstanding the acknowledged effectiveness of Queensland's response capability, there are areas that still need to be improved. Weaknesses remain in the situational awareness and intelligence-gathering capability and the information and communication systems of State agencies and local councils.

The interoperability of the communications systems of police and the emergency response agencies remains problematic. This issue was similarly exposed in the Victorian natural disasters; however, unlike the Comrie review (2011:8) into the Victorian floods, it was disappointing that the QFCOI made no specific recommendations in relation to information and communications systems. Instead, it included a statement of support for 'the move towards interoperability between Queensland's public safety agencies, both in narrowband communications and through the establishment of a whole government wireless network' (QFCOI 2012:399). The cost of this, however, would be substantial. In the current fiscal environment, a specific recommendation would have provided a much stronger case for giving priority to investment in this network, which would enhance public safety objectives for the emergency response agencies in their normal operations.

The assumptions underlying disaster management planning remain too narrow. Queensland's preparatory thinking has been informed by previous experiences where significant flooding, storm and cyclonic events have occurred (for example, Cyclone Larry in 2006). Experiences in other States and from overseas have further honed these capabilities. Still, the flooding of 2010–11 exposed deficiencies in local planning and preparation and the variability in the capacities of different councils, as recognised by many councils themselves and reinforced in the QFCOI's interim report.

Moreover, international experiences, from hurricanes like Katrina or earthquakes in Haiti, Japan or New Zealand, or the tsunamis in Aceh, Sumatra and Samoa, and the oil spill in the Gulf of Mexico, should alert policymakers and emergency management agencies that our planning assumptions have been too narrow (see Boin and 't Hart 2010:360). Training (including scenario-based exercises) must focus not only on particular skills, but also on the roles and relationships of those involved in the disaster management system.

The Challenge Ahead

The NSDR creates an imperative for all the actors involved in emergency and disaster management (governments, businesses, individuals and communities) to move beyond the traditional emphasis on response and recovery towards activities and initiatives that will build resilience to natural disasters and other emergencies. Frequent and severe natural disaster events occurring with some frequency—such as bushfires, floods and cyclones—underscore the salience of the policy directions endorsed by COAG.

'Disaster resilience is a long-term outcome, which will require long-term commitment. Achieving disaster resilience will require achieving sustained behavioural change' (COAG 2011:3).

The challenge to our national, State and Territory leaders, though, is obvious. They need to embrace the necessary behavioural change. It is time for the aspiration of building resilience to be supported through policy changes and resourcing priorities. COAG cannot advocate for a resilience-based approach to disaster management and then continue to deny the reality that the critical policy gap with the NSDR is the failure of successive federal and State governments to recognise and address their funding responsibilities. Local communities and individuals urgently need assistance to reduce their exposure to natural disasters by investment in mitigation and adaptation initiatives. The missed opportunity of the QFCOI to contribute to these important policy debates is lamentable.

References

Attorney-General's Department. 2011. *National Partnership Agreement on Natural Disaster Resilience*, 14 October. Available from: <http://www.em.gov.au/npa>.

Bell, P. 2012. 'McClelland Talks Sense on Disaster Mitigation', Media release, 4 April (Brisbane: Local Government Association of Queensland). Available from: <http://lgaq.asn.au/web/guest/news/-/asset_publisher/pG32/content/mcclelland-talks-sense-on-disaster-mitigation?redirect=%252Fweb%252Fguest%252Fnews>.

Boin, A. and 't Hart, P. 2010. 'Organising for Effective Emergency Management: Lessons from Research', *Australian Journal of Public Administration*, 69(4):357–71.

Bureau of Transport and Regional Economics. 2002. *Benefits of Flood Mitigation in Australia*, Report No. 106 (Canberra: Bureau of Transport and Regional Economics). Available from: <http://www.bitre.gov.au/publications/2002/files/report_106.pdf>.

Comrie, N. 2011. *Review of the 2010–11 Flood Warnings and Response*, December 2011 (Melbourne: Government of Victoria). Available from: <http://www.floodsreview.vic.gov.au/images/stories/documents/review_20101011_flood_warnings_and_response.pdf>.

Council of Australian Governments (COAG). 2011. *National Strategy for Disaster Resilience*, February 2011 (Canberra: Council of Australian Governments). Available from: <http://www.em.gov.au/Documents/1National%20Strategy%20for%20Disaster%20Resilience%20-%20pdf.PDF>.

Council of Australian Governments (COAG). 2012. *Communique*, 13 April (Canberra: Council of Australian Governments).

Ferris, E. and Petz, D. 2012. *The Year that Shook the Rich: A Review of Natural Disasters in 2011* (Washington, DC: The Brookings Institution).

Goode, N., Spencer, C., Archer, F., McArdle, D., Salmon, P. and McClure, R. 2011. *Review of Recent Australian Disaster Inquiries* (Melbourne: Monash Injury Research Institute). Available from: <http://www.em.gov.

au/AboutAGD/Authorityandaccountability/Committeesandcouncils/ Documents/Review%20of%20Recent%20Australian%20Disaster%20 Inquiries%20-%20final%20report.PDF>.

McClelland, R. 2012. 'Federal MP Questions Disaster Funding, Labor's Future', *The World Today*, ABC Radio National, 2 April.

Queensland Floods Commission of Inquiry (QFCOI). 2011. *Interim Report*, August 2011 (Brisbane: Government of Queensland). Available from: <http:// www.floodcommission.qld.gov.au/__data/assets/pdf_file/0006/8781/QFCI-Interim-Report-August-2011.pdf>.

Queensland Floods Commission of Inquiry (QFCOI). 2012. *Final Report*, March 2012 (Brisbane: Government of Queensland). Available from: <http://www. floodcommission.qld.gov.au/__data/assets/pdf_file/0007/11698/QFCI-Final-Report-March-2012.pdf>.

Queensland Reconstruction Authority. 2011. *Rebuilding a Stronger, More Resilient Queensland* (Brisbane: Government of Queensland).

Rose, A., Porter, K., Dash, N., Bouabid, J., Huyck, C., Whitehead, J., Shaw, D., Eguchi, R., Taylor, C., McLane, T., Tobin, L., Ganderton, P., Godschalk, D., Kiremidjian, A., Tierney, K. and West, C. 2007. 'Benefit–Cost Analysis of FEMA Hazard Mitigation Grant', *Natural Hazards Review*, 8(4):97–111. Available from: <http://research.create.usc.edu/cgi/viewcontent.cgi?article=1014&context=pu blished papers 2007>.

Victorian Bushfires Royal Commission. 2010. *Final Report*, July (Melbourne: Government of Victoria).

19. The Role of Post-Disaster Institutions in Recovery and Resilience: A comparative study of three recent disasters

James Smart

Dealing with natural disasters and their after-effects is among the most difficult tasks governments face. Their harm is pervasive, affecting the financial, social, environmental and human welfare of a country. Managing them often requires coordination between local authorities, businesses, neighbourhood groups and volunteer organisations; but effective management can reduce a disaster's long-term impact.

Governments are concerned with four areas of disaster management, commonly known as the four rs. First, they can reduce societal vulnerability and build resilience through *reduction* of known risks. Second, *readiness* is established by building and maintaining capability. Third, these capabilities are marshalled to *respond* to immediate human needs. Fourth, *recovery* alleviates immediate societal suffering and improves citizens' long-term prospects by building *resilience* against future disasters.

This chapter places its focus on the fourth area, recovery and resilience, but an effective recovery owes much to the other areas. Good institutions provide the adaptive capacity that lets communities recover from natural disasters, which is particularly clear when three natural disasters in Australia and New Zealand are reviewed

- Victoria's bushfires in 2009
- Queensland's flooding from 2010 to 2011
- Canterbury's earthquakes from 2010.

These cases demonstrate the importance of flexible management, evidence of institutional learning before and after disasters, the role of community engagement, response to insurance issues and the building of resilience.[1]

---

1   The full working paper on which this chapter is based, including all references, is available on the Institute of Governance and Policy Studies website: <http://igps.victoria.ac.nz/publications/publications/show/334>.

Why Disaster Response Matters

Effective government-led responses often require changes to service delivery and the agencies that deliver them. Existing agencies may be improperly equipped for the tasks that confront them, but implementing changes can take time. Governments unable to respond with the swiftness demanded by citizens can quickly increase societal uncertainty and pessimism. Individuals and businesses may leave the area and financial intermediaries may no longer provide insurance and loans. Declining institutional quality presents greater challenges to governments already unable to drive the recovery process. Changes to those institutions that reinforce community capacity are vital to restore functionality. They should be able to learn from their operational environment, integrate experience and adapt accordingly.

Disasters are exacerbated by policy failure (Birkland 2006). Retrospective inquiries that examine policy choices during disaster response are often instructive, but may also encourage catharsis and relieve perceived injustice among affected people (Bovens 2007). If their recommendations are taken seriously, lessons learned can inform community decision-making during recovery and reduce the effects of future disasters.

As with other crises, optimising the level of resources for disaster recovery is hard. Physical destruction and its proportionality to the economy are unhelpful as metrics to policymakers. Two dynamics are important in the short run. First, capital stock is usually required to produce goods and services. Output will be lower if capital is destroyed, though rebuilding capital will increase output. The net effect of these dynamics is ambiguous; their timing will differ.

Reconstruction is likely to be uneven and much delayed after the initial loss. The mixture of outputs will differ, as seen in labour markets. A destroyed bakery will be unable to produce bread, but may employ a builder to replace its building. This sudden change in the required skill mix could push the economy up against structural limitations, such as the number of trained builders.

The economic impact of disasters is hard to predict during the event, with two competing narratives. Medium-term growth could be lower if structural limits to reconstruction are reached, and if a disaster increases the perceived risk of investing. Medium-term growth could be higher if new capital is superior in quality to old—one prevailing effect in climatic disaster recovery (Skidmore and Toya 2002). On average, ambiguity appears to triumph. Carvallo et al. (2011) find no significant effect on the long-run economic growth of disaster-affected countries.

Most important in this analysis are the human costs, both direct and indirect. The scale and effectiveness of the response have long-term implications for recovery. Seventeen years after Hurricane Iniki hit the Hawaiian island of

Kauai in 1992, the island's population had not recovered from post-disaster emigration (Coffman and Noy 2009). The fiscal cost of reconstruction borne by governments can lead to major challenges beyond the immediate disaster time frame, particularly if pre-disaster debt is high and capital flight is a genuine risk (Noy 2009). Governments facing these issues may not have the capacity to help communities recover.

Major disasters often result in high stock costs, giving insurance an important recovery role. Insurers may assume that the risk of a high-cost event in the near future is very low but the probability of a disaster is difficult to integrate into actuarial models. Individual destructive events expected to occur with a very low probability impose high, near-simultaneous costs after a disaster. The concurrent timing of these tail events often results in higher than anticipated losses for insurance companies, risking their solvency (Kousky and Cooke 2009).

Ideally, insurance markets help smooth financial costs over a lifetime and improve individual welfare; so individuals who neglect to take out insurance will face relatively higher costs after a disaster. Governments may be tempted to intervene through direct assistance, but some individuals may see such assistance as a quasi-permanent replacement for private insurance. Insurance take-up could be discouraged and dependency on the state would grow— behaviour known as *moral hazard*.

Reconciling the desire to assist risk-takers and the cost of moral hazard is a Samaritan's dilemma. Complex recovery efforts frequently highlight a lack of consensus on values (Hischemoller and Hoppe 1996). It is not clear whether the immediate suffering of citizens is a greater issue than future welfare loss created by moral hazard. These problems demand political solutions, but building consensus requires time. Governments may be unwilling or unable to provide that time, to the detriment of new social rules and expectations that develop.

Responses in Victoria, Queensland and New Zealand

Australia and New Zealand are both developed economies, sharing a British heritage with similar political and legal institutions, most notably the Westminster parliamentary system; however, their constitutions have important differences. Australia's provides defined roles and responsibilities for Federal and State governments, while local governments provide a third tier of designated responsibilities and roles during disasters. New Zealand has no level between central and local (or regional) government. Local governments raise a modest level of revenue, mostly through property tax, concentrating most of New Zealand's disaster response capacity in Wellington.

Disasters have affected both countries since 2009. Bushfires burned across Victoria for more than a month in early 2009, particularly affecting rural communities. For three summer months in 2010–11, heavy rains brought extensive flooding to Queensland, compounded by damage from Cyclone Yasi. Meanwhile, since September 2010, New Zealand has been faced with a series of seismic events in the Canterbury region, including a severe earthquake on 22 February 2011. All three disasters were followed by large-scale government responses.

Table 19.1 Scale of Disasters

	Killed	Estimated damage (US$billion)^A	Affected people
Victorian bushfires	173	1.3 (0.1 % of GDP)	9954
Queensland floods	35	15.9 (1.1 % of GDP)	200 000
Canterbury earthquakes	185	16.5 (9.8 % of GDP)	301 500

Note A: CRED defines estimated damage as direct (for example, damage to infrastructure, crops, housing) and indirect (for example, loss of revenue, unemployment and market destabilisation).

Sources: Centre for Research on the Epidemiology of Disasters (CRED). n.d. <www.cred.be>; International Monetary Fund (IMF). 2011. *Australia: Article IV Consultation. Country Report No.11/300*, June; World Bank 2011, *Queensland: Recovery and Reconstruction in the Aftermath of the 2010/2011 Flood Events and Cyclone Yasi* (Washington, DC: The World Bank); Victorian Bushfire Reconstruction and Recovery Authority (VBRRA) 2011, *Legacy Report* (Melbourne: Victorian Bushfire Reconstruction and Recovery Authority).

Australia

Australia's State governments are responsible for emergency services, public schools, infrastructure and policing. The Commonwealth Government collects the most significant source of public revenue: direct taxes. State revenue largely comprises other taxes, particularly property taxes. State expenditures are far larger than revenue, resulting in high levels of fiscal imbalance, compensated by large grants from the Federal Government.

Federal and State governments negotiate funding arrangements after disasters. The National Disaster Relief and Recovery Arrangements (NDRRA) specify four funding categories of emergency assistance. These are individual relief (Category A), restoration of public assets (Category B), a community recovery package (Category C) and acts of relief or recovery that alleviate damage in 'exceptional' circumstances (Category D). Federal assistance is dependent on the scale of the fiscal cost of relief. For Categories A, B and C, if the first threshold is passed the Commonwealth provides 50 per cent of State expenditure.[2] For

---

2   That is, 0.225 per cent of the State's total general government sector revenue and grants in the financial year two years prior to the relevant financial year.

expenditure exceeding the second threshold, the Commonwealth provides 75 per cent in excess of the second threshold.[3] For Category D, the Commonwealth has discretion over the rate of its assistance.

The Australian Emergency Management Handbook Series includes a book on 'Community Recovery'. Community recovery focuses on five environments: social, built, economic, financial and natural. It argues that successful recovery is dependent on understanding the context, recognising complexity, using community-led approaches, ensuring coordination of all activities, employing effective communication and acknowledging capacity limits.

Victoria

Bushfires quickly spread and rapidly intensified, devastating several communities across Victoria on 7 February 2009. Worst affected were the towns of Kinglake and Marysville, both in Murrindindi Shire. With 173 deaths and 4300 buildings destroyed, it was the worst bushfire in Victorian history (VBRRA 2011).

By 10 February, the Victorian Government set up the Victorian Bushfire Reconstruction and Recovery Authority (VBRRA) to coordinate reconstruction. An order-in-council, a mechanism that lets the executive modify existing legislation, established the authority, which would act as a unit under the Department of Premier and Cabinet. The expected lifespan of the Victorian Bushfire Reconstruction and Recovery Authority (VBRRA) was not widely publicised, so as not to detract from the authority's work (VBRRA 2011). The authority was given broad terms of reference; policies were formed by a new, dedicated committee in the Victorian cabinet.

The authority's main function was to coordinate the Victorian Department of Human Services (DHS) and other Victorian service-delivery departments by delegating specific services under the recovery plan. The VBRRA worked with all levels of government: Commonwealth Government agencies, Victorian Government, local councils, especially the Murrindindi Shire Council, and non-governmental organisations.

The early establishment of the VBRRA increased the tempo of recovery, but this advantage would have been lost if staffing requirements were not quickly satisfied. Fewer than 20 staff comprised the initial start-up team sourced from the Australian Defence Force (ADF) and Victorian Government departments. In March 2009, Christine Nixon, who had been the chief commissioner of Victoria Police during the time of the fires, became head of the VBRRA.

---

3   That is, 1.75 times the first threshold.

Approximately A$1 billion was made immediately available for the recovery (Department of Treasury and Finance 2009). The Federal Government funded A$266 million under the NDRRA, while private donations to the Victorian Bushfire Appeal Fund totalled A$395 million (Victoria Bushfire Appeal Fund 2012). The total budget for the VBRRA over its life was A$21.2 million, the majority going to Victoria's service-delivery agencies.

The strategic recovery framework was developed from both Australian and international experience. In line with best practice, the recovery plan focused on local communities, with four broad headings. The 'people' heading included rebuilding community assets, such as recreational facilities and halls, temporary housing and counselling. 'Reconstruction' involved community and State-owned buildings, infrastructure and provision of building advice to residents. 'Economy' combined a number of support packages for business investment stimulus. 'Environment' aimed to restore the natural environment to its pre-bushfire condition, protect endangered animals and stabilise land.

The VBRRA (2011) cited evidence that community involvement could improve individual health and wellbeing. The authority conducted 29 community meetings, attended by approximately 4400 people. These meetings gave the authority legitimacy and established clear recovery requirements. The authority encouraged the formation of community groups, Community Recovery Committees (CRCs), to develop recovery plans for their areas. While the VBRRA would provide guidance and templates for CRC planning, CRCs established priorities and wrote recovery plans, which the VBRRA combined into a Statewide recovery plan. Nearly 800 CRC projects were funded.

The rebuilding of Marysville showcases the recovery process undertaken in Victoria (VBRRA 2009). The Victorian Bushfire Appeal Fund disbursed A$29 million in grants to Marysville within eight months. Temporary housing was built for the local community, while a Rebuilding Advisory Centre provided advice to residents on rebuilding homes. Residential reconstruction was accelerated by the Victorian Government's amendment of the *Victorian Building Regulations* so destroyed homes could be rebuilt without planning permits. The residential building standards were changed so new structures could withstand a severe bushfire event. A temporary marketplace provided businesses with interim trading facilities. Around 600 people contributed to the town's Urban Design Framework, identifying immediate needs such as regenerating commerce and locating a petrol station, and 'catalyst projects' that would stimulate economic recovery.

After 7 February, the Premier of Victoria announced the formation of a royal commission to investigate the causes of and immediate response to the disaster. The commission's terms of reference required it to improve the resilience of Victoria to future bushfire events. It was chaired by Bernard Teague, a former judge of the Supreme Court of Victoria. On 31 July 2010, the commission delivered its final report, with 67 recommendations. They spanned Victorian bushfire safety policy, emergency management and fireground response, to planning and building, land management and the organisation of fire services. These recommendations affected State institutions (for example, the Country Fire Authority) and State regulations, and access to Commonwealth resources (for example, aerial resources owned by Emergency Management Australia and the Department of Defence). In areas of high fire risk, the commission recommended a 'retreat and resettlement' plan for affected communities.

A pressing issue was the distribution of donations received through the relief effort. These funds were distributed through DHS at the direction of an independent advisory panel; however, there was no consensus on whether the uninsured should receive more from the fund than insured homeowners. Some insured homeowners questioned whether the uninsured deserved greater pity. One argued, 'I think we should all get the same'.

Insurance status did not affect fund payout eligibility for damaged and destroyed homes; however, payouts were partially dependent on the circumstances of the applicant. For destroyed homes and contents, payouts were a maximum of A$45 000, with an additional A$40 000 depending on need. For damaged homes, payouts were a maximum of A$35 000, of which A$20 000 was based on need. Other payouts were available, such as transitional support, psychological support packages and support for exceptional hardship and severe injury.

The VBRRA was intended as a temporary institution to direct immediate recovery needs. The Victorian Government intended the authority's life to be approximately 18 months, but it was lengthened to two years. To plan for its closure, transition risks were identified, mitigation plans were put in place and it was ensured that permanent government departments could enact the recovery plan. One risk was the expiration of staffing contracts that might disrupt the work of the authority in its final months, but this was alleviated through staff retention and planned redeployment. The VBRRA was officially disbanded on 30 June 2011.

Prior to the VBRRA's closure, there were concerns that the pace of reconstruction was slow. Two years after 7 February, 41 per cent of homes had been rebuilt; some expected recovery to take up to five years. Stelling et al. (2011) conducted a number of interviews with informants and focus groups in the Beechworth region. Communities felt they had been brought together and their networks were strengthened after the fires; but they also believed that over time these bonds would weaken as community members left, and resentment stemming from some decisions taken during and after the fires lingered. Nevertheless, community resilience against future event appears to have been built. Participants in the study believed their communities were far better prepared for bushfire events than before 2009.

Queensland

In 2010, the Southern Oscillation climate pattern saw the strongest La Niña pattern since 1976, bringing above-normal wet weather to Queensland. Flooding began in December 2010 and increased on 23 December. Cyclone Tasha, a category one cyclone, brought further rain and damage on 24–25 December. By the end of the rains, more than 99 per cent of Queensland was declared 'disaster affected'. Cyclone Yasi, a category five cyclone, compounded flood damage in northern Queensland on 3 February 2011.

In 2006 Queensland had experience of recovering from meteorological disasters when Cyclone Larry caused A\$1.5 billion of damage in the north of the State. Recovery was steered by a task force, led by General Peter Cosgrove, former chief of the Australian Defence Force. General Cosgrove was also an internationally recognised logistics expert, whose arrival in the area instantly lifted morale. Recovery was generally successful.

The *Disaster Management Act 2003* was amended in 2010 following a review of Queensland's disaster management arrangements (Government of Queensland 2011). The State Disaster Management Group (SMDG) is the key policy and decision-making body for Queensland's disaster management. Recovery required Statewide coordination and management of large resources. The amendments to the 2003 Act let the Queensland Government establish a designated recovery authority to prioritise agency response and recovery funding.

The initial change to institutional settings came soon after the December flooding, and was at first similar to the Victorian experience. The State Government established a Flood Recovery Taskforce and a special cabinet committee to coordinate responses. The task force was headed by Major General Mick Slater, then commander of the Australian 1st Division, in Brisbane. The choice of military leadership echoed Queensland's task force in the aftermath of Cyclone Larry, enabling transfer of operational lessons from that event.

Enabling legislation soon followed. On 21 February 2011, the task force was absorbed into a new statutory authority, the Queensland Reconstruction Authority (QldRA), with the passing of the *Queensland Reconstruction Authority Act* (*QldRA Act*). The QldRA had clear functions. It decided recovery priorities, worked closely with communities, collected information about property and infrastructure, shared data with all levels of government, coordinated and distributed financial assistance, and facilitated flood mitigation.

The QldRA board comprised Major General Slater, two members nominated by the Australian Government,[4] one nominated by the Local Government Association of Queensland[5] and three with expertise and experience in engineering and planning.[6] The authority's chief executive was Graeme Newton, formerly of Queensland Water Infrastructure. The board reported directly to the Premier of Queensland, Anna Bligh.

The QldRA estimated the rebuild cost at A$6.8 billion (QldRA 2011a); 75 per cent would be provided by the Federal Government under the NDRRA and 25 per cent would come from the State Government. Road reconstruction took 70 per cent of the QldRA's budget, with the majority of the residual going to grants aimed at primary producers, small businesses and non-profit organisations.[7] The QldRA reconstruction framework was based on six lines: human and social; economic; environmental; building recovery; roads and transport; community liaison and communication. Six subcommittees in these areas were established with unique concepts of operation.

The QldRA was directed by its enabling legislation to ensure 'Queensland and its communities effectively and efficiently recover from the impacts of disaster events' (QldRA 2011a:47). Its powers were broad, having power to acquire land, carry out works and implement development schemes for declared projects. It could also close roads, overrule council development decisions and decide the fate of damaged infrastructure.

The QldRA had recovery and reconstruction phases. Recovery would be completed by 30 June 2011 and reconstruction by the end of 2012 (Government of Queensland 2012). The QldRA's operations were to be transferred to other agencies after two years.[8] The recovery effort made substantial progress in the first six months (see Table 19.2). Most of the work repaired damaged infrastructure, while the QldRA focused on the capability of affected areas to withstand future flooding by building resilience, improving damaged structures and incorporating local government in the rebuilding effort in all six reconstruction areas. More specific plans included storm tide-prone area reconstruction (QldRA 2011c) and improvements to electrical infrastructure (QldRA 2011d).

---

4   Brad Orgill, head of the Building the Education Revolution Implementation Taskforce, and Glenys Beauchamp, secretary of the Department of Regional Australia, Regional Development and Local Government.
5   Brian Guthrie, former CEO of Townsville City Council.
6   Kathy Hirschfeld, a former oil executive; Steve Golding, former director-general of Main Roads; and Jim McKnoulty, a local government planning expert.
7   Provided by the Queensland Rural Adjustment Authority (QRAA).
8   Section 139 of the *QldRA Act*.

Table 19.2 Damage Impact and Recovery Statistics

	November 2010 – March 2011	As at September 2011
Roads	9170 km of Queensland's road network affected	8482 km of Queensland's road network recovered
Rail	4748 km of Queensland's rail network affected	4596 km of Queensland's rail network recovered
Bridges and culverts	89 State-owned bridges and culverts with major damage	89 State-owned bridges and culverts recovered
Schools	411 Queensland schools affected	411 Queensland schools operating
National parks	138 national parks closed due to natural disaster	123 national parks reopened
Premier's Disaster Relief Appeal	More than A$276 m donated, with more than A$251 m distributed to individuals	
Personal hardship and assistance grants	More than A$121 m in grants paid to small businesses, primary producers and non-profit organisations. More than A$12 m in concessional loans to small businesses and primary producers	
Sport Flood Fight Back Scheme	More than A$13 m in funding for infrastructure and/or equipment to assist organisations to re-establish sport and recreation services	

Source: Adapted from QldRA (2011b).

The QldRA exercised its powers most visibly in reconstructing Grantham, a town west of Brisbane. Declaring it a 'reconstruction area' in April 2011, the authority created a 'development scheme' for the town, in consultation with local residents.[9] The scheme enabled the QldRA to override planning instruments, plans and policies made under any Act. In May 2011, the Lockyer Valley Regional Council purchased 937 ha of land on higher ground and offered a 'swap deal' to Grantham residents. By December 2011, the Grantham Reconstruction Area was in effect, with the QldRA arguing the scheme would sweep away 'regulatory hurdles' that would otherwise hinder progress.

The flooding led to a significant rise in insurance premiums. One estimate suggested average home and contents premiums rose by 12 per cent, with flood-affected areas seeing average increases of up to 41 per cent (*Insurance News* 2011). Some homeowners were surprised to discover they were not covered for flood damage. Because insurers lacked a common definition of a flood event, the Federal Government subsequently mandated a standard definition for flooding for all insurance policies.

The Federal Government provided approximately A$5 billion of the reconstruction fund, some 50 per cent of the total, imposing a flood levy on individuals with incomes of more than A$50 000. One senator cited moral

---

9   Per sections 62–5 of its enabling legislation.

hazard as a reason for initially withholding his support because the Queensland Government's insurance fund did not have reinsurance. His eventual support was conditional on mandatory insurance for State governments against disasters and States losing access to NDRRA funding if insurance cover for State assets was deemed inadequate.

In June 2011, the World Bank (2011) reported on the Queensland reconstruction effort, concluding that it met many good-practice standards, while commending the QldRA on its 'build back better' focus. It argued that the response saved lives, quickly provided funding to individuals and communities, and management of the recovery and reconstruction was effective.

New Zealand

New Zealand has two institutions designed to deal automatically with disaster recovery. First, the Earthquake Commission (EQC), a crown entity, provides partial insurance for natural disasters. The EQC is funded by levies on home insurance and purchases cover with reinsurance companies. After a natural disaster, the EQC pays out the first NZ$100 000[10] of damage suffered on insured houses, with private insurers covering the residual.[11] Prior to the first Canterbury earthquake, the EQC's assets were approximately NZ$6 billion (EQC 2010). Second, Civil Defence and Emergency Management (CDEM), a ministry, coordinates the initial response after a state of emergency is declared.

CDEM can declare two types of emergency. A local emergency empowers only subsidiary groups in the affected area to respond. A national emergency provides response powers to all CDEM groups simultaneously, and was not used before 2010.

The first Canterbury earthquake struck at 4:35 am on 4 September 2010. It was New Zealand's most damaging earthquake since the 1931 Napier earthquake, but caused no reported deaths because the Christchurch city centre was largely deserted. A local emergency was then declared. The event caused damage of approximately NZ$5 billion. Insured homeowners were eligible to lodge damage claims with the EQC immediately.

Fears that existing legislation would slow the recovery process encouraged the Government to expand its powers. The Government faced few constraints on its capacity to amend legislation or intervene in the affairs of specific localities. A local MP, Gerry Brownlee, was appointed Minister for Earthquake Recovery. Within two weeks, legislation was passed in the form of the *Canterbury*

---

10   Plus goods and services tax.
11   The EQC's cover does not apply to businesses.

Earthquake Response and Recovery (CERR) Act. It provided for orders-in-council for the recovery. Brownlee argued this power was necessary to remove bureaucracy and speed up the recovery process.

On 14 September 2010, the Canterbury Earthquake Recovery Commission (CERC) was established under the Act to enable better coordination between local and central governments. CERC advised on potential orders-in-council to the minister. CERC had seven commissioners, three of whom were the mayors of Christchurch City, Selwyn District and Waimakariri District; one was from Environment Canterbury, the regional authority, and three were appointed by the minister. CERC's life was limited to about 18 months, after which it would disband and orders-in-council applying to Canterbury would expire.

This response was severely challenged by the earthquake of 22 February 2011, resulting in 185 fatalities, most due to building collapses. The earthquake's proximity to the city caused more damage to buildings than the September earthquake and liquefaction damaged land to a far greater extent.[12] Consequently, the Civil Defence Minister declared a national state of emergency. The second earthquake scaled up the challenge facing the Government. The EQC determined that the February earthquake was a new event,[13] enabling homeowners to claim against new damage suffered. The Government set aside an additional NZ$5.5 billion for reconstruction costs as part of the 2011 budget.

Because the orders-in-council were scheduled to expire in April 2012, the *CERR Act* was replaced with the *Canterbury Earthquake Recovery (CER) Act*. This legislation provided much wider and more significant powers. The Act and associated orders-in-council extended the period in force to 2016 and the Minister for Earthquake Recovery was empowered to 'suspend, amend or revoke' a number of local council plans and 'suspend or cancel' resource consents granted under the *Resource Management Act*. These powers enabled a recovery strategy to be developed by November 2011 in conjunction with Christchurch City Council, Selwyn and Waimakariri District Councils and Environment Canterbury.

The most important change was the establishment of a new government department: the Canterbury Earthquake Recovery Authority (CERA). The Act gave CERA strong powers and a budget of NZ$25.5 million for the first two years. Roger Sutton, previously chief executive of a regional electricity distribution company, was appointed to head the authority.[14] CERA decided reconstruction

---

12 Liquefaction is the surfacing of liquefied sand and water from below the ground due to shaking during an earthquake.

13 Prior to the February earthquake, there had been four such 'new events' including the initial September earthquake.

14 CERA was immediately active, with deputy State Service commissioner John Ombler as acting chief executive.

priorities, expropriated land with compensation, entered premises with notice to undertake works and closed roads. It also used its power to demolish and dispose of buildings.

The authority took control of public works from CDEM on the expiration of the national state of emergency on 1 May 2011. CERA coordinated the drafting of the recovery strategy for Greater Christchurch, which complemented Christchurch City Council's draft recovery plan for the CBD. The recovery strategy, released in October 2011, referred to 15 plans along four lines of reconstruction: economic, social, natural and buildings. Each plan would involve several stakeholders, including central and local government bodies, non-governmental organisations, such as the region's principal *iwi*, Ngāi Tahu, and business organisations.

Damaged housing was an immediate concern for CERA. Many residents questioned rebuilding on land that had suffered liquefaction. Geotechnical information needed refreshing after the earthquake. The risk of significant aftershocks deterred rebuilding in the short term and reluctance by insurance companies to offer new policies compounded the issue. CERA's response was to divide the city's land into several areas. Most areas were designated 'green', with lesser degrees of risk for future liquefaction, which allowed for rebuilding; however, land repair in 'red' areas would be 'prolonged and uneconomic'. The Crown would compensate residents in red areas for loss of their homes at the council's last valuation of their property.[15]

Continuing seismic activity seriously impeded recovery operations. After September 2010 the concentration of earthquakes shifted eastward, with several damaging more buildings. Liquefaction continued to cause problems near the Avon River, despite many areas being designated by CERA as suitable for rebuilding. By 8 February 2012, the EQC recognised 15 different events, allowing affected insurance holders to claim against new damage; however, the region has not suffered further damage comparable with that of the September 2010 or February 2011 earthquakes.

Seismic uncertainty depressed the supply of insurance, throttling quick home and business reconstruction. Alan Bollard and Mike Hannah (2011) argued that the CERA changes, land remediation and reassessment of damage on buildings complicated the insurance process, as geotechnical and policy uncertainties have discouraged insurers from increasing their exposure to Canterbury.

Excessive claims from the February 2011 earthquake resulted in one domestic provider, AMI, requiring nationalisation. Other insurers anticipated higher

---

15   This was 2007 for Christchurch, and 2008 for Waimakariri.

reinsurance costs, increased their premiums and sought to minimise exposure to the rebuild. Bad loans and the risk of business disruption created uncertainty for banks and other financial institutions.

The earthquakes placed immense pressure on the EQC's capacity. Additional claims by individuals were made as already damaged homes suffered more damage from aftershocks. Cowan and Simpson (2011) argue liability estimates and loss allocation were complex because no existing models were calibrated for events of this type and liability for land damage was difficult to estimate. Furthermore, the EQC had to meet complex legal requirements, and it coordinated more than a dozen agencies from the private sector and government to meet geotechnical demands. On 11 October 2011, the Government announced that the insurance levy used to finance the EQC would be tripled.

Monetary and fiscal policy responses were swift. The Reserve Bank of New Zealand (RBNZ) decreased its official cash rate by 50 basis points in the immediate aftermath of the February earthquake. Public finances were put under pressure by the earthquakes. Earthquake-related public expenditure was approximately NZ$13.6 billion in the 2010–11 financial year[16] (Bollard and Hannah 2011). The earthquakes coincided with increases in government debt stemming from the late 2000s economic downturn. In response, the Government has set a target of returning to budget surplus by 2015.

The Government established a royal commission of inquiry to investigate buildings that caused injury on 22 February 2011, especially the CTV Building and PGC House, and those that failed after being deemed safe following the September 2010 earthquake. Furthermore, the Government is investigating the adequacy of current legal and best-practice requirements. In October 2011, an interim report with geotechnical and building design recommendations was released, and the final report was due for release in late 2012.

After the November 2011 general election, the National Party formed a coalition government with several minor parties. CERA compiled a *Briefing to the Incoming Minister* summarising the recovery process and future challenges. It identified seismic uncertainty as a major issue in recovery of the CBD and the primary cause of landowners delaying decisions to repair or rebuild. It acknowledged that 'managing the pace and timing of its contribution to the recovery is the single greatest risk CERA faces' (CERA 2011). It also noted that CERA's work program might require increased future funding and defended the recovery process to date, arguing that economic activity and employment were above expectations and that the foundation was set for recovery.

---

16   Year ended 30 June 2011.

Discussion

The three cases show points of similarity and difference. While each government created recovery agencies to coordinate the recovery, they had different functions and powers. They were tasked with community engagement yet citizens were empowered to make decisions to different degrees. The cases display clear evidence of institutional learning as recovery progressed and the complexity of insurance issues after disaster.

Choice of Agency Type

The recovery agency in Victoria was not complemented with legislative powers, an apparently deliberate strategic decision that let the Government coordinate recovery quickly. The bushfires took place over a relatively short period compared with the disasters in Queensland and Canterbury. The marginal benefits of waiting for new legislation to be drafted, passed and enacted justified the immediate establishment of a recovery authority. It is also clear that there was considerable goodwill for the VBRRA in the initial stages of recovery. In contrast, Queensland and Canterbury experienced repeated events that exhausted the institutions initially set up to cope with them. Recovery authorities with more and greater powers were deemed necessary in those cases.

Queensland and New Zealand designed recovery authorities with strong powers that circumvented existing regulations. Queensland's institutional response was specifically cited in a New Zealand cabinet minute proposing the creation of CERA. The agencies' powers are remarkably similar, but there are important differences. CERA is a government department while the QldRA was created as a statutory body. The QldRA had a board and its minister was the premier rather than a portfolio minister. In New Zealand, Brownlee had the advantage of being a senior minister in cabinet, indicating more direct control and influence over the recovery process.

Although both agencies faced big challenges, they faced very different issues. With the exception of small towns, the QldRA's funding was primarily focused on the restoration of services and rebuilding infrastructure, while respecting established use of premises. Christchurch, facing more complex recovery demands, granted authority to the Minister for Earthquake Recovery to change resource consents granted under the *Resource Management Act*.

An effective command structure requires leadership capable of rapport with the affected community. All three cases reveal a similar preference. An outstanding example for the Australian responses to draw on was the Queensland Government's appointment of General Cosgrove, former chief of the

ADF, to lead its response to Cyclone Larry in 2006. In 2011, the Queensland Government appointed high-level ADF officers to head recovery coordination. Military involvement signals an effective response to a traumatised community and managing the logistics of recovery. In Victoria the appointment of a public figure gave the VBRRA significant capital, which was important given the lack of enabling legislation. In New Zealand, Roger Sutton became a high-profile figure in the immediate response phase.

Community Engagement

All three approaches involve the public in decision-making; yet public participation does not always diffuse power from government to citizens. Arnstein's (1969) ladder of citizen participation describes eight 'rungs', ranging from non-participation to 'citizen power'. In Hirschman's (1970) framework of 'exit, voice and loyalty', participation that does not empower citizens may lead them to exit the process, impoverishing decision-makers' information base.

The VBRRA acknowledged that community-led recovery was difficult when individuals were still undergoing personal recovery, and it was not until later that the model changed from 'token' consultation to creating partnerships with CRCs. The VBRRA adopted most of the projects identified and prioritised by CRCs.

In New Zealand, the *CER Act* mandates the minister to appoint a community forum and 'have regard' to their information and advice. This has not been sufficient to build consensus on complex issues in Christchurch. Ostrom (1986) outlines a consultative institutional model with several rules under which the participatory game is played. When *authority rules* constrain decision-makers, a more effective process is likely. Merely having regard to a forum's information and advice concentrates power with the central government. *Boundary rules* specify how participants are selected. Unlike Victoria, where the membership of CRCs was self-selecting, Christchurch's sole community forum, with only 38 members, was appointed by the minister. The *pay-off rules* distribute cost and benefits to participants. The draft CERA recovery plan for Greater Christchurch received 304 submissions and it is unclear if it was influenced by other means of community participation. Community forum minutes record that participants reported an 'attitudinal problem' within Christchurch City Council that left them feeling disempowered (CERA 2011).

It is unclear if the participatory process has built consensus. Hisschemoller and Hoppe (1996) describe a lack of consensus on knowledge, norms and values as an *intractable controversy*. Controversies come into existence if viewpoints of certain groups or interests are not taken seriously by policymakers (1996:49). They become serious if there is considerable policy and geotechnical uncertainty.

Community engagement was mandated in the *CER Act* to develop the recovery plan for Greater Christchurch. It is unlikely that the time frame was sufficient to build consensus on some of the more complex issues facing the region.

Queensland's Grantham land swap was also contentious. Some residents preferred to remain in the flooded valley despite the known risks; however, residents were not compelled to accept the deal offered by the Lockyer Valley Regional Council. In Christchurch, issues were acute when compulsion was used. This ranged from dissatisfaction over building restrictions to unhappiness with the land zoning of homes. Such intractable controversies are a serious obstacle that New Zealand has yet to overcome.

Institutional Learning and Adaptive Change of Rules

The VBRRA *Legacy Report* (2011) outlines a number of lessons arising from the authority's operations. Aligning the recovery body with the highest level of government provides authority. Statutory powers can speed up progress on unanticipated issues, especially if they cannot use other government agencies' existing powers. Broad terms of reference, though necessary in complex recovery situations, generate uncertainty. The recovery body must be flexible as recovery moves from immediate issues towards more enduring, long-term issues.

The QldRA appeared to take on some of these lessons. First, the enabling legislation clearly defined its functions and gave it considerable powers. Second, its board reported directly to the Queensland premier. Third, the QldRA had clear steps to move from recovery to reconstruction before transitioning to other agencies. Permanent government agencies were involved in subcommittees in the six areas of reconstruction, and their priorities were decided by the QldRA.

Creating CERA was the clearest adaptation in New Zealand. Establishing the department outside Wellington indicated government recognition that in a crisis it is important to be close to the people affected. CERA (2011) made explicit note of lessons it had learned from local and international experience, including: building the capacity of the community-led response, devolving decision-making to the local level, focusing on those most affected by the disaster, and ensuring government agencies worked in a holistic, joined-up way.

Insurance Issues and Building Resilience

Moral hazard was a clear problem in Victoria and Queensland. In Victoria the high level of donations made distribution a complicated process. In the end, the uninsured did not receive special treatment, though increased need among those individuals may have led to greater access to funding. This approach has far less potential to distort individual incentives than alternatives. Queensland's floods highlighted moral hazard among intra-governmental actors, with the Federal Government resorting to compulsory State disaster insurance.

New Zealand's permanent disaster institutions adequately coped with the issue of moral hazard for home insurance. The EQC reduced risk exposure for private insurers without encouraging homeowners to neglect taking up insurance. The Government refused to extend the EQC's coverage to those without insurance and has not yet offered compensation for uninsured red-zoned land. It is not yet clear if moral hazard issues will result from the nationalisation of AMI. Nevertheless, the reduced supply of private insurance in the Canterbury region has slowed the pace of recovery.

All three cases show a clear commitment to mitigating the risk of future disasters. Inquiries investigated the causes of and response to the disaster, the failure of buildings and infrastructure, and delivered recommendations to reduce the risk of reoccurrence. Victorian building codes were strengthened and the capacity of standing institutions for disaster response was increased. Queensland's issues relating to flood preparedness were delivered quickly. In New Zealand, the royal commission's interim report delivered recommendations that informed early decision-making on rebuilding and repair work in Christchurch.

Conclusion

Despite differences in the three approaches to disaster recovery there are similarities. Institutional responses dealt with the disaster effectively and quickly, and avoided the feedback loop between poor institutions and higher crisis levels. While it is too early to judge the success of the recovery effort in Christchurch, large-scale unemployment, homelessness and poverty have been avoided. Despite parts of the CBD remaining closed to the general public, Christchurch continues to function relatively well.

In its evaluation of the Queensland recovery effort, the World Bank (2011) highlighted a number of features important in good recovery practice. First, the recovery effort built on planned responses to disaster. Second, governments introduced specific agencies to deal with recovery. Third, they showed a commitment to community engagement, particularly in longer-term strategic planning. Fourth, all worked with local government in recovery planning. Fifth, relief and recovery arrangements were already in place, with the World Bank specifically citing the NDRRA. Sixth, the recovery effort attempted to ensure that mitigation of risk was incentivised and moral hazard was avoided. Seventh, technical advice was provided to individuals trying to rebuild. Eighth, efforts were made to understand policy failures that exacerbated the disaster, and to recommend changes to mitigate future risk. Many of these good-practice principles are also evident in the Victorian and Canterbury recovery efforts.

Successful institutions are constrained by their context, ever changing in a crisis situation. Governments showed an ability to learn from past experiences and as the recovery process moved ahead. Where institutions, both public and private, struggle to cope with the demands disasters impose on their capacity, it is important that these institutions are supported to maintain the tempo of recovery. Optimising the level of resources that are used in recovery and reconstruction is hard, and an under-resourced recovery can create new problems that last for years after the disaster. Early engagement and ensuring that the demands on government are kept to a manageable level are the clearest lessons of the three cases.

References

Arnstein, S. 1969. 'A Ladder of Citizen Participation', *AIP Journal*, 35(4):216–24.

Birkland, T. A. 1997. *After Disaster: Agenda Setting, Public Policy and Focusing Events* (Washington, DC: Georgetown University Press).

Birkland, T. A. 2006. *Lessons of Disaster: Policy Change after Catastrophic Events* (Washington, DC: Georgetown University Press).

Bollard, A. and Hannah, M. 2011. Tale of two crises, Speech to Canterbury Employers' Chamber of Commerce, Christchurch. Available from: <http://www.rbnz.govt.nz/speeches/4659119.html>.

Bovens, M. 2007. 'Public Accountability', in E. Ferlie, L. E. Lynn and C. Pollitt (eds) *The Oxford Handbook of Public Administration* (Oxford: Oxford University Press).

Buchanan, J. M. 1975. 'The Samaritan's Dilemma', in E. Phelps (ed.) *Altruism, Morality and Economic Theory* (New York: Russell Sage Foundation).

Canterbury Earthquake Recovery Authority (CERA). 2011. *Briefing to the Incoming Minister*, December (Christchurch: Canterbury Earthquake Recovery Authority). Available from: <http://cera.govt.nz/about-cera/briefing-for-incoming-minister>.

Carvallo, E., Galiani, S., Noy, I. and Pantano, J. 2011. *Catastrophic Natural Disasters and Economic Growth*, IDB WP Series No. IDB-WP-183 (Washington, DC: Inter-American Development Bank).

Centre for Research on the Epidemiology of *Disasters* (CRED). n.d. <www.cred.be>.

Coffman, M. and Noy, I. 2009. *A Hurricane's Long-Term Economic Impact: The Case of Hawaii's Iniki*, Working Paper No. 09-5, June (Manoa: Department of Economics, University of Hawai'i). Available from: <http://www.economics. hawaii.edu/research/workingpapers/workingpapers.html>.

Cowan, H. and Simpson, I. 2011. Planning for disasters and responding to unforeseen complexity: the first large test for the New Zealand Earthquake Commission, 12th Hazards Conference, 29 September – 1 October, Surfers Paradise, Qld.

Department of Treasury and Finance. 2009. *2009 State Budget: Building jobs, Building Victoria*, 5 May (Melbourne: Government of Victoria). Available from: <http://www. budget.vic.gov.au/domino/Web_Notes/budgets/budget09.nsf/d6e571e551bef80eca 2572bb002bcea7/5d0390e6678ff38fca2575ac00574fd5!OpenDocument>.

Earthquake Commission (EQC). 2011. *Earthquake Commission Annual Report 2009–2010* (Wellington: Earthquake Commission).

Folke, C., Colding, J. and Berkes, F. 2003. *Synthesis: Building Resilience and Adaptive Capacity in Social-Ecological Systems* (Cambridge: Cambridge University Press).

Government of Queensland. 2011. *Disaster Readiness Update*, November (Brisbane: Department of the Premier and Cabinet). Available from: <http:// www.premiers.qld.gov.au/publications/categories/reports/assets/disaster- readiness-update.pdf>.

Government of Queensland. 2012. *Complete Budget Paper 5—Service Delivery Statements* (Brisbane: Government of Queensland). Available from: <http:// www.budget.qld.gov.au/budget-papers/2011-12/bp5-2011-12.pdf>.

Hirschman, A. O. 1970. *Exit, Voice and Loyalty: Responses to Decline in Firms, Organisations, and States* (Cambridge, Mass.: Harvard University Press).

Hisschemoller, M. and Hoppe, R. 1996. 'Coping with Intractable Controversies: The Case for Problem Structuring in Policy Design and Analysis', *Knowledge and Policy*, 8(4):40–60.

Insurance News. 2011. 'Queensland Sees Highest Rise in Residential Premiums', *Insurance News*, 24 October. Available from: <http://www.insurancenews. com.au/local/queensland-sees-highest-rise-in-residential-premiums>.

International Monetary Fund (IMF). 2011. *Australia: Article IV Consultation. Country Report No.11/300*, June.

Kousky, C. and Cooke, R. M. 2009. *Climate Change and Risk Management: Challenges for Insurance, Adaptation and Loss Estimation*, RFF Discussion Paper No. 09-03-REV (Washington, DC: Resources for the Future).

Noy, I. 2009. 'The Macroeconomic Consequences of Disasters', *Journal of Development Economics*, 88:221–31.

Ostrom, E. 1986. 'An Agenda for the Study of Institutions', *Public Choice*, 48(1):3–35.

Queensland Reconstruction Authority (QldRA). 2011a. *Operation Queenslander: The State Community, Economic and Environmental Recovery and Reconstruction Implementation Plan 2011–2013* (Brisbane: Queensland Reconstruction Authority).

Queensland Reconstruction Authority (QldRA). 2011b. *Rebuilding a Stronger, More Resilient Queensland* (Brisbane: Queensland Reconstruction Authority).

Queensland Reconstruction Authority (QldRA). 2011c. *Planning for a Stronger, More Resilient North Queensland. Part 1—Rebuilding in Storm Tide Prone Areas: Tully Heads and Hull Heads* (Brisbane: Queensland Reconstruction Authority.

Queensland Reconstruction Authority (QldRA). 2011d. *Planning for a Stronger, More Resilient Electrical Infrastructure. Improving the Resilience of Electrical Infrastructure during Flooding and Cyclones* (Brisbane: Queensland Reconstruction Authority).

Skidmore, M. and Toya, H. 2002. 'Do Natural Disasters Promote Long-Run Growth?', *Economic Inquiry*, 40(4):664–87.

Stelling, A., Millar, J., Boon, H., Cottrell, A., King, D. and Stevenson, B. 2011. *Recovery from Natural Disasters: Community Experiences of Bushfires in North East Victoria 2003 to 2009*, ILWS Report No. 65 (Albury, NSW: Institute for Land, Water and Society, Charles Sturt University). Available from: <http://www.riv. csu.edu.au/research/ilws/research/reports/docs/65_Bushfire_Recovery.pdf>.

Victoria Bushfire Appeal Fund. 2012. *December 2012 Progress Report* (Melbourne: Department of Human Services). Available from: <http://www.dhs.vic.gov. au/__data/assets/pdf_file/0017/760220/VBAF-December-2012-Report.pdf>.

Victorian Bushfire Reconstruction and Recovery Authority (VBRRA). 2009. *Rebuilding Marysville & Triangle* (Melbourne: Victorian Bushfire Reconstruction and Recovery Authority).

Victorian Bushfire Reconstruction and Recovery Authority (VBRRA). 2011. *Legacy Report* (Melbourne: Victorian Bushfire Reconstruction and Recovery Authority).

World Bank. 2011. *Queensland: Recovery and Reconstruction in the Aftermath of the 2010/2011 Flood Events and Cyclone Yasi* (Washington, DC: The World Bank).

20. Governing the Canterbury Earthquake Recovery, 2010–2011: The debate over institutional design

Rachel Brookie

The sequence of earthquakes in Christchurch shattered its residents' preconceived notions about the location and magnitude of such events. By March 2012, Canterbury had endured more than 10 000 aftershocks, of which more than 3000 were noticeable. The quakes not only shook infrastructure, buildings and people, but also governance arrangements and institutional design for recovery.

This chapter first describes the relevant impacts of these events. Second, it briefly examines literature on the governance of response to and recovery from major disasters and on community engagement in disaster recovery. Third, it describes and clarifies the country's existing framework for disaster response and recovery before the quakes. Fourth, it evaluates the evolving governance arrangements created to manage the recovery from the quakes. Finally, it discusses the inadequacies in institutional design and lessons highlighted by the quakes.

This chapter argues that the existing statutory framework for long-term recovery was inadequate. The governance arrangements created after the quakes addressed a number of concerns, but also generated problems. Future arrangements must provide an institutional framework that addresses both immediate response and adequate statutory and policy support for long-term recovery.[1]

Background: A series of unfortunate events

Canterbury was struck by three major, and hundreds of minor, earthquakes between 4 September 2010 and 22 February 2011. They resulted in liquefaction, damage to buildings and infrastructure, and the third major quake took 185 lives.

---

1   A longer version of this chapter was originally published as a working paper. It is available on the IPGS website: <http://igps.victoria.ac.nz/publications/files/27b07e4270b.pdf>.

In March 2011, the Government predicted the repair work would cost NZ$20 billion (Bollard and Ranchhod 2011). Others argued the figure could reach NZ$30 billion (NZPA 2011). In December 2011, Treasury estimated the combined cost of the two largest earthquakes to be equivalent to about 10 per cent of GDP (Bollard and Ranchhod 2011). While all sources emphasise uncertainty surrounding their estimates, the *Treasury Budget Policy Statement 2012* (Treasury 2011) stated that rebuilding Canterbury was the biggest economic undertaking in New Zealand's history, having a severe impact on government finances.

Two large aftershocks on 13 June 2011 caused further damage. Canterbury was faced with 124 km of damaged water mains, 300 km of damaged sewer pipes and 50 000 road surface defects. More than 1200 central city buildings were severely damaged and more than 100 000 residential houses require repair or rebuilding (CERA 2011a).

On 23 December 2011, 11 quakes of magnitude 4.0 to 6.0 resulted in further damage and liquefaction and added about NZ$300 million to the Government's operating deficit. By mid January 2012, Canterbury had experienced 9500 quakes, an average of one quake of more than magnitude 3.0 every four hours.

This ranks as one of the most costly natural disasters for insurers worldwide since 1950 (Doherty 2011). As at December 2011, the estimated total net cost to the Crown was NZ$13.5 billion (Doherty 2011). The Earthquake Commission (EQC), the New Zealand Government-owned provider of national disaster insurance to residential property owners, has received 156 670 claims as a result of the September 2010 quake, 156 543 claims as a result of the February 2011 quake, and by February 2012 received 434 797 claims for all seismic events.

In summary, in mid January 2012, 500 days after the first quake, 892 buildings had been demolished and NZ$2.78 billion in EQC claims paid out (Greenhill 2012). As at 10 February 2012, the EQC reports there have been 15 major earthquake events that allow insurance holders to make a claim. Continued seismic activity has constrained recovery activities.

Looking at the Literature

Defining Response and Recovery

The most important terms in the disaster literature are summarised as the four 'rs'—*reduction, readiness, response* and *recovery*—and are defined in the National Civil Defence and Emergency Management (CDEM) Plan.[2] James Rotimi (2010) finds that the *response* phase is the emergency or crisis period that ends when

---

2 These definitions are available in James Smart's Chapter 19, this volume.

there are no more search and rescue operations and all safety evaluations are completed. *Recovery* involves initiating activities after impact and extending them until the community's capacity for self-help is restored. Rotimi (2010:34) describes *recovery* 'as the totality of activities, carried out at the post-impact stage at some point after the initial crisis time period of disasters, to progressively reinstate damages made to every facet of a community's environment'. It starts at day one of the emergency and ends when the community's capacity for self-help is restored. The *response* and *recovery* phases overlap.

Literature on the Governance of Major Disasters

International literature shows that the recovery phase shares many principles with the other 'rs'. As with risk reduction and response, recovery requires an approved government policy, an enabling national system, appropriate tools and advocacy among all the actors including civil society. Decentralisation, links between local and national governments and a holistic approach to managing disasters are also needed.

The United Nations Development Programme document *Post-Disaster Recovery: Guiding Principles* (UNDP 2006:10) sets out appropriate institutional arrangements for recovery. Roles and responsibilities should be clearly defined within a country's broader risk reduction, disaster preparedness and contingency planning processes. Experience suggests recovery and reconstruction efforts are best mounted on existing institutional frameworks and, if necessary, enabled with faster mechanisms for recovery. If a new structure for recovery is to be put in place, its objective should be achieving cohesion, coordination and consensus among different disaster stakeholders. The new structure should focus on:

> The definition of recovery/development policies, priorities and strategic guidelines, formulation/implementation/oversight of recovery proposals, monitoring of progress, establishing a permanent dialogue and consensus space with civil society, opposition parties, private sector, international cooperation agencies, donors and lending agencies, maintain transparency, accountability and good governance in the process as well as a strategic communications and information campaign. (UNDP 2006)

The document also states that the main challenge in devising an institutional arrangement for recovery and reconstruction is to find a rapid implementation mechanism that does not undermine the existing institutional framework or affect ongoing good-governance mechanisms. It also notes that in the aftermath of a major disaster, implementation capacity is a major recovery planning issue.

Local authorities often lack the capabilities and resources to address adequate preparation for disasters and to deal with their short and long-term implications. Therefore, local authorities may require central government support, and substantial linkages must be established between local and national levels—this includes support with resources and efficient coordination achieved by collaboration.

Literature on Community Engagement in Disaster Recovery

Community involvement in recovery activities contributes beneficially to the success of long-term recovery. Engaged communities can identify 'workable solutions to the range of problems recovery presents, sharing and delegation of duties, securing community "buy in" to the process, and building trust' (Vallance 2011:20).

Some writers argue that community participation by 'deliberative methods' is more practicable in the recovery phase than in the response phase. Community panels, citizens' juries, deliberative polling, consensus conferences and planning cells[3] promote high levels of community engagement in decision-making, bring communities together to achieve understanding of an issue or problem and find common ground that will ideally lead to a decision. Successful deliberative processes depend on three elements: *influence*—the process should have the ability to influence policy and decision-making; *inclusion*—the process should ideally be representative, inclusive and encourage equal opportunity to participate; and *deliberation*—the process should provide open discussion, access to information and movement towards consensus (Millen 2011). Such methods facilitate trust in governance, whatever the decision-making structure may be. They can improve effective communication and recovery outcomes as they engage local knowledge. This results in appropriate, detailed, contextual plans and policies. Millen argues deliberative methods should be embedded in recovery and community engagement processes.

Effective engagement, which aims to facilitate communities owning their own recovery, is a crucial element, integrating social, economic and environmental goals and ideals.

---

3   For further information on deliberative methods, see Millen (2011).

The New Zealand Disaster Response and Recovery Framework

The Response and Recovery Framework Prior to September 2010

This section will outline the New Zealand disaster response and recovery processes—including legislation, policies and agencies—that existed prior to the Canterbury earthquakes.

The National CDEM Strategy sets out the New Zealand vision to encourage resilience, where communities understand and manage their hazards. This approach centres New Zealand's emergency management system on the community—the first level of response in the event of a disaster.

The *Civil Defence and Emergency Management (CDEM) Act 2002* takes an 'all hazards, multi-agency approach' across the four rs. The Act and the CDEM strategy, plan and guide set out the structure for the management of the four rs.

The Ministry of Civil Defence and Emergency Management (MCDEM) is responsible for disaster response and recovery at a national level; however, planning for and implementation of disaster response is led at a local level through CDEM groups, which are partnerships between local authorities, fire, police, health services, government departments and lifeline utilities (such as water and power providers). CDEM groups coordinate planning programs and other activities for civil defence and emergency management, providing the basis for the integration of national and local civil defence emergency management planning and the alignment of local planning with the national strategy and plan.

Local authorities in CDEM groups must prepare for and be able to *respond* to disasters. CDEM groups, through local authorities, implement emergency response activities at the local level through Emergency Operations Centres (EOCs), normally located in council buildings. The Central Government intervenes when an event exceeds local capacity.

New Zealand, unlike most other Western nations, does not have specific stand-alone organisations that manage disasters. Nor is there a national body for disaster risk reduction that combines all sector coordination and collaboration. Instead, the disaster management system is based on day-to-day organisational responsibilities and planning together with other agencies to coordinate an approach to disasters. It is highly devolved: local authorities and their communities lead the response and recovery.

In a large-scale disaster, coordination is managed on a continuum. The CDEM group works at the regional level, while the Officials Committee for Domestic and External Security Coordination (OCDESC) synchronises the whole-of-government disaster response and recovery at the national level. The OCDESC comprises chief executives of government agencies and relevant officials and is administered by the Department of Prime Minister and Cabinet.

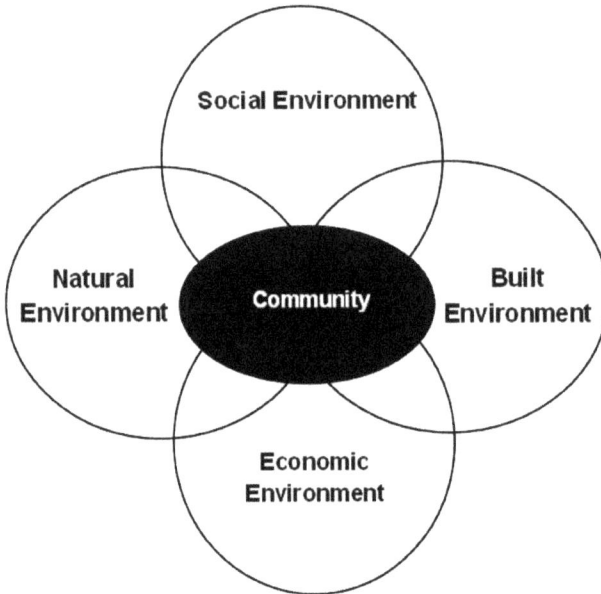

Figure 20.1 Ministry of Civil Defence and Emergency Management's 'Focus on Recovery'

Source: Ministry of Civil Defence and Emergency Management (MCDEM). 2009. *Section 25. Recovery* (Wellington: Government of New Zealand).

When a state of national emergency is declared, the control of emergency management operations by the director of CDEM is supported by a range of enabling powers. Powers may include: evacuating and entering premises, closing roads, giving directions, requisitioning powers, carrying out inspections and undertaking works to make roads and structures safe. The director also controls the exercise and performance of the powers of CDEM groups and group controllers. Such powers may be exercised only during a declared state of emergency, after which the provisions that enable response and some recovery activities cease to apply.

Recovery

The MCDEM's 'Focus on Recovery' outlines a holistic framework for recovery, which centres on the statement that recovery is best achieved when the affected community exercises a high degree of self-determination. It encompasses the social, built, economic and natural environments, integrating recovery activities with the community at the centre.

The environments are represented by task groups charged with recovery. Sub-task groups may be set up for larger-scale recovery. Task groups are coordinated by a recovery manager. Communication and regular meetings between the groups and the recovery manager are crucial. Information derived from these groups should be communicated to the media and all agencies (MCDEM 2009b).

As the scale of the recovery and level of complexity increase so does the institutional response. The civil defence 'national recovery management structure' demonstrates the recovery task groups being undertaken in parallel at local, regional and national levels. These are coordinated at the *readiness* phase, so all actors know how to respond when an emergency occurs. In practice, central government is involved with a local response—for example, MCDEM officials are designated to assist by liaising with relevant government agencies.

The director of CDEM coordinates the recovery. This includes advising the Minister of Civil Defence of needed government assistance, providing information to the OCDESC, and preparing and implementing a 'recovery action plan'. The director coordinates activity through a national recovery manager, who will, where necessary, establish a National Recovery Office to ensure activity is coordinated and the recovery function is implemented. Other tasks of the National Recovery Office include: coordinating agencies, determining priorities and major areas of recovery, formulating recovery policies and strategies, and monitoring recovery activities.

Under the Act, recovery activity is focused on CDEM groups, but the Act empowers the MCDEM to manage recovery if the minister is satisfied the CDEM group cannot manage on its own. A recovery coordinator may also be appointed to manage the work of agencies and ensure that government assistance and actions are coordinated. The recovery coordinator, appointed for up to 28 days, will be responsible to, and funded by, the Director of Civil Defence.

In an emergency the CDEM Group Recovery Manager coordinates the recovery activity in the region. The Local Recovery Manager, who may be appointed indefinitely, coordinates the recovery activity in a particular local authority area with the CDEM Group Recovery Manager. Tasks and responsibilities for all of these actors are outlined in the guide to the National CDEM Plan (MCDEM 2009a).

Community Engagement

CDEM community engagement best-practice documents acknowledge that effective recovery programs depend on the number of competent people involved. CDEM documents explain that the context of the disaster provides for the designation of the level and process of engagement. The response will depend on the nature of the task, the type and impact of the disaster, and the affected community (MCDEM 2010). While effective engagement in disaster recovery management includes public meetings, community representation and inclusion of representatives from community organisations in decision-making, public participation in New Zealand after disasters generally takes the form of consultation—a low level of public engagement. The EQC, a crown entity, is also involved by providing natural disaster insurance cover to those who have home and/or contents insurance. Funded through a levy, the EQC covers up to NZ$100 000 for damage to dwellings, and up to NZ$20 000 for damage to contents. Private insurers pay the residual amount. The EQC also provides limited cover for damage to residential land. Land cover is unique internationally.

Disasters and recovery involve other legislation and regulations in New Zealand. The *Building Act 2004* governs the construction of new buildings and alteration and demolition of existing buildings. The *Resource Management Act (RMA) 1991* designates management of the environment.

Criticism of the Pre-Earthquake Recovery Framework

New Zealand has effective, modern and well-resourced emergency services for dealing with small-scale localised emergencies, but has significant gaps and deficiencies with respect to dealing with nationally significant disasters.

Rotimi (2010), indicating that practical problems in legislation could constrain recovery, focused on the inadequacy of statutory powers to coordinate recovery. Only months before the first quake, he outlined deficiencies in the recovery legislation and supporting framework.

1. The *CDEM Act* addresses recovery only during the state of emergency.

2. There are likely to be resource shortages during recovery.

3. Institutional capacity mandated in recovery activities is concerning, and local councils' duties and obligations during an emergency and recovery are unclear.

4. The *CDEM Act* covers only the first 28 days of a recovery, and is confusing about responsibility for reconstruction/recovery. The powers of the appointed recovery coordinator should extend beyond a declared emergency period.

5. It is difficult to understand who coordinates reconstruction and how this is done.

6. A strict implementation of the *EQC Act* could prevent property owners from receiving damage compensation—for example, the EQC may refuse compensation if a building is on land notified as subject to natural hazards.

7. Strict application of the *RMA* would slow recovery and consent applications would overwhelm local councils' capabilities.

In summary, in an emergency, the existing model for disaster recovery in New Zealand envisaged that the MCDEM had extra short-term powers to enact response and early recovery activities. Long-term recovery was not supported by legislative powers. Local authorities—through CDEM groups—would have to lead the recovery.

Rotimi concluded that though the statutory basis for the coordination of recovery activities was under government review, it was inadequate.

Looking at Recovery

The following sections outline the debate surrounding, and the results of, the governance arrangements following the earthquakes.

September 2010: A local emergency

A state of local emergency was declared initially by the mayors of Christchurch City, Selwyn District and Waimakariri District. It permitted actions unavailable in normal circumstances, including suspending normal and essential services.

In Wellington, the MCDEM activated the National Crisis Management Centre (NCMC) where the National Director of Civil Defence coordinated the response to the earthquake. CDEM groups in Christchurch, Waimakariri and Selwyn implemented response activities and were expected to lead the recovery.

The EQC received 156 670 claims for damage to houses and land. Unsafe buildings were cordoned off and an overnight curfew was established for parts of Christchurch City. Up to 75 per cent of the city's power was disrupted by the quake, but 90 per cent had been restored on the same day. Citycare[4] connected as many water connections in three days as it would normally do in a year.

Gerry Brownlee was appointed the minister responsible for the Christchurch earthquake recovery, leading a cabinet committee on Canterbury reconstruction to coordinate the Government's response. On the day before the state of emergency ended, the Government introduced the Canterbury Earthquake Response and Recovery (CERR) Bill. It would enable the Executive to use orders-in-council[5] to amend almost all legislation, if needed, to respond to and recover from the earthquake. The Bill also established the Canterbury Earthquake Recovery

---

4   A provider of maintenance and management services across New Zealand's infrastructure.
5   An order-in-council is made without the approval of Parliament, allowing legislative changes to be made and assented to quickly.

Commission (CERC) to advise ministers about proposed orders-in-council and to liaise between central and local governments. The *Canterbury Earthquake Response and Recovery (CERR) Act* was passed with multi-party support and without select committee examination.

The *CERR Act* allowed amendments to legislation that were required to ensure 'that the Government has adequate statutory power to assist with the response to the Canterbury earthquake' until the state of emergency was lifted (Government of New Zealand 2010). When the state of emergency was lifted all special powers accorded to the MCDEM would expire and routine procedures would resume.

CERC was established, consisting of the three local mayors, a regional council (Environment Canterbury) representative, an engineer and the former director-general of the Ministry of Agriculture and Forestry as chair.

The Recovery from the September Earthquake

Within two days the CDEM recovery mechanisms were up and running. Leaders had been appointed for the social, built, economic and natural environments, reporting to a designated coordinating executive group (Dalziel 2011). Despite this, and despite the wideranging powers the Act provided, local people within months complained that the recovery process had stalled.

Lianne Dalziel, a Christchurch MP, attributed slow progress to inadequate processes, undue haste and lack of rigorous scrutiny during the creation of the Act and CERC. CERC, intended only as an advisory group, created confusion over to whom the leaders of the recovery functions were reporting and who was in charge of the overall recovery. The Christchurch City Council (CCC) did not, as recommended in the CDEM recovery plan, appoint a recovery manager to focus on coordination and communication, nor did it develop recovery planning processes (Dalziel 2011).

Before the earthquake, Christchurch City mayor Bob Parker faced a serious challenge to re-election and voters expressed dissatisfaction with the performance of the council and its chief executive. After the earthquake Parker displayed exactly the communication skills needed to reassure the citizens and was re-elected.

In October the recovery phase was under way and the CDEM framework called for leadership, coordination and steering from the CCC, which should at the same time resume 'business as usual'. The CCC resumed business-as-usual processes, which effectively stalled recovery activities by, for example, not fast-tracking consents for rebuilding. Many argued there was no visible engagement from the CCC with the public over how recovery should be handled, and it left the EQC and CERC to take charge.

In contrast, the Selwyn and Waimakariri district councils placed community engagement at the core of all decision-making and communication (Dalziel 2011). Before the quake they had active and well-funded community boards. Shortly after the earthquake, a hub office for Waimakariri was set up, with agencies involved in the recovery establishing offices there. This enabled the recovery agencies to know the situation on the ground and residents to get information. Waimakariri community engagement was seen as successful. In comparison it took until mid November 2010 for the CCC to hold the first 'community meetings', by which time the lack of communication angered residents. With CERC lacking capacity for action, and the CCC failing to develop recovery plans, the recovery process ground to a halt. By the time of the February quake, residents, MPs and business owners demanded the Minister for Earthquake Recovery use his powers under the *CERR Act* to speed up the recovery.

Rethinking the Framework for Recovery Following the February 2011 Earthquake

A state of local emergency was again declared immediately after the earthquake on 22 February 2011. Then, on 23 February, New Zealand's first state of national emergency was declared. This empowered the Director of Civil Defence to direct the *response* on a national basis, mostly from Christchurch. National and international teams joined the local CDEM groups in the search for survivors.

With the CBD cordoned off and damage to homes and infrastructure across the city, the state of national emergency remained until 30 April 2011. By then, the Government had implemented new governance arrangements to meet the scale of the disaster. Whole hillsides had slipped away, liquefaction reappeared and many roads were impassable.

Lessons had been learned after the September earthquake: recovery was a long-term activity that needed to commence quickly, and could not be just about infrastructure—social and economic contexts were equally, possibly more, important. The Government also considered lessons from international experience, where status-quo arrangements were insufficient to cope with major disasters and a new authority was needed to lead the recovery effort. The Government noted no single existing central or local government agency at that time had the powers to manage the recovery, nor was the *CERR Act* framework sufficient for long-term recovery.

The *Canterbury Earthquake Recovery Act 2011* (*CER Act*) was introduced, and passed by Parliament under urgency on 14 April, after a one-day select committee process. The Act extended the Executive's power to modify legislation through orders-in-council to five years. It disbanded CERC, replacing it with the Canterbury Earthquake Review Panel as the advisor to the minister. It created a new government department, the Canterbury Earthquake Recovery Authority (CERA), to report to the Minister for Earthquake Recovery. CERA was to lead and coordinate the recovery efforts of the three councils, Environment Canterbury, central government departments and crown entities, infrastructure providers, business, construction firms and the local community.

CERA had the power to decide reconstruction priorities, compulsorily acquire land, enter premises, undertake works and demolish and dispose of dangerous buildings. CERA, given a five-year mandate, began operations with the Deputy State Services Commissioner as interim head. On 13 June, the former head of the electricity distribution network Orion took over as CEO. The 2011 budget allocated NZ$25.5 million over two years to set up CERA. An additional NZ$5.5 billion was committed over six years for the Canterbury Earthquake Recovery Fund.

The cabinet paper *Proposed Governance Arrangements* (Government of New Zealand 2011a) noted that departments are the default option for the governance of functions and powers requiring a high degree of ministerial control, including where there is exercise of the significant coercive powers of the state. Officials argued that the departmental form would have 'a leadership structure that is able to act decisively and quickly and be closely aligned with the Government's priorities' (Government of New Zealand 2011a). Officials decided against establishing an advisory board, which would impact on the clear line of accountability from the CEO to the minister.

CERA was given nine months to create a recovery strategy as a road map for effective, timely and well-coordinated recovery for Greater Christchurch. The CCC was tasked with developing a recovery plan for the Christchurch CBD, to be signed off by the minister.

The Minister for Earthquake Recovery has extensive powers to coordinate activity needed to effect the recovery and oversee policy and legislative process. Under the *CER Act*, a four-person independent review panel advises the minister.

The *CER Act* also mandated a community forum to provide information and advice to the minister on earthquake recovery matters, meeting at least six times annually. International experience reinforced the importance of community engagement during the recovery, and the forum would give the opportunity for the minister 'to encourage meaningful participation by community representatives in the process' (Government of New Zealand 2011a). While the Act suggested 20 members, the minister appointed 38 from a cross-section of the Canterbury community, representing business and ethnic interests, as well as residents' associations and groups. An eleventh-hour change in Parliament made CERA subject to the *Official Information Act*.

Key Issues: Governance

Despite cabinet papers citing international best practice of instituting a layer of governance between the authority and the politicians, CERA was made a government department. The Government considered an alternative option to set up CERA as an independent crown entity. Crown entities normally have an arm's-length relationship with ministers but cabinet preferred a strong relationship between the minister and CERA and strong coordination across portfolios and agencies embodied in the departmental form (Government of New Zealand 2011a). Additionally, it seems likely that cabinet wanted the whole process directly driven by a minister, given the political and fiscal risks involved; however, this approach raised the risk of political priorities driving aspects of the recovery rather than the needs of the affected communities.

Professor Bruce Glavovic, the Massey University holder of the Earthquake Commission chair in natural hazards planning, expressed concerns that instead of following best practice CERA was 'untried, untested'; New Zealand was 'inventing their own recipe' (McCrone 2011).

Although the CDEM mechanism was bypassed by the introduction of CERA, the *CER Act* mirrors the 'holistic' approach advocated in the MCDEM literature, being centred on the four environments mentioned earlier.

Reflecting on Rotimi's Concerns

Several of Rotimi's concerns about the adequacy of the statutory and regulatory framework to manage disaster recovery have been realised. Government inaction before the earthquakes has now been addressed for Canterbury only by CERA.

First, the problem that the *CDEM Act* enables statutory powers only for short-term recovery, during the declared state of emergency, was addressed by CERA, which empowered recovery activities for five years.

Rotimi's second concern—that there are likely to be shortages of resources during recovery—is hard to determine at this early stage of rebuilding. The reality is that extensive rebuilding is just beginning. The Government has acknowledged that there are skills shortages in the construction industry. Third, Rotimi suggested the institutional capacities of local councils in recovery activities would be insufficient. These concerns, evident in Christchurch post September 2010, have arguably increased since February 2011. The CCC's institutional capacity has been diminished by flawed relationships, ineffective processes and political infighting. The communication procedures and management of the CCC have become a major issue, generating significant protest action.

There were calls for the councillors to be replaced with government-appointed commissioners. At the end of February 2012, the CCC was operating with a crown observer to help the council address governance issues and ensure it functions well enough to support the recovery. The crown observer introduced another layer of central government involvement into the governance of council business, but was made with the agreement of the council.

Rotimi's fourth concern—of confusion over who should take charge during reconstruction and recovery—has been addressed by the clear reporting lines provided in the *CER Act*. All roles and responsibilities designated after the state of emergency was lifted are available on the CERA and CCC websites. The CCC is responsible for the Central City Plan, which was well received by the public. CERA is responsible for the recovery strategy document, policy, planning and the majority of work in Christchurch to date: demolitions. CERA also has overall control of the direction of the recovery, for which the most important decisions are made by the Minister of CER and cabinet. The *CER Act* gave the minister the ability to suspend, amend, cancel or delay any council plans and policies, which must be consistent with CERA's recovery strategy and be signed off by the minister.

The role of the CCC in the recovery effort with CERA could have been neglected. In its comment on the draft recovery strategy of October 2011, the CCC was 'concerned that appropriate governance arrangements have yet to be established to ensure that recovery activities are integrated and well-coordinated and that decisions are made with the right level of input from others' (CCC 2011). The CCC acknowledged CERA had the lead role; however, the CCC did not think it was appropriate that the council did not have a governance role in the preparation of the draft strategy (CCC 2011).

Fifth, Rotimi's concerns about the coordination of recovery activities have been addressed by CERA, which is responsible for coordination and planning for infrastructure, economic recovery and the welfare rebuild. Again, the CCC (2011) had concerns, calling for greater clarity about how recovery work and decisions should be coordinated in CERA's recovery strategy, and asked that the affected local authorities be involved in the development of each recovery plan. This tends to support media reports and blog comments that some residents feel the major recovery actors are not communicating and coordinating their activities with one another and so are hindering recovery.

The coordination of reconstruction has been addressed by the EQC awarding Fletcher Construction a bulk contract for rebuilding approximately 50 000 moderately or seriously damaged properties. This means residents do not have to compete for the services of a limited number of building contractors, but now compete for attention within the Fletcher organisation.

Rotimi's sixth concern, about the inadequacies of the *EQC Act*, has been realised. The *EQC Act* had not envisaged multiple events within such a short time (Cowan and Simpson 2011). As at 10 February 2012, the EQC had dealt with 15 claimable events.

In September 2011, the EQC and the Insurance Council sought a declaratory judgment in the High Court as to whether EQC liability would be limited to NZ$100 000 for claims relating to an aggregate of events, or whether its cover would reinstate after each major quake. The court found that EQC cover (and therefore its liability of up to NZ$100 000) would reinstate after each major quake. This decision provided certainty, but it also added a large amount of liability to the Government.

Due to the unforeseen 'widespread and locally catastrophic liquefaction' (Cowan and Simpson 2011), EQC liability for restoration of the land in Canterbury has become much more complex, involving complicated engineering and legal considerations not anticipated when the *EQC Act* was passed. Decisions about zoning and the future designation of properties have become much more difficult and time-consuming.

There has been concern at the slow rate of EQC settlements. As at mid February 2012, 85 794 EQC claims from all events, including aftershocks, had been resolved.

Insurance has been the most urgent and significant issue holding back the progress of recovery. The continual sequence of aftershocks has made rebuilding decisions much harder. The susceptibility to risk of liquefaction in some areas added to this uncertainty.

EQC cover applies only when property owners are insured, and there are problems with the availability and pricing of earthquake cover as well as concerns about slow payouts from private insurers. Insurers able to arrange reinsurance cover are finding that costs have increased as much as four or five times (Grant 2011). As the increased cost to insurers is largely being passed on to consumers, earthquake insurance may become increasingly unavailable and unaffordable.

The quakes have wiped out the NZ$6 billion reserve of the Natural Disaster Fund, which underpins the EQC. The Government provided back-up financial support for AMI when it seemed the costs of the quakes might exceed AMI's reinsurance and reserves. Business interruption insurance has been crucial for many businesses' survival, but for most businesses this insurance ran out on 22 February 2012.

Seventh, Rotimi was concerned that a strict application of the *Resource Management Act* would slow the recovery. The *RMA* was amended by orders-in-council under both the *CERR Act* and the *CER Act*. These orders eased time frames for approval of consents by councils and introduced a range of amendments to address specific problems, such as faster resource consent processes to allow repairs to electrical system damage. Rotimi noted that consent applications would overwhelm local councils' capabilities during any post-disaster recovery. While it is unclear if this has happened, the CCC (2012) announced an additional 69 full-time staff to deal with consent issues. The real surge on consents will occur when rebuilding starts in earnest.

CERA has responsibility for zoning of land designated as 'green', 'orange', 'red' or 'white'. As at June 2011, the residential green zone contained around 100 000 homes that, subject to some further investigation about liquefaction risk, could begin the repair/rebuild process. Repair/rebuild of about 10 000 homes in the residential orange zone was on hold pending further assessment. The residential red zone contained about 5000 homes, many built on land prone to liquefaction, where remediation was judged likely to be 'prolonged and uneconomic'. In June 2011, the Government announced it would offer to buy out red-zoned insured residential homes at recent rateable value. The cost of the buyout was estimated to be between NZ$485 and NZ$635 million, which would come out of the NZ$5.5 billion earthquake recovery fund. As at February 2012, some homeowners were yet to hear the fate of their properties.

Community Engagement

Community engagement was at the centre of recovery policies before the quakes; however, the structure of CERA, combined with a faltering CCC, might overlook the opportunity for higher levels of community engagement. This section will consider the potential for, and progress of, community engagement in disaster recovery in Canterbury.

CERA's structure was initially criticised for being top-down, centralised and bureaucratic, in contrast with the ideals of the recovery management being bottom-up, decentralised and community led. CERA's arrangements were described as having the appearance of community engagement but the reality of ministerial control. CERA's draft recovery strategy supports the holistic framework for recovery advocated by the MCDEM, which places the community at the centre of all the task groups. Weak implementation, however, could undermine international lessons about the value of community engagement in recovery.

The Christchurch community forum design may compromise effective engagement, as its members may struggle to represent the views of the city's 400 000 people. Confusion about how the forum can influence the minister and what its role is generally—according to the CCC (2011), its role is unclear in the draft recovery strategy—diminishes the Government's assertion that it would encourage meaningful participation by community representatives in the recovery process.

The scale of community consultation by the CCC has improved recently. The community contributed 106 000 ideas to help inform the direction for the draft plan, generated from various initiatives and conversations. The CCC worked closely with Ngāi Tahu, Environment Canterbury and CERA during the development of the draft plan; however, there is still some criticism that the CCC is not generating higher levels of community engagement.

The community forum's 3 November 2011 meeting notes indicate that the CCC understands its people less than Waimakariri or Selwyn councils (CERA Community Forum 2011). This is probably a function of the CCC's size, but also reflects the perceived unwillingness in the CCC to delegate to the community.

A community's recovery may demand more engagement than would normally be expected; however, it was not clear whether the views expressed in eight CERA community workshops influenced the preparation of the recovery strategy. While there was a commitment in the draft strategy to engage and collaborate in the recovery, the draft recovery strategy does not define how this will occur. Submissions on the strategy suggest CERA should more proactively encourage community engagement at every stage—planning, implementation, monitoring and review—and at levels beyond consultation.

Much of the literature supporting community engagement seems to 'assume that the state will be both willing and able to accept post-disaster input from communities who are themselves willing and able to participate in the recovery process' (Vallance 2010:20). This assumption may not be valid. Vallance (2011) suggests recovery authorities struggled to connect adequately with affected communities for some time in Canterbury. In early February 2012, only 79 written comments on the draft central city plan had been received (The Press 2012). The reasons for the difference between these numbers and the 106 000 ideas generated for the creation of the same plan and the number of protestors who demonstrated over the pay increase for the council's CEO are matters for further study. Community engagement is, however, more suited to the recovery phase than the response phase. It has yet to be seen whether the recovery will truly benefit from comprehensive community engagement.

Discussion

New Zealand has four options to govern future large-scale disasters. First, the pre-quake legislative arrangements could be reinstituted. Second, a CERA-style model could be replicated. Third, significant amendments to the pre-quake framework could be made. Fourth, there could be a new and completely different model for disaster management and recovery.

The difficulties with the first two options have been indicated above, and the fourth would be difficult at the design and legislative stages. The pre-quake framework had many strengths, with most weaknesses related to the recovery phase. So there is a good case for amending the pre-quake framework for recovery after exceptional events.

Amendments to the Framework for Recovery

CDEM

New provisions should be added to the *CDEM Act* to support long-term recovery management after a state of emergency has been dissolved. Rotimi (2010) notes that this would require a more proactive role by the MCDEM. Furthermore, recovery planning and management should be strengthened across all involved sectors.

That enabling powers for long-term recovery were not considered prior to the quakes was an oversight. This must be addressed with due regard to democratic and constitutional norms.

The position of a national recovery coordinator to facilitate recovery planning and management initiatives should be made permanent (Rotimi 2010) to reflect the important, long-term nature of recovery management after a disaster.

In large-scale disasters central government intervention may always be necessary, as city councils probably lack the capability and resources to meet needs in the years following a disaster. A small permanent agency, having recovery powers like those of CERA, could be considered. This could involve extending the role of the MCDEM into the recovery phase; however, any such agency is likely to be inactive for long periods and could attract problems when clarifying who pays for localised disaster recovery. The MCDEM and other agencies involved in recovery could have a scale-up plan that would be triggered in a Canterbury-scale scenario.

If local authorities are to manage long-term recovery, they may require extra powers to enable recovery activities. Furthermore, if there is substantial damage to council-owned land and investments, as well as population flight, how will councils fund the recovery?

The events in Christchurch indicate that disasters will overwhelm councils. Rotimi (2010) recommends the development of memoranda of understanding between agencies. These should outline how recovery can be achieved through collaborative efforts.

Rotimi recommends greater alignment of the *CDEM Act* with the *RMA* and *Building Act* so all recovery-related provisions and activities avoid conflicting implementation of recovery tasks. The amendments to legislation provided by orders-in-council provide policymakers with a number of potential areas that will need to be aligned and addressed. Some of these issues were considered in evidence provided to the Canterbury Earthquakes Royal Commission.

Any change to legislation should take best-practice literature into account. The current devolved model of recovery assumes local authorities know their communities best, which gives the best opportunity for community engagement; however, Christchurch shows that the institutional capacity of local authorities after major disasters will be overwhelmed, which is likely to be true both for institutional capacity in general and their ability to engage with their communities. Also, opportunities for higher-level engagement may be discouraged. There are calls in Christchurch for recovery actors to move beyond tokenistic approaches to community consultation and embrace higher levels of community engagement. If people do not feel involved in the future of their city then those who can might leave.

A significant focus of disaster management is on planning for recovery, but how do you plan for the unexpected? This question should be studied. Institutional arrangements ought to be flexible enough to deal with a large range of disasters of different scales, as well as with emergent policy issues.

The people of Christchurch will largely have to work within the institutional arrangements that currently exist; however, they should be able to have a substantial say in their future.

Resource Management Act

The *RMA*'s procedural requirements and other provisions for wide consultation might hinder fast recovery. Rotimi proposed the scale of consultation and public notification be limited to permit a speedy approval process. Procedural requirements can delay essential works, as the complete collapse of seven previously damaged heritage buildings in the February quake showed. Approval to demolish them required an engineering report and resource consent, which would take months. In February the facades of the buildings collapsed, killing 12 people. Demolition of buildings is now allowed if they pose an immediate danger to human safety. Heritage protection remains an issue for legislators, especially in balancing the need for public consultation with the need for safety.

The *RMA* should be amended but procedures should not hinder the purpose of sustainable management of resources. The Government intends to amend the *RMA* to give greater weight to managing the risks of natural hazards. This should include a review of consents given to land that is prone to issues like liquefaction.

The EQC

A 2009 review of the EQC suggested it was not prepared for a major national disaster. Furthermore, there was widespread confusion about what its role would be, with the Government expecting agencies like the EQC to be more 'directly involved in the response and recovery than their mandate and capability allows' (Heather 2011). This led to the EQC having more contact with private insurers, and in case of a major quake aiming to settle 80 000 claims in 12 months.

The EQC was overwhelmed by the scale of the Canterbury quakes. In February 2012, there were huge disparities between the approaches of private insurance companies and the EQC in assessing the damage to homes. For example, private insurers' policies say that they will reinstate the property 'as new'. The *EQC Act* provides that they will reinstate the property 'substantially the same as when new'. This disparity could mean the difference between repair and demolition (Wright 2012).

Changes to the *EQC Act* should address these issues. The EQC should plan for multiple events and large numbers of claims. Its financial viability will also need to be examined. The EQC levy paid annually by homeowners has already tripled. EQC advice to the incoming minister in November 2011 suggested changes, including removing contents insurance cover, introducing variable premiums depending on house size or hazards risk, automatic adjustment of premiums and payout caps, and increasing the excess on claims.

With the costs of damage rising, the viability of the EQC model will become difficult, especially given the government guarantee to meet the EQC's shortfall. As the cost of insurance in disaster-prone areas becomes increasingly unaffordable, it is likely more people will choose not to insure their homes and EQC cover will not apply. In this situation, the problem of moral hazard arises, particularly if the public expects the Government will take on residual risk. Additionally, as outlined earlier, provisions in the *EQC Act* allow for cover not to apply to high-risk land or notified earthquake-prone buildings. A stricter application of the Act in the future may be harsh, but fiscally necessary.

Conclusion

An evaluation of the pre-quake framework for recovery now confirms that the legislative support for long-term recovery was inadequate. The new governance arrangements following the quakes had flaws. The legislation addressing recoveries in both cases were rushed because the Government was dealing with disasters of unprecedented scale.

The disasters raise several wider implications. How is the cost of the Canterbury quakes and the role of government altering expectations and incentives for the future? Will we become less insured and does this effectively increase the fiscal risk for governments? Will local governments expect future recovery projects will be centrally planned as Canterbury is? How will the 'shelf plan' for the next major event balance collaboration with executive management? How does that affect the democratic deficit in local government? How important is it to have an effective legislative framework in place when future governments will be able to legislate to meet the needs of the disaster?

The role of councils leading long-term recovery needs further evaluation. While councils may theoretically provide the opportunity for effective community engagement, their capability to lead recovery is questionable.

New Zealand's framework for recovery needs to be future-proofed. Though we cannot prevent most natural disasters, we can try minimising their impact and create governance arrangements to maximise recovery. The process for learning from disaster and recovery should consider not only institutional understandings, but also citizen expectations of what should be done better next time. Crucially, we must find ways to imbed learning from disasters into institutional memory.

References

Bollard, A. and Ranchhod, S. 2011. Economic impacts of seismic risk: lessons for Wellington, Speech delivered to the Rotary Club of Wellington and Victoria University of Wellington Organisational Effectiveness in Times of Seismic Risk Conference, Wellington.

Canterbury Earthquake Recovery Authority (CERA). 2011a. *Briefing to the Incoming Minister* (Christchurch: Canterbury Earthquake Recovery Authority).

Canterbury Earthquake Recovery Authority (CERA). 2011b. *Draft Recovery Strategy for Greater Christchurch* (Christchurch: Canterbury Earthquake Recovery Authority). Available from: <http://cera.govt.nz/sites/cera.govt. nz/files/common/draft-recovery-strategy-for-greater-christchurch.pdf>.

Canterbury Earthquake Recovery Authority (CERA) Community Forum. 2011. *Minutes of the Meeting of the CERA Community Forum*, 3 November (Christchurch: Canterbury Earthquake Recovery Authority). Available from: <http://cera.govt.nz/sites/cera.govt.nz/files/common/community-forum-meeting-notes-20111103.pdf>.

Christchurch City Council (CCC). 2011. *Draft Recovery Strategy Comments from Organisations* (Christchurch: Christchurch City Council). Available from: <http://cera.govt.nz/sites/cera.govt.nz/files/common/draft-recovery-strategy-comments-from-organisations.pdf>.

Christchurch City Council (CCC). 2012. Council streamlines consent process, Media release (Christchurch: Christchurch City Council). Available from: <http://www.ccc.govt.nz/thecouncil/newsmedia/mediareleases/2012/201202032.aspx>.

Cowan, H. and Simpson, I. 2011. Planning for disasters and responding to unforseen complexity: the first large test for the New Zealand Earthquake Commission, Presentation to 12th Biennial Aon Benfield Hazards Conference, Surfers Paradise, Qld.

Dalziel, L. 2011. Turning disaster into opportunity, Keynote address, Australian and New Zealand Institute of Insurance and Finance Conference, Auckland.

Department of Labour (DOL). 2011. *Employment Opportunities in Canterbury*, December (Wellington: Government of New Zealand). Available from: <http://www.dol.govt.nz/publications/research/employment-opportunities-canterbury/eoc.pdf>.

Doherty, E. 2011. *Economic Effects of the Canterbury Earthquakes*, Parliamentary Library Research Paper (Wellington: Government of New Zealand).

Geddis, A. 2011. An open letter to New Zealand's people and their Parliament, 28 September (North Dunedin: Faculty of Law, University of Otago).

Geonet. 2011. 'Christchurch Badly Damaged by Magnitude 6.3 Earthquake', *GNS Science*, 22 February. Available from: <http://geonet.org.nz/news/feb-2011-christchurch-badly-damaged-by-magnitude-6-3-earthquake.html>.

Government of New Zealand. 2010. *Canterbury Earthquake Response and Recovery Bill 2010* (Wellington: Government of New Zealand). Available from: <http://www.legislation.govt.nz/bill/government/2010/0215/latest/whole.html>.

Government of New Zealand. 2011a. *Cabinet Paper 1: Proposed Governance Arrangements* (Wellington: Government of New Zealand). Available from: <http://cera.govt.nz/sites/cera.govt.nz/files/common/cabinet-paper-1-proposed-governance-arrangements-march-2011.pdf>.

Government of New Zealand. 2011b. *Cabinet Paper 2: Proposed Powers—Annex 2—Regulatory Impact Statement* (Wellington: Government of New Zealand). Available from: <http://cera.govt.nz/sites/cera.govt.nz/files/common/cabinet-paper-2-proposed-powers-annex-2-regulatory-impact-statement-march-2011.pdf>.

Government of New Zealand. 2012. *Summary of Crown Observer Proposal* (Wellington: Government of New Zealand). Available from: <http://www.beehive.govt.nz/sites/all/files/Crown_Observer_Proposal.pdf>.

Grant, J. 2011. 'One Year On—The Future of Earthquake Insurance for Residential Properties', *interest.co.nz*, 5 September. Available from: <http://www.interest.co.nz/insurance/55212/one-year-future-earthquake-insurance-residential-properties>.

Greenhill, M. 2012. 'Life on the Edge of a Raw Nerve', *stuff.co.nz*, 17 January. Available from: <http://www.stuff.co.nz/national/christchurch-earthquake/6266653/Life-on-the-edge-of-a-raw-nerve>.

Heather, B. 2011. 'Extent of Damage Never Imagined', *stuff.co.nz*, 4 September. Available from: <http://www.stuff.co.nz/national/christchurch-earthquake/5559040/Extent-of-disaster-never-imagined>.

International Association for Public Participation (IAP2). 2004. *IAP2 Public Participation Spectrum* (Wollongong, NSW: IAP2). Available from: <http://www.iap2.org.au/sitebuilder/resources/knowledge/asset/files/36/iap2spectrum.pdf>.

McCrone, J. 2011. 'Over the Top?', *The Press*, 23 April. Available from: <http://www.stuff.co.nz/the-press/news/christchurch-earthquake-2011/4920414/Over-the-top>.

Millen, D. 2011. *Deliberative Democracy in Disaster Recovery: Reframing Community Engagement for Sustainable Outcomes* (Sydney: University of Western Sydney).

Ministry of Civil Defence and Emergency Management (MCDEM). 2005a. *Focus on Recovery: A Holistic Framework for Recovery in New Zealand* (Wellington: Government of New Zealand).

Ministry of Civil Defence and Emergency Management (MCDEM). 2005b.*New Zealand's Response to the 1994 Yokohama Strategy and Plan of Action for a Safer World: National Information Report*, United Nations International Strategy for Disaster Reduction (Geneva: UNISDR). Available from: <http://www.unisdr.org/2005/wcdr/preparatory-process/national-reports/New-Zealand-report.pdf>.

Ministry of Civil Defence and Emergency Management (MCDEM). 2008. *National Civil Defence Emergency Management Strategy* (Wellington: Government of New Zealand).

Ministry of Civil Defence and Emergency Management (MCDEM). 2009a. *Guide to the National Civil Defence Emergency Management Plan 2006*, Rev. edn (Wellington: Government of New Zealand). Available from: <http://www.civildefence.govt.nz/memwebsite.nsf/Files/The-Guide-2009-revision/$file/summary-of-sections.pdf>.

Ministry of Civil Defence and Emergency Management (MCDEM). 2009b. *Section 25. Recovery* (Wellington: Government of New Zealand).

Ministry of Civil Defence and Emergency Management (MCDEM). 2010. *Community Engagement in the CDEM Context—Best Practice Guideline for Civil Defence Emergency Management Sector* (Wellington: Government of New Zealand).

New Zealand Press Association (NZPA). 2011. 'Christchurch Quake Could Cost $30b', *3news.co.nz*, 11 March. Available from: <http://www.3news.co.nz/Christchurch-quake-could-cost-30B/tabid/423/articleID/201875/Default.aspx>.

Rotimi, J. 2010. An examination of improvements required to legislative provisions for post disaster reconstruction in New Zealand, PhD Thesis (Christchurch: University of Canterbury).

The Press. 2012. 'Recovery Plan Attracts Fewer than 20 Comments', *The Press*, Last updated 1 February 2012. Available from: <http://www.stuff.co.nz/the-press/news/christchurch-earthquake-2011/6344439/Recovery-plan-attracts-fewer-than-20-comments>.

Treasury. 2011. *Budget Economic and Fiscal Update* (Wellington: Government of New Zealand). Available from: <http://www.treasury.govt.nz/budget/forecasts/befu2011>.

United Nations Development Programme (UNDP). 2006. *Post-Disaster Recovery: Guiding Principles* (New York: UNDP Bureau for Crisis Prevention and Recovery—Disaster Reduction Unit). Available from: <http://www.undp.org/cpr/disred/documents/publications/regions/america/recovery_guidelines_eng.pdf>.

United Nations International Strategy for Disaster Reduction (UNISDR). 2005. *Governance: Institutional and Policy Frameworks for Risk Reduction* (Geneva: UNISDR). Available from: <http://www.unisdr.org/2005/wcdr/thematic-sessions/WCDR-discussion-paper-cluster1.pdf>.

Vallance, S. 2011. 'Early Disaster Recovery: A Guide for Communities', *Australian Journal of Disaster Recovery & Trauma Studies*, 2011–12:19–25.

Wright, M. 2012. 'EQC, Insurers to Join Forces on Assessments', *stuff.co.nz*, Last updated 1 February 2012. Available from: <http://www.stuff.co.nz/national/christchurch-earthquake/6344433/EQC-insurers-to-join-forces-on-assessments>.

21. Seismic Shifts: The Canterbury earthquakes and public sector innovation

John Ombler and Sally Washington

The Canterbury earthquakes had a huge impact on government services. The scale of the 22 February 2011 event meant that many public servants could not access their damaged buildings, forcing many to work remotely from home or co-located in buildings that remained functional. Some departments deliberately redeployed staff to help where they were needed most, including to work with non-governmental organisations (NGOs) and in the community. The tenacity of those public servants and their commitment to serving the public, despite their own personal and family disruptions, were commendable. Sometimes the choice of where to work in the early days was determined on the basis of where there was functional plumbing.

Government departments with a presence in Canterbury were asked to document the impacts of the earthquakes on their staff and operations, and how they had responded to that disruption. Putting all those responses together produced a tome of A3 sheets that revealed some innovative approaches to public service delivery and design. When these examples were presented to ministers, they asked for more of the same, not only in Canterbury but also nationwide.

The earthquakes showed the agility and resilience of the public service in times of crisis. This will help our ability to be ready and able to respond to future crises. They also provided a 'perfect storm' for innovation. The innovative responses to the disaster revealed some new ways of working that offer lessons about how to improve public service design and delivery, not only in response to a disaster but in a business-as-usual context. The Canterbury innovations provide live demonstrations of what New Zealand's Better Public Services (BPS)[1] program is trying to achieve.

This chapter discusses the Canterbury innovations and the lessons they offer for public service design and delivery. We argue that building innovation capability is an important component of future-proofing the state.

---

1   For a description of the Better Public Services program, including the Prime Minister's 10 Result Areas, see: <http://www.ssc.govt.nz/better-public-services>.

The Canterbury Innovations Project

The State Services Commission (SSC) took the lead on a project to ensure the public sector took full advantage of the lessons from the Canterbury innovations. Key partners in that project are the Canterbury Earthquake Recovery Authority (CERA) and the Christchurch Government Leaders Group, comprising senior leaders from government agencies based in Christchurch. The project is now an integral part of the BPS program. It sits at the interface of two of the Government's top priorities (see Box 21.1)—delivering better public services and rebuilding Christchurch—and should contribute to the two economic priorities.

Box 21.1

Government priorities
• Responsibly manage the Government's finances
• Build a competitive economy
• Deliver better public services
• Rebuild Christchurch

The project provides early practical examples of BPS made real. Too often we tell agencies what to do without giving them guidance or shoot them down when they get it wrong. We need to also celebrate success and share examples of where they have got it right, including as a way to inspire other agencies to follow suit. The Canterbury innovations project is designed to

- showcase and sustain the innovations, draw the lessons from them and apply them, where appropriate, to business elsewhere
- promote Christchurch as an innovation zone, applying deliberate and coordinated capability to help drive the Christchurch rebuild, and to prototype models of service delivery and design for the rest of the country as demonstrations of BPS
- draw lessons from Christchurch to help build innovation capability across the state services.

Showcasing Christchurch Innovations and Applying the Lessons Elsewhere

The Christchurch innovations project began with four case studies demonstrating examples of innovative public service delivery and/or design emerging in response to the earthquakes. The organisations involved in the initiative, the value added by the initiative, what the innovation demonstrated in terms of better public services, its potential scalability and next steps for the initiative were the subjects of a report to cabinet and published case studies, which are all available on the SSC's website.[2]

The initial four case studies covered the following.

- *The Canterbury District Health Board (CDHB) eShared Care Record View (eSCRV):* A secure online system for sharing patient information between health professionals—invaluable in a disaster when paper records were irretrievable and access to usual health providers was disrupted. The eSCRV was co-produced by the CDHB and a range of private health providers, ensuring buy-in and that the service met the needs of users.

- *Recover Canterbury:* A joint venture between the Canterbury Development Corporation, the Canterbury Employers Chamber of Commerce and several government agencies including Inland Revenue, which supports earthquake-affected businesses with advice, mentoring, referrals (to government as well as professional services) and grants. Users of the service report not knowing, or caring, whether they were dealing with public or private sector staff— they just recognised Recover Canterbury as a vital support and a successful brand.

- *Justice Services Recovery:* Including centralised court scheduling and the use of alternative facilities that enabled the maintenance of court proceedings despite significant damage to infrastructure. Co-location of justice agencies and community-based organisations is also being explored, building on agencies' shared experience at Ngā Hau e Whā marae following the earthquakes.

- *Earthquake Support Coordination Service (ESCS):* Co-production between government agencies and NGOs to provide support for families and households following the earthquakes.

The innovations were significant in their own right; but more importantly, they offer lessons for the future design and delivery of public services in New Zealand.

Citizen/Business-Centric Service Design: Designing services around the user

Citizen-centric service design—building services around people's needs—was a constant theme running through the case studies. Both Recover Canterbury and the ESCS used a tailored support model, with clients assessed on need and offered varying levels of support, from 'light touch' to full wrap-around

---

2   <http://www.ssc.govt.nz/christchurch-innovations>.

services based on that assessment—a triage approach to service provision. Both examples provided a coordinated service with multiple access points; there was 'no wrong door'. The sustainability of these models and the cost and benefits in different policy contexts will need to be evaluated over time. They provide live demonstrations of channel strategies for providing services and information (online, telephone, in person, and so on).

Building services around citizen needs was a key theme of the BPS Advisory Group's report.[3] The Christchurch experience will help inform options for BPS Results 9 and 10 aimed at improving government interactions with New Zealanders.

Co-Production: Making the most of available capability

The BPS Advisory Report argued that citizen/business participation is a powerful driver for delivering better services and value for money and that more use could be made of best-sourcing to drive improved performance in New Zealand state services. Christchurch provides practical examples of the value of co-production.

CDHB's eSCRV was the product of multiple stakeholders, public and private, coming together to design and agree on a mutually beneficial system (funded by CDHB). Recover Canterbury and the ESCS are further examples of co-production and tapping the best expertise available, whether public, private or community based, with funding and form following the desired function.

The ESCS demonstrated a new approach to contracting with NGOs, involving providing funding to backfill the roles of staff seconded into the ESCS rather than the standard 'contract-for-service' approach.

Co-Location: The foundation for joined-up services

Co-location and secondments to other agencies changed how public servants thought about their work and their operating environment. In Christchurch staff gained valuable insights from the opportunity to see how other agencies operate, and for those staff working in Recover Canterbury and the ESCS, a better understanding of the business and community sectors respectively. For example, interviews conducted with Inland Revenue Department (IRD) and Work and Income staff (Inland Revenue/Communications and Inquiry National Research Unit 2011) revealed that they now see joined-up government service

---

3   The advisory group's report is available on the SSC website: <http://www.ssc.govt.nz/better-public-services>.

as the way of the future. Despite differences in organisational culture and functions, they recognised similarities in customers and types of services and the potential to realise efficiencies by sharing information and facilities while providing clients with the best possible assistance available. The Christchurch experience confirms the value of co-location for frontline services and provides a practical example of how common results have the power to break down agency silos.

Information Sharing and Use of Technology Drives Better Services and Improves Efficiency

The Christchurch innovations show multiple examples of information sharing and the use of technology to drive better services, with improved outcomes as the driver and efficiency the by-product.

Faster treatment, less duplication of diagnostic procedures and reduced acute admissions are some of the efficiencies facilitated by shared access to patient records, without the associated cost of having to design a central database or replace existing IT systems in CDHB's eSCRV.

The ESCS shared client information (with a consent process)[4] between government agencies and with the community partners involved. Recover Canterbury similarly involved sharing information across agencies. This facilitated faster and better referrals and better services to clients.

Centralised venue location, a centralised inbound calling function and text messaging were used to enable essential court services to be maintained following the earthquakes; the initiatives provided a practical application of work under way in the Ministry of Justice and are being fed into future justice sector planning.

We have stressed the need to maintain the enabling environment in Christchurch to support and to monitor the current and emerging initiatives over time. This is crucial for testing the sustainability of those innovations and future iterations and for assessing their ongoing value including in other contexts. Some might be appropriate to an emergency situation and the transition phase but have diminishing returns under business as usual. Moreover, agencies such as Inland Revenue deployed staff and resources into the emergency response

---

4   Sharing of personal information is allowed in emergency situations under the *Privacy Act*. The Privacy Commissioner communicated the Christchurch Earthquake (Information Sharing) Code 2011 (Temporary) to clarify the conditions under which personal information could be shared. The Privacy Commissioner has since commissioned research into the use of the code (<http://privacy.org.nz/christchurch-earthquake-information-sharing-code-2011-temporary/>), the results of which will feed into the development of a new code of practice applicable to any national emergency.

in Christchurch that would need to be redeployed under business as usual. Agencies have been asked to monitor and evaluate the initiatives to assess how they can be applied to their business elsewhere. A further report to cabinet on sustaining innovation in Christchurch government services will be prepared in late 2012.

Christchurch as an Innovation Zone and a Harbinger of Better Public Services

The need to build new infrastructure in Christchurch offers a once-in-a-lifetime opportunity to redesign government services and to test innovative models of service delivery. This should build on the lessons learned post earthquakes—for example, to maximise the opportunities for co-location and to design services around user needs. Several big opportunities stand out.

Rebuilding Education Facilities in Greater Christchurch.

The rebuilding of education facilities in Greater Christchurch offers a unique opportunity to test new approaches to governance, provision of school facilities and property (shared infrastructure/facilities with other community services), building on some of the interim arrangements introduced following the earthquakes, such as shared campuses and the use of portacoms for early childhood education. The focus for renewing the education network will be on strengthening the delivery of education including through sharing property and facilities and better transitions between learning stages, from early childhood to tertiary education. As in other service areas, the aim is to build back better rather than to simply replace what was there before.

Office Accommodation for Government Services in Christchurch: Trialling Functional Leadership

Government agencies' needs for new accommodation in Christchurch provide the opportunity to develop innovative accommodation arrangements that are both more efficient and galvanise cross-agency work seeded during co-location following the earthquakes. There are two key phases of work: securing government office accommodation for regional management and corporate support functions in the CBD rebuild, and a longer-term service delivery network (in-person public interface sites). Christchurch provides an opportunity to operationalise and test the value of functional leadership[5] that is a major component of the leadership stream of the BPS program.

Shared Front of House: Prototyping service transformation and BPS Result 10

Decisions about the Government's overall property strategy provide a limited window to implement some different approaches to face-to-face service delivery in Christchurch. Evidence from existing initiatives in Christchurch, and from similar front-of-house consolidation in other jurisdictions, confirms that integrated government service delivery has benefits for citizens as well as for agencies. These models put citizens at the forefront; services are designed around meeting their needs efficiently and effectively. Moving from an agency-centred service delivery approach to a citizen-centred one requires consideration of issues such as the alignment of technology, work practices, business processes and employment agreements. There is a significant opportunity in Christchurch to experiment with different delivery models and to trial a number of short-term options in the interim phase, before longer-term accommodation options are fixed. These opportunities allow for some prototyping of options for BPS Result 10.[6]

Justice and Emergency Services: Opportunities for co-location

Police, New Zealand Security Intelligence Service (NZSIS) and Department of Internal Affairs (DIA) Fire Service, as well as ambulance and local government Civil Defence and Emergency Management (CDEM) are working together to co-locate and integrate some areas of service delivery into a shared campus in the CBD. It involves a rethink of infrastructure and property arrangements and an analysis of the synergies between agencies. Synergies between the justice sector and emergency services are sought through shared custodial services, shared office accommodation, shared emergency operations centres and a suite of shared facilities, as well as enhanced emergency management capabilities and processes for anticipating responses to a range of events. Drawing on arrangements following the earthquakes, several other examples of co-location in this sector are already operational.

---

5   Cabinet mandates have been given to three chief executives to assume leadership for driving greater cross-government efficiencies and effectiveness. Functional leader mandates relate to three functional areas: property, procurement and information and communication technology (ICT).

6   For a description of BPS results related to improving interaction with government, see: <http://www.ssc. govt.nz/bps-interaction-with-govt>.

Taken together, these projects (alongside the rebuilding of hospital facilities) represent significant capital investment and a key part of the Christchurch rebuild. A deliberate and coordinated approach to the rebuilding and redesign process is required. The Canterbury Government Leaders Group has built the foundations for ongoing cross-agency coordination. The willingness to try new things in Christchurch means there is scope to test new approaches to service provision, including delivery of BPS results. Christchurch can serve as an innovation zone for BPS, where new models of service delivery and design can be tested, prototypes developed and debugged, and the scalability to the state services assessed.

Embedding Innovation across State Services: From 'innovation by necessity' to 'innovation by design'

Most of the Christchurch initiatives were 'innovation by necessity'; the status quo was not an option. Christchurch public servants innovated and continue to operate in a difficult and challenging environment. Christchurch can, however, offer lessons about what enables innovation to flourish in a public sector context.

Leadership and Permission are Crucial Enablers of Innovation

People on the ground in Christchurch could innovate because they had explicit permission from senior leadership to 'do whatever it takes'. The tolerance for risk-taking was higher because the risk of not trying something new was greater, although this was not uniform across agencies (some regional staff had stronger decision rights than others; inconsistent regional boundaries had a further impact on the ability to act without referring to head office).

Permission and clear goals articulated by senior leadership are key enablers of innovation; top-down sponsorship enables bottom-up innovation. A study of high-performing innovative public and private sector organisations and sectors (Albury 2011) concluded that a key characteristic of those organisations is having leadership that is passionate about goals, but is permissive about how to reach them. Innovation is not just a question of unleashing creativity or coming up with bright ideas. 'Innovation by design' requires investment in capability, a focus on users, expertise in the use of innovative methods, as well as strong mandates to experiment and to take bounded, informed and well-managed risks. It requires engagement with staff at the front line where new ideas are often generated.

Capability in Innovation Tools and Methods is Essential for Making it Happen

A number of the Christchurch initiatives were enabled by pre-existing innovation capability and experience in applying innovation tools, methods and disciplines to problems. The Inland Revenue service design team based in Christchurch was instrumental in several of the innovations (in particular, Recover Canterbury and proposals for the shared front of house). Inland Revenue has developed a service design capability over the past seven years. Service design as a method has a strong focus on the customer and their experience as the starting point for designing services, and is a recognised method for driving innovation in the public (and private) sector.

Similarly, the CDHB has established a reputation for investing in innovation. Its overall shared vision was developed through a process that included 'Showcase', a series of participatory workshops and the showcasing of innovative ideas and models of care, involving more than 2000 stakeholders, providers, consumers and health professionals. The earthquakes expedited the implementation of the shared care record, which was in development prior to that time, but the organisational foundations for innovation were well entrenched.

Inland Revenue and the CDHB are exploring the potential to co-locate their service design functions in Christchurch in order to share skills and knowledge. This could provide a prototype to inform the development of some future cross-agency innovation capability at the national level. Drawing on these exemplars, the SSC is preparing a case study on innovation capability that will test those organisations against the characteristics derived from the international literature about what makes for an organisation that enables and supports innovation. The intention is for this work to offer lessons to other agencies wishing to enhance their ability to be innovative.

Walking the Talk

In a small attempt to walk the talk, and inspired by CDHB's Showcase, the SSC decided to try something innovative itself. We decided to forgo the usual cabinet committee briefing process in favour of an experiential session dubbed 'Seismic Shifts' to brief ministers on the initial and emerging Canterbury innovations. The session—something between a trade show and speed dating—involved public servants from Canterbury coming to Wellington to tell their own stories about how they had responded to the earthquakes. They used visual props, including videos of users of the innovative services. The timing was such that ministers could choose only four of the eight booths to sit at. A bell was rung at five-minute intervals, signalling a move to the next booth. On leaving the session, ministers were handed tent cards that subsequently ended up on several of their desks. That two-sided card had messages on each side about how to enable and how to stop innovation (see Box 21.2). A further Seismic Shifts session was held for senior officials. We received positive feedback from minsters about the session. It was a more powerful way of informing them about the Canterbury innovations than a dry paper or briefing from Wellington officials.

Box 21.2

Seismic Shifts
How to stop innovation
- Demand people think differently and expect it to happen
- Create silos of thinking
- Punish failure

Lessons for fostering transformation
- Focus on the citizen
- Clear goals, flexible process
- Encourage frontline engagement

The Next Steps

We need to maintain the enabling environment in Christchurch to keep the momentum of innovation going. Christchurch has the potential to provide a model of twenty-first-century innovative and responsive state services. Agencies are being asked to report to central agencies and ministers about what new things they are trying in Christchurch, including prototyping options for BPS results. We also want to ensure that the lessons from Christchurch are taken elsewhere around the country. That does not mean simply taking a cookie-cutter approach to up-scaling initiatives from Christchurch to another part of New Zealand. It means taking the essence of that innovation and grafting it to local conditions. It also means agencies developing their capability to enable and support new innovation, to seek new and better ways of doing things.

The challenge for the centre is to take the lessons from Christchurch to drive BPS work to embed innovation in a business-as-usual context. Canterbury was about disruptive innovation or innovation by necessity. We need to create a seismic shift in activity, behaviour and capability to achieve innovation by design. An innovative public sector is one that is agile, responsive and ready for whatever comes its way. Building innovation capability is an important strategy for future-proofing the state.

References

Albury, D. 2011. 'Creating the Conditions for Radical Public Service Innovation', *Australian Journal of Public Administration*, 70(3):227–35.

Inland Revenue/Communications and Inquiry National Research Unit. 2011. *Inland Revenue and Ministry of Social Development Staff Views of Joined Up Government Service in Christchurch*, November (Wellington: Inland Revenue/ Communications and Inquiry National Research Unit).

22. Examining the Public Sector's Responses to the Canterbury Earthquakes

Lyn Provost, Henry Broughton and Andrea Neame

This chapter describes the Auditor-General's program of work examining how public agencies performed during the recovery from the earthquakes that hit Canterbury in 2010 and 2011, especially the 7.1 magnitude earthquake of 4 September 2010 and the 6.3 magnitude earthquake of 22 February 2011, which killed 185 people.

The Role of the Auditor-General

An auditor-general's role is to provide assurance about the public money spent by public agencies. The Office of the Auditor-General (OAG) fulfils this role in four ways

- statutory, annual financial audits, and audits of service performance reporting
- the controller function
- performance audits
- inquiries.

The Auditor-General is responsible for the audits of about 4000 public entities. Audit New Zealand (an operational business unit of the Auditor-General) and audit firms carry out annual audits on the Auditor-General's behalf. Annual audits form most of the Auditor-General's output. The Auditor-General carries out performance audits and inquiries at her discretion, with reference to an annual plan of work that is presented to Parliament.

Our Future Needs: Is the public sector ready?

As Auditor-General, I have a firm belief that we should, wherever we can, help to improve the public sector. New Zealand has a public sector I am proud of, but I believe it can always be better. The focus of our 2012–13 work has been on our future needs. Is the public sector ready to meet future needs? An overriding need for New Zealand is to rebuild Christchurch, our second-largest city.

Our Response to the Canterbury Earthquakes

The past 18 months and the 12 000 earthquakes and aftershocks in Canterbury have been a journey for us and many others. In many countries, the Auditor-General would be busy during the emergency response phase to a natural disaster because of the increased risk of fraud, theft and corruption when significant public money and aid pour into a region. New Zealand is, however, fortunate to have a transparent and relatively corruption-free public sector, with operating controls and systems generally effective. Reviews of the response phase were carried out soon after the 4 September 2010 and 22 February 2011 earthquakes, and we saw no need to duplicate this work. During the response phase, we focused largely on our core work of annual audits.

A few hundred of the 4000 audits we carry out every year are around Christchurch. We were pragmatic when public agencies asked us about accountability and reporting requirements. For example, we exempted about 40 schools from producing annual reports. The schools' priority was to get functioning again and focus on their students.

Many of our audit opinions on financial statements for 2011–12 drew attention to uncertainties about liabilities and asset valuations of public entities.

Agencies did their best to account for liabilities and damage from the earthquakes but, in many instances, ongoing change and a lack of information meant uncertainty was unavoidable. Indeed, uncertainty was a consistent theme right through to the financial statements of the Government, where, for the first time, we drew attention to uncertain matters. The statements included estimates of

- the Earthquake Commission's liability for damage to home contents, houses and residential land
- the 60 per cent infrastructure costs that transfer from local to central government
- the Government's guarantee for what is additional to the Earthquake Commission's Natural Disaster Fund[1]
- the cost of houses in the residential red zone (earthquake-damaged land and properties in Christchurch the Government agreed to buy and clear).

The scale of public expenditure that the recovery and rebuild entails (it is forecast that about NZ$15 billion of public funds will go to the Christchurch

---

1   There is a NZ$1.5 billion excess for each earthquake event. If the required Earthquake Commission payout exceeds the total of the excess and reinsurance (NZ$4 billion), the remainder of the payout is met by the commission up to the limit of the Natural Disaster Fund. If the payout exceeds those assets, a crown guarantee requires that the Government pays the remainder.

recovery and rebuild) as well as the unique and uncertain context of that expenditure meant we needed to think carefully about how we could best use our limited discretionary powers.

We set up a small team led by two managers: one from our local government team and the other from our central government team. The team visited Christchurch regularly, meeting public officials, community groups and people affected by the earthquakes. The team visited the Red Zone, meeting homeowners and people demolishing houses. The team met tradespeople repairing the houses as part of the Earthquake Commission's Homes Repair Programme.

Always we were conscious of the need to keep in mind that many of the people working in the public sector in Canterbury had suffered through thousands of earthquakes. We listened and reflected on what we heard to inform our decisions about what work we should do.

Learning from Audit Offices Overseas

As well as visiting Canterbury regularly, we also carried out desk research into the work of audit offices in other countries in response to natural disasters. This included the work of the Chinese National Audit Office (CNAO) following the Wenchuan earthquakes in 2008. The CNAO carried out a 'real-time audit' of the response and reconstruction that involved literally thousands of auditors over a three-year period. The audit involved tracking and auditing every step of the reconstruction effort, from preliminary planning, project development and commissioning, to completion of projects (CNAO n.d.).

We looked at the Queensland Audit Office's performance audit of the systems and processes involved in the national partnership agreement for natural disaster reconstruction and recovery (Auditor-General of Queensland 2011). The aim of this work was to provide assurance to the Queensland Parliament and public about the State's systems to deliver the funding and services to the community as provided for in the agreement.

The US Government Accountability Office (GAO) has looked at the government response to many natural disasters, such as Hurricane Katrina, to gather and learn lessons. The GAO has compiled the key areas of learning from this work, which proved to be a useful resource for us to consider the key lessons and the key principles to an effective recovery effort.[2]

---

2   See the US Government Audit Office website: <www.gao.gov>.

We drew on the work of the UN Development Programme, the World Bank and the Organisation for Economic Cooperation and Development (OECD) to identify key themes for an effective government response and recovery to a natural disaster (OECD 2004; UNDP n.d.; World Bank 2011). These include

- public confidence and trust, gained through being transparent and communicating openly
- clear relationships between different levels of government to manage risks of duplicating work and poor coordination
- recovery authorities focusing strongly on gaining and maintaining cohesion, coordination and consensus.

An Assessment Framework Helps to Prioritise our Discretionary Work

We used the World Bank's report on the Queensland Recovery Authority to create a framework to structure our thinking about the New Zealand Government's performance in the recovery from the Canterbury earthquakes (World Bank 2011). This framework has 25 criteria for an effective recovery and rebuild from a natural disaster, which we put into a spreadsheet that we could regularly revise as the recovery moved into different stages. This living document has informed our thinking about how we structure our work program.

Through balancing what we have listened to, looking at the assessment criteria and talking to people throughout the public sector, we identified four areas of priority for our work in Canterbury.

- *Accountability and responsibility:* Who is doing what? Who is accountable?
- *Funding and finance:* How much will the recovery and rebuild cost the taxpayer and ratepayer? How will costs be shared?
- *Procurement and monitoring:* Are services being properly procured, and is the money being used appropriately?
- *Insurance:* How have the earthquakes affected the way public agencies insure assets?

Table 22.1 summarises the main issues under each theme, as well as the type of audit response.

Table 22.1 Priority Themes, Main Issues to Address and Audit Response

Theme	Summary of main issues	Audit response
Accountability and responsibility	Complexity, heightened risk of duplication	Regular reports on roles, responsibilities and funding First report presented to Parliament in October 2012
Funding and finance	A wide range of new appropriations and funding arrangements in place to finance the recovery and rebuild Central government and local government contributions; private sector funding; insurance and reinsurance; complex and expensive	Controller function Report on roles, responsibilities and funding Regular tracking of costs Annual audit of financial statements
Procurement and monitoring	Significant contracts for the demolition, repair, and rebuilding of homes, infrastructure, and the central business district	Annual audits of financial statements and service performance
	Earthquake Commission's Canterbury Home Repair Programme—large-scale procurement and project management. More than 80 000 repairs	Performance audit, 2013
	Repair and rebuilding of horizontal infrastructure—mainly waterpipes and roads—delivered through an alliance model of five contractors working with Christchurch City Council, the Canterbury Earthquake Recovery Authority, and the New Zealand Transport Agency	Performance audit, 2013
Insurance and the public sector	The increasing cost of insurance has been expensive for public entities throughout New Zealand	Parliamentary report (June 2013) on the results of a survey of all public entities by our auditors

Source: Authors' summary.

Roles, Responsibilities and Funding

Our first piece of discretionary work has been to map and describe the roles and responsibilities of the key public entities involved in the recovery.

In October 2012, we published *Roles Responsibilities, and Funding of Public Entities after the Canterbury Earthquakes* (Office of the Auditor General 2012), which provides an objective view of how the recovery is being run. In doing so, it describes how the recovery is being carried out, the roles of agencies, how the recovery is being funded and what the main risks and challenges are—for the agencies involved and for Cantabrians. We intend to provide updates on these matters at appropriate intervals.

The report included mapping the relationships between public sector entities, private companies and Te Rūnanga Ngāi Tahu (the local *iwi*) in meeting the challenges of the Canterbury earthquake recovery. This was represented in a complex diagram that can be sourced from the OAG website.[3] In drawing this diagram, we aimed to focus on the fact that the accountability needs to be understood from the viewpoint of people living in Canterbury. The recovery and rebuild effort involves significant funding, large-scale projects and contracts, and many entities with interacting roles and responsibilities.

The diagram shows the many organisations involved and the complexity of the recovery and rebuild. It is important to manage complexity effectively. Complexity can bring opportunities as well as challenges. For example, the State Services Commission has identified many good examples of public entities working in new and more effective ways in response to the earthquakes.

To sum up, during our visits to Canterbury, we heard often about how the private sector, the public sector and *iwi*[4] are working together, and we saw much evidence of this.

Each agency has roles and responsibilities. These need to be clear to the agencies and their staff, as well as to their partners. Accountability needs to be clear, although that need not be agency by agency. Accountability can be by task and by outcome. People need to work together to be able to achieve outcomes that contribute to recovery. In fact, the agenda of better public services is challenging us all to think about how we work together to collaborate on shared outcomes.

We consider that for the recovery to be effective and efficient it is important that all the agencies involved know what each is doing. If there is a lack of clarity, there is a risk that their work might not be mutually supportive, could lack direction and could be wasteful because of duplication. Accountability could be unclear and, in the end, the effective use of public spending could be put at risk. Because rebuilding in a changing environment is complex, leaders in Canterbury must continually monitor and take appropriate action to manage these risks.

As the rebuild in Canterbury changes, we will update our diagram regularly and ensure that we keep monitoring any changes. I have no doubt it will evolve

---

3   This diagram can be found at http://www.oag.govt.nz/2012/canterbury/2012/canterbury/docs/figure1.pdf.
4   *Iwi* are Māori tribes.

as new ways of working together and more collaboration become apparent or take place between agencies and Wellington and Canterbury and between the public and private sectors.

References

Auditor-General of Queensland. 2011. *National Partnership Agreement for Natural Disaster Reconstruction and Recovery. Performance Management Systems Audit*, Report to Parliament No. 7 2011 (Brisbane: Auditor-General of Queensland).

Chinese National Audit Office (CNAO). n.d. *Introduction to the Real-Time Audit of the Wenchuan Post-Earthquake Recovery and Reconstruction Projects.* Available from: <www.cnao.gov.cn>.

Office of the Auditor-General. 2012. *Roles Responsibilities, and Funding of Public Entities after the Canterbury Earthquakes*, Parliamentary Paper, October (Wellington: Office of the Auditor-General).

Organisation for Economic Cooperation and Development (OECD). 2004. *Large-Scale Disasters: Lessons Learnt* (Paris: OECD).

United Nations Development Programme (UNDP). n.d. *Post-Disaster Recovery Guidelines (Version 1)* (New York: Bureau for Crisis Prevention and Recovery).

World Bank. 2011. *Queensland Recovery and Reconstruction in the Aftermath of the 2010/11 Flood Events and Cyclone Yasi* (Washington, DC: The World Bank).

Name Index

Subject Index

www.ingramcontent.com/pod-product-compliance
Lightning Source LLC
Chambersburg PA
CBHW041119280326
41928CB00061B/3377